THE SOCIAL WORKER

by William Berwick

The Social Worker © 2024 William Berwick
All rights reserved.

This book is independently published by the author. No part of this book may be reproduced, distributed, or transmitted in any form or by any means, including photocopying, recording, or other electronic or mechanical methods, without the prior written permission of the author, except in the case of brief quotations embodied in critical reviews and certain other non-commercial uses permitted by copyright law.

Dedication

To all the social workers and advocates who tirelessly support vulnerable children and families. Your dedication and compassion inspire us all.

Acknowledgements

I would like to express my deepest gratitude to the following individuals and organizations for their support and encouragement throughout the writing of this book:

- The Johnson Family Foundation, for their unwavering support and belief in my work.
- My family and friends, for their love, patience, and understanding.
- Dr. Collins, for providing invaluable guidance and support.
- My colleagues and mentors, for their collaboration and inspiration.
- The community members and volunteers, for their dedication and commitment to making a difference.

Thank you all for being a part of this journey.

Epigraph

"Compassion is the basis of morality."
— Arthur Schopenhauer

Introduction

Welcome to "The Social Worker," a story that delves into the life of Emily Johnson, a dedicated social worker whose unwavering commitment to child welfare transforms the lives of countless vulnerable children and families. This novel is not just a tale of one woman's journey, but a tribute to the resilience, compassion, and advocacy that define the human spirit.

As the author, I have drawn inspiration from my own experiences and observations in the field of social work. Through Emily's story, I aim to shed light on the often unseen and uncelebrated efforts of those who work tirelessly to make a difference in their communities. Emily's journey is a testament to the power of dedication and the profound impact one individual can have on the lives of many.

In writing this book, I hope to inspire readers to recognize the importance of empathy, support, and advocacy in creating a brighter future for all. Whether you are a social worker, an advocate, or simply someone who believes in the power of positive change, I invite you to join Emily on her journey and discover the strength that lies within each of us.

Thank you for embarking on this journey with me. I hope "The Social Worker" resonates with you and leaves a lasting impression.

Table of Contents

Chapter 1: Introduction to Emily's Family 1
Chapter 2: Signs of Trouble 11
Chapter 3: The Breaking Point 21
Chapter 4: Taken into Care 32
Chapter 5: The Foster Home 43
Chapter 6: Adjusting to a New Life 57
Chapter 7: The Court Hearing 74
Chapter 8: Building Trust 91
Chapter 9: A New Family 109
Chapter 10: Healing and Growth 127
Chapter 11: Looking Back 146
Chapter 12: Moving Forward 164
Chapter 13: Mentorship and Leadership 182
Chapter 14: Personal Life and Relationships 200
Chapter 15: Legacy and Impact 217
Chapter 16: Expanding Horizons 235
Chapter 17: Personal Fulfilment 254
Chapter 18: Continuing the Mission 271

Chapter 1
Introduction to Emily's Family

Emily's story begins in a small, worn-out house on the outskirts of town. Her family, though once filled with hope and dreams, has been overshadowed by the dark clouds of alcoholism and depression. Emily's father, once a hardworking man, has succumbed to the bottle, seeking solace in alcohol to escape the harsh realities of life. His once bright eyes now dull, he spends his days in a haze, the clinking of bottles a constant background noise in their home.

Emily's mother, overwhelmed by the weight of her own untreated depression, finds it difficult to provide the nurturing care that Emily desperately needs. Once a vibrant woman with a love for life, she now spends most of her days in bed, the curtains drawn tight against the world outside. The house, once filled with laughter and warmth, has turned into a place of tension and neglect.

Emily, a bright and curious child, often finds herself caught in the crossfire of her parents' struggles. She watches her father stumble through the door late at night, the smell of alcohol heavy in the air. She hears her mother's quiet sobs from the bedroom, a sound that has become all too familiar. Despite the chaos around her, Emily clings to the small moments of joy and normalcy, hoping for a better future.

The neglect Emily experiences is not always overt. It's in the small things – the empty fridge, the unwashed clothes, the forgotten birthdays. It's in the way her parents' eyes glaze over when she tries to tell them about her day at school, their minds elsewhere. It's in the way she learns to fend for herself, making her own meals and getting herself ready for school each day.

Emily's home life is a stark contrast to the world outside. At school, she excels, her teachers praising her intelligence and curiosity. She finds solace in books, losing herself in stories of far-off places and happy families. But no matter how hard she tries, she can't escape the reality of her home life. The weight of her parents' struggles hangs heavy over her, a constant reminder of the life she wishes she could leave behind.

As Emily grows older, the neglect takes its toll. She becomes withdrawn, her once bright smile fading. She stops inviting friends over, embarrassed by the state of her home and her parents' behaviour. She learns to hide her pain, putting on a brave face for the world while inside she feels like she's falling apart.

Despite everything, Emily remains hopeful. She dreams of a better life, one where her parents are happy and healthy, and where she can be a child again. She holds onto the belief that things will get better, that one day her family will find their way out of the darkness. But for now, she takes it one day at a time, finding strength in the small moments of joy and the hope for a brighter future.

Emily's daily life at home is a stark contrast to the world outside. Each morning, she wakes up to the sound of her father's snores and the sight of her mother's empty bed, a reminder of the long nights spent in a depressive haze. The kitchen is often bare, with only a few cans of food and stale bread to sustain her. Breakfast is a luxury she rarely enjoys, and she often goes to school on an empty stomach, her hunger pangs a constant companion throughout the day.

The neglect Emily faces is pervasive and unrelenting. Her clothes are often dirty and ill fitting, hand-me-downs from charity shops or donations. She learns to wash her own clothes in the sink, using whatever soap she can find, and hangs them to dry on a makeshift clothesline in her room. The house itself is in disrepair, with peeling wallpaper, broken furniture, and a persistent smell of dampness that permeates every corner.

Basic care is a rarity in Emily's life. Her parents, consumed by their own struggles, often forget to provide the essentials. She learns to fend for herself, making simple meals from whatever scraps she can find and ensuring she has clean clothes for school. Bathing is infrequent, and she often feels self-conscious about her appearance and hygiene. The lack of care extends to her emotional well-being as well. Her parents are distant and unresponsive, their minds clouded by their own issues. Emily craves their attention and affection, but it is rarely given.

Despite the neglect, Emily finds small moments of solace in her daily routine. She escapes into the world of books, losing herself in stories of far-off places and happy families. She excels at school, finding comfort in the structure and predictability of the classroom. Her teachers praise her intelligence and curiosity, unaware of the struggles she faces at home.

Emily's resilience is remarkable. She navigates her daily life with a quiet determination, finding ways to cope with the neglect and make the best of her situation. She dreams of a better future, one where she is loved and cared for, and where her parents are happy and healthy. Until then, she takes it one day at a time, finding strength in the small moments of joy and the hope for a brighter future.

Emily, despite her young age, develops a remarkable set of coping mechanisms to navigate the neglect and chaos of her home life. She quickly learns to take on responsibilities that far exceed those of a typical child, driven by a need to survive and maintain some semblance of normalcy.

One of Emily's primary coping strategies is her ability to fend for herself. She becomes adept at preparing simple meals from the limited food available, often making do with whatever scraps she can find. She learns to be resourceful, using her creativity to turn basic ingredients into something edible. Breakfast might be a piece of toast with a smear of jam, while dinner could be a can of soup heated on the stove. These small acts of self-care provide her with a sense of control and independence.

In addition to feeding herself, Emily takes on the responsibility of managing the household chores. She washes her own clothes in the sink, scrubbing them with whatever soap she can find and hanging them to dry on a makeshift clothesline in her room. She tidies up the house as best she can, sweeping the floors and picking up after her parents. These tasks, though burdensome, give her a sense of accomplishment and help her maintain a semblance of order in her chaotic environment.

Emily also finds solace in routines. She establishes a daily schedule for herself, waking up early to get ready for school and ensuring she completes her homework each evening. This structure provides her with a sense of stability and predictability, something she desperately needs amidst the unpredictability of her home life. School becomes a sanctuary for her, a place where she can escape the neglect and focus on her studies.

To cope with the emotional neglect, Emily turns to books and writing. She loses herself in the pages of novels, finding comfort in the stories of characters who face and overcome their own challenges. Writing becomes an outlet for her emotions, a way to express her thoughts and feelings when there is no one else to listen. She fills notebooks with poems and stories, pouring her heart onto the pages.

Despite the heavy burden she carries, Emily remains hopeful. She dreams of a better future, one where she is loved and cared for, and where her parents are happy and healthy. She holds onto this hope, using it as a source of strength and motivation. Her resilience is remarkable, and she continues to find ways to cope and thrive despite the neglect she faces.

The emotional toll on Emily is profound and pervasive, shaping her sense of self and her view of the world. The neglect she experiences at home leaves her feeling isolated and abandoned, emotions that weigh heavily on her young shoulders.

Emily often feels an overwhelming sense of loneliness. Despite being surrounded by people at school and in her neighbourhood, she feels disconnected and alone. Her parents, consumed by their own struggles, are emotionally unavailable, leaving Emily without the support and affection she craves. She watches other children with their parents, feeling a pang of envy and sadness as she longs for the same kind of love and attention.

The lack of emotional support from her parents leads to feelings of abandonment. Emily struggles with the idea that she is not worthy of love or care, internalizing the neglect as a reflection of her own value. This belief erodes her self-esteem, making her feel insignificant and unimportant. She often wonders what she did wrong to deserve such treatment, blaming herself for her parents' inability to provide the care she needs.

Emily's emotional pain manifests in various ways. She becomes withdrawn and quiet, preferring to keep to herself rather than risk rejection or disappointment. Her once bright and curious nature dims, replaced by a cautious and guarded demeanour. She finds it difficult to trust others, fearing that they too will abandon her or let her down.

Despite these challenges, Emily finds ways to cope with her emotions. She turns to books and writing as a means of escape and expression. Through reading, she immerses herself in worlds where characters face and overcome their own struggles, finding solace in their stories. Writing becomes an outlet for her feelings, allowing her to articulate her pain and process her experiences.

Emily also finds comfort in small moments of joy and normalcy. She cherishes the rare instances when her parents show her affection or when she experiences kindness from others. These moments, though fleeting, provide her with a glimmer of hope and remind her that she is capable of being loved and valued.

The emotional impact of neglect leaves lasting scars on Emily, shaping her into a resilient yet vulnerable individual. She carries the weight of her experiences with her, but she also holds onto the hope that things will get better. Her strength and determination to overcome her circumstances are a testament to her resilience and the enduring power of hope.

Amidst the neglect and chaos of her home life, Emily finds solace in small moments of joy and comfort. These brief instances provide her with a glimmer of hope and a respite from her daily struggles.

One of Emily's cherished moments is when she plays with her favourite toy, a worn out teddy bear named Mr. Snuggles. Despite its tattered appearance, Mr. Snuggles is a source of comfort for Emily. She often talks to the bear, sharing her thoughts and feelings, finding a sense of companionship in its silent presence. Holding Mr. Snuggles close, she feels a warmth and security that is otherwise missing from her life.

Another source of joy for Emily is her interactions with a kind neighbour, Mrs. Thompson. An elderly woman with a gentle demeanour, Mrs. Thompson often greets Emily with a warm smile and a kind word. She occasionally invites Emily over for tea and biscuits, providing a brief escape from the neglect at home. These visits are a highlight for Emily, as she basks in the warmth and care that Mrs. Thompson offers. The simple act of being noticed and valued by someone makes a significant difference in Emily's life.

Emily also finds comfort in nature. She loves spending time outdoors, exploring the nearby park and immersing herself in the beauty of the natural world. The rustling of leaves, the chirping of birds, and the gentle breeze provide a soothing backdrop to her thoughts. She often takes long walks, finding peace and solace in the quiet moments surrounded by nature. Hiking and cycling become her favourite activities, allowing her to escape the confines of her home and experience a sense of freedom.

Books are another source of joy for Emily. She loses herself in the pages of novels, transported to different worlds where characters face and overcome their own challenges. Reading becomes a refuge, a way to escape the harsh realities of her life and find comfort in the stories of others. She often visits the local library, where the librarian, Mrs. Green, recommends books and encourages her love for reading. These interactions and the stories she discovers provide Emily with a sense of connection and inspiration.

Despite the neglect she faces, Emily's resilience shines through in these small moments of joy. They provide her with the strength to endure and the hope for a better future. Each moment, whether it's playing with Mr. Snuggles, receiving a kind word from Mrs. Thompson, exploring nature, or losing herself in a book, helps Emily navigate the challenges of her life and find a sense of peace and comfort.

As time passes, the neglect Emily faces at home worsens, leading to more severe consequences for her physical and emotional well-being. The once sporadic instances of neglect become a constant, pervasive presence in her life, eroding her sense of security and stability.

The lack of food becomes more pronounced. The kitchen, already sparse, often has nothing but a few cans of expired goods and stale bread. Emily's meals become even more infrequent and inadequate, leaving her perpetually hungry and malnourished. Her physical health begins to deteriorate, and she frequently feels weak and fatigued. The hunger pangs that once came and went now gnaw at her constantly, making it difficult for her to concentrate at school or find joy in activities she once loved.

Basic care and hygiene continue to decline. Emily's clothes, already worn and ill fitting, become increasingly tattered and dirty. She struggles to keep herself clean, as the household lacks basic supplies like soap and clean water. Her appearance becomes a source of embarrassment and shame, further isolating her from her peers. The neglect extends to her medical needs as well. Minor illnesses and injuries go untreated, and Emily learns to endure pain and discomfort in silence.

The emotional neglect Emily experiences also intensifies. Her parents, consumed by their own struggles, become even more distant and unresponsive. The rare moments of affection and attention she once received disappear entirely. Emily feels increasingly invisible and unimportant, her self-esteem plummeting as she internalizes the neglect as a reflection of her own worth. The emotional toll manifests in anxiety and depression, and she often feels overwhelmed by a sense of hopelessness and despair.

The worsening neglect also has severe consequences for Emily's education. Her once stellar performance at school begins to decline as the stress and instability at home take their toll. She finds it difficult to focus on her studies, and her grades suffer as a result. The teachers, noticing the change, express concern, but their efforts to help are often thwarted by the lack of support from Emily's parents. The school becomes another source of stress, as Emily struggles to keep up with her peers and fears falling further behind.

Socially, Emily becomes more withdrawn and isolated. The neglect at home makes it difficult for her to form and maintain friendships. She stops inviting friends over, embarrassed by the state of her home and her parents' behaviour. Her interactions with others become strained, and she often feels like an outsider, unable to relate to her peers who lead more stable and nurturing lives.

Despite the escalating neglect, Emily's resilience remains remarkable. She continues to find small moments of joy and solace, clinging to the hope that things will get better. Her strength and determination to survive and overcome her circumstances are a testament to her enduring spirit. However, the worsening neglect leaves deep scars, shaping her into a resilient yet vulnerable individual who carries the weight of her experiences with her.

Emily's inner world is a complex tapestry of thoughts and feelings, shaped by the neglect and challenges she faces at home. Despite the chaos around her, she harbours a rich inner life that provides her with a sense of solace and escape.

Emily often retreats into her imagination, creating vivid worlds where she feels safe and loved. In these imagined places, she is free from the burdens of her daily life, surrounded by caring figures who provide the affection and support she craves. These daydreams offer her a temporary respite from the harsh realities of her existence, allowing her to experience moments of joy and comfort.

Her thoughts are often filled with questions and uncertainties. She wonders why her parents are unable to care for her and what she might have done to deserve such neglect. These questions weigh heavily on her mind, leading to feelings of self-doubt and insecurity. Emily struggles with the idea that she is not worthy of love or attention, internalizing the neglect as a reflection of her own value.

Despite these negative thoughts, Emily also possesses a remarkable sense of hope and resilience. She dreams of a better future, one where her parents are happy and healthy, and where she can experience the love and care she longs for. This hope serves as a beacon of light in her darkest moments, giving her the strength to endure and persevere.

Emily's inner world is also a place of creativity and expression. She finds solace in writing, using it as an outlet for her emotions. Her notebooks are filled with poems and stories that reflect her inner struggles and desires. Through writing, she is able to articulate her pain and process her experiences, finding a sense of release and understanding.

Books play a significant role in Emily's inner life. She loses herself in the pages of novels, finding comfort in the stories of characters who face and overcome their own challenges. These stories provide her with a sense of connection and inspiration, reminding her that she is not alone in her struggles. The characters become her companions, offering her guidance and hope.

Emily's inner world is a testament to her resilience and strength. Despite the neglect and challenges she faces, she maintains a rich and vibrant inner life that provides her with the comfort and hope she needs to endure. Her thoughts and feelings are a reflection of her enduring spirit and her unwavering belief in a better future.

As Emily navigates her increasingly difficult life, subtle signs begin to hint at the challenges that lie ahead. The once sporadic arguments between her parents become more frequent and intense, their voices echoing through the thin walls of their home. The tension in the house is palpable, and Emily can sense that something is about to change.

Emily's father, whose drinking has steadily worsened, starts to disappear for days at a time, leaving Emily and her mother to fend for themselves. His absences create a void that is filled with uncertainty and fear. Emily's mother, already struggling with depression, becomes even more withdrawn and unresponsive. The weight of their combined struggles begins to take a toll on Emily, who feels increasingly isolated and overwhelmed.

At school, Emily's teachers notice a change in her behaviour. Once a bright and engaged student, she now appears distracted and distant. Her grades begin to slip, and she often seems lost in thought, her mind preoccupied with the troubles at home. Concerned, her teachers reach out to her, but Emily is reluctant to share the full extent of her struggles, fearing the consequences of revealing her family's secrets.

Despite her efforts to maintain a sense of normalcy, Emily's coping mechanisms start to falter. The small moments of joy that once provided solace become harder to find, and the weight of her responsibilities feels increasingly burdensome. She begins to experience frequent nightmares, waking up in a cold sweat, her heart pounding with fear. These dreams, filled with images of abandonment and loss, foreshadow the challenges that are soon to come.

The signs of trouble are not lost on Emily's few friends and neighbours. Mrs. Thompson, the kind neighbour who has always looked out for Emily, notices the deepening shadows under her eyes and the growing sadness in her demeanour. She tries to offer support, but Emily, wary of burdening others, keeps her distance. The sense of impending crisis hangs heavy in the air, a silent but ever-present reminder of the storm that is about to break.

    As the neglect at home escalates, Emily's resilience is put to the test. She finds herself at a crossroads, struggling to hold onto hope while facing the harsh realities of her situation. The intervention that will soon take place is hinted at through these subtle signs, setting the stage for the pivotal moments that will shape Emily's journey and ultimately lead her towards a path of redemption and healing.

Chapter 2
Signs of Trouble

Emily's teachers begin to notice subtle yet concerning signs of neglect that gradually become more apparent over time. Initially, it's the small things that catch their attention. Emily's clothes, once neat and clean, start to appear worn and dirty. Her hair, usually brushed and tidy, becomes unkempt and tangled. These changes in her appearance are the first red flags that something is amiss at home.

As the days go by, Emily's behaviour also starts to shift. She becomes increasingly withdrawn and quiet, a stark contrast to the bright and engaged student she once was. In class, she seems distracted, her mind often wandering far from the lessons being taught. Her teachers notice that she frequently stares out the window, lost in thought, and struggles to concentrate on her schoolwork. Her once excellent grades begin to slip, and she falls behind in her assignments.

During playtime and lunch breaks, Emily isolates herself from her peers. She no longer joins in the games and activities she used to enjoy. Instead, she sits alone, often with a book in hand, using it as a shield to avoid interaction. Her teachers observe her eating habits as well. Emily often brings little to no food for lunch, and when she does have something to eat, it's usually a small, inadequate portion. The sight of her picking at a meagre meal or going
without food altogether raises further concerns.

Emily's physical health also starts to show signs of neglect. She appears tired and lethargic, with dark circles under her eyes indicating a lack of proper sleep. She occasionally comes to school with minor injuries or illnesses that go untreated, such as cuts, bruises, or persistent colds. These physical symptoms, combined with her deteriorating appearance and behaviour, paint a troubling picture for her teachers.

The teachers, deeply concerned for Emily's wellbeing, try to reach out to her. They ask gentle questions, hoping to understand what might be happening at home. However, Emily, wary of revealing too much, often responds with vague or evasive answers. She fears the consequences of exposing her family's struggles and the potential repercussions for herself and her parents.

Despite their best efforts, the teachers feel increasingly helpless as they watch Emily's situation worsen. They discuss their concerns among themselves and consider the best course of action to support her. The signs of neglect are clear, and they know that intervention may be necessary to ensure Emily's safety and well-being.

Emily's neighbours, though not fully aware of the extent of her struggles, begin to notice troubling signs that something is amiss. Mrs. Thompson, the kind elderly woman next door, is one of the first to sense that Emily's situation is deteriorating. She often sees Emily walking to school alone, her clothes increasingly worn and her demeanour more withdrawn. Mrs. Thompson's heart aches for the young girl, but she feels uncertain about how to intervene without overstepping boundaries.

Other neighbours also observe changes in Emily's behaviour and appearance. Mr. and Mrs. Patel, who live across the street, notice that Emily's once cheerful greetings have become rare. They see her sitting alone on the front steps of her house, looking lost in thought. The Patels discuss their concerns with each other, wondering if they should reach out to Emily's parents or contact someone who can help. However, they hesitate, fearing that their involvement might make things worse for Emily.

The neighbourhood children, who used to play with Emily, also sense that something is wrong. They notice that she no longer joins their games and often seems tired and sad. They miss her presence but are unsure how to approach her, sensing that she is dealing with something beyond their understanding.

Despite their growing concerns, the neighbours feel a

collective sense of helplessness. They are unsure of the best course of action and worry about the potential repercussions of getting involved. Some consider calling social services, but the fear of causing more harm than good holds them back. They hope that the situation will improve on its own, but the signs of neglect become harder to ignore.

Mrs. Thompson, in particular, struggles with her conscience. She wants to help Emily but is unsure how to do so without intruding. She decides to keep a closer eye on the young girl, offering small acts of kindness whenever possible. She invites Emily over for tea and biscuits, hoping to provide a brief respite from her troubles. During these visits, Mrs. Thompson gently tries to learn more about Emily's home life, but Emily remains guarded, reluctant to share too much.

The neighbours' concerns grow as they witness the escalating neglect. They feel a sense of responsibility to do something but are paralyzed by uncertainty and fear. The signs of trouble are clear, and they know that intervention may be necessary to ensure Emily's safety and well-being. However, the path to helping her is fraught with challenges, and they struggle to find the right way to make a difference.

Emily's struggles at home inevitably spill over into her school life, creating a host of challenges that make it difficult for her to keep up with her schoolwork and maintain social interactions. The neglect she faces at home leaves her physically and emotionally drained, impacting her ability to focus and perform well in her studies.

In the classroom, Emily's teachers notice a marked decline in her academic performance. Once a bright and engaged student, she now struggles to concentrate on her lessons. Her mind often wanders, preoccupied with worries about her home life. She finds it difficult to complete her assignments on time, and her grades begin to slip. The once enthusiastic learner now appears disinterested and detached, her passion for learning overshadowed by the weight of her responsibilities and the emotional toll of neglect.

Emily's difficulties are not limited to academics. Her social interactions also suffer as a result of her home situation. She becomes increasingly withdrawn, isolating herself from her peers. During playtime and lunch breaks, she often sits alone, preferring the company of a book to the bustling playground. The other children, sensing her distance, are unsure how to approach her, and Emily's friendships begin to wane.

The lack of proper nutrition and sleep further exacerbates Emily's struggles. She often comes to school hungry and tired, her energy levels depleted. This physical exhaustion makes it even harder for her to keep up with her schoolwork and participate in class activities. Her teachers notice her frequent yawns and the dark circles under her eyes, signs of the neglect she endures at home.

Emily's emotional state also takes a toll on her social interactions. She feels a deep sense of shame and embarrassment about her home life, which makes her reluctant to open up to others. She fears judgment and rejection, so she keeps her struggles to herself. This isolation only deepens her feelings of loneliness and abandonment, creating a vicious cycle that is difficult to break.

Despite these challenges, Emily tries her best to maintain a semblance of normalcy. She puts on a brave face, determined not to let her struggles show. She continues to attend school regularly, finding solace in the structure and routine it provides. Her teachers, aware of her difficulties, offer support and encouragement, but they are limited in what they can do without knowing the full extent of her situation.

Emily's resilience is remarkable, but the ongoing neglect at home makes it increasingly difficult for her to thrive at school. Her struggles with academics and social interactions are a reflection of the broader challenges she faces, highlighting the urgent need for intervention and support.

Despite their growing concerns, Emily's teachers and neighbours make small but significant attempts to help her, though their efforts are often accompanied by hesitations and uncertainties.

Mrs. Thompson, the kind neighbour who has always looked out for Emily, takes the initiative to offer her support. She invites Emily over for tea and biscuits more frequently, hoping to provide a safe and comforting space for her. During these visits, Mrs. Thompson gently tries to learn more about Emily's home life, but Emily remains guarded, reluctant to share too much. Mrs. Thompson senses the depth of Emily's struggles but feels unsure about how to intervene further without overstepping boundaries.

Emily's teachers, deeply concerned about her declining performance and appearance, also try to offer support. Mrs. Green, her homeroom teacher, begins to check in with Emily more regularly, asking how she's doing and offering a listening ear. She provides extra help with schoolwork, hoping to ease some of the academic pressure Emily faces. Despite these efforts, Mrs. Green feels limited in what she can do without knowing the full extent of Emily's situation at home.

Mr. Patel, another neighbour, notices Emily's frequent absences from school and her increasingly dishevelled appearance. He decides to speak with her parents, hoping to understand what might be going on. However, when he approaches Emily's father, he is met with hostility and denial. Mr. Patel leaves the conversation feeling frustrated and helpless, unsure of how to proceed without causing more harm.

The school counsellor, Ms. Johnson, also becomes involved after noticing the changes in Emily's behaviour. She invites Emily to her office for regular check-ins, creating a safe space for Emily to talk about her feelings. Emily appreciates the support but remains cautious, fearing that revealing too much could lead to unwanted consequences. Ms. Johnson, aware of the delicate situation, tries to build trust with Emily while considering the best way to provide further assistance.

Despite these small attempts to help, the teachers and neighbours are often hesitant to take more decisive action. They worry about the potential repercussions for Emily and her family, fearing that their involvement might make things worse. The signs of neglect are clear, but the path to intervention is fraught with challenges and uncertainties.

These small acts of kindness and support, though limited, provide Emily with moments of comfort and reassurance. They remind her that there are people who care about her well-being, even if they are unsure how to help. The hesitations and uncertainties of those around her highlight the complexity of her situation and the urgent need for a more comprehensive intervention.

As the neglect at home worsens, Emily's sense of isolation

deepens, creating an emotional chasm that becomes increasingly difficult to bridge. The once vibrant and curious child now feels like a shadow of her former self, struggling to connect with those around her.

At school, Emily's isolation is palpable. She no longer participates in class discussions or group activities, preferring to sit quietly at her desk, lost in her thoughts. Her teachers notice her withdrawal and try to engage her, but their efforts are often met with silence or a forced smile. Emily's classmates, sensing her distance, gradually stop inviting her to join their games and conversations. The playground, once a place of laughter and camaraderie, now feels like a foreign land where Emily is an outsider.

Emily's isolation extends beyond the classroom. She stops attending birthday parties and social gatherings, finding it easier to avoid the awkward questions and pitying looks. The few friends she once had drift away, unable to understand the depth of her struggles. Emily's loneliness becomes a constant companion, a heavy weight that she carries with her everywhere she goes.

At home, the isolation is even more pronounced. Her parents, consumed by their own issues, are emotionally unavailable. The house, once filled with the sounds of family life, is now eerily quiet. Emily spends most of her time alone in her room, finding solace in books and writing. She pours her heart into her journal, expressing the pain and loneliness she feels but cannot share with anyone else.

The lack of emotional support takes a toll on Emily's mental health. She begins to experience feelings of worthlessness and despair, questioning her own value and purpose. The neglect and isolation erode her self-esteem, making it difficult for her to believe that she deserves love and care. Emily's once bright and hopeful outlook on life dims, replaced by a sense of resignation and hopelessness.

Despite her growing isolation, Emily clings to small moments of connection. She cherishes the rare instances when a teacher offers a kind word, or a neighbour shows her a small act of kindness. These fleeting moments provide her with a glimmer of hope, reminding her that she is not entirely alone. However, they are not enough to fill the void left by the absence of meaningful relationships and emotional support.

Emily's struggle to connect with others is a reflection of the broader challenges she faces. The neglect at home creates a barrier that is difficult to overcome, isolating her from the world around her. Her growing sense of isolation highlights the urgent need for intervention and support, as she navigates the difficult path of finding her place in a world that often feels indifferent to her pain.

As the neglect at home worsens, the physical signs become increasingly apparent, painting a stark picture of Emily's deteriorating condition. These signs are not only visible to those around her but also serve as a constant reminder of the hardships she endures.

One of the most noticeable signs is Emily's persistent hunger. Her once healthy frame becomes gaunt and frail, her cheeks hollow and her eyes sunken. The lack of proper nutrition leaves her perpetually hungry, and she often goes to school on an empty stomach. Her teachers notice her frequent yawns and the way she struggles to stay awake during lessons. At lunchtime, Emily's meagre meals, if she has any at all, consist of small portions of stale bread or a few crackers. The other children, with their packed lunches and snacks, look on with concern and pity.

Emily's physical appearance also reflects the neglect she faces. Her clothes, already worn and ill-fitting, become increasingly tattered and dirty. She often wears the same outfit for several days in a row, the fabric stained and frayed. Her hair, once brushed and tidy, is now unkempt and tangled, a clear sign that she lacks the basic care and attention she needs. The lack of hygiene is evident, and Emily becomes self-conscious about her appearance, further isolating herself from her peers.

Bruises and minor injuries start to appear more frequently on Emily's body. These marks, often the result of accidents or rough play, go untreated and become more noticeable over time. Her teachers and neighbours notice the bruises on her arms and legs, the cuts and scrapes that never seem to heal properly. When asked about them, Emily offers vague explanations, unwilling to reveal the true extent of her neglect. The physical pain, though significant, is overshadowed by the emotional toll it takes on her.

The neglect also affects Emily's overall health. She becomes more susceptible to illnesses, her immune system weakened by the lack of proper nutrition and care. She frequently suffers from colds, coughs, and other minor ailments that linger for weeks without proper treatment. Her energy levels are consistently low, and she often feels fatigued and lethargic. The physical symptoms of neglect are a constant burden, making it difficult for her to focus on her studies or enjoy the activities she once loved.

Despite these visible signs, Emily tries to maintain a sense of normalcy. She puts on a brave face, determined not to let her struggles show. However, the physical signs of neglect are hard to hide, and they serve as a stark reminder of the challenges she faces every day. The worsening neglect leaves deep scars, both physical and emotional, highlighting the urgent need for intervention and support.

Despite the overwhelming challenges and neglect she faces, Emily's resilience shines through as she strives to maintain a sense of normalcy in her life. Her inner strength and determination are remarkable, allowing her to navigate the difficulties with a quiet grace and resolve.

Emily's resilience is evident in her daily routines. She wakes up early each morning, determined to start her day on a positive note. She takes care of herself as best as she can, washing her face and brushing her hair, even if her resources are limited. She packs her school bag meticulously, ensuring she has all her books and supplies ready. This routine provides her with a sense of stability and control, a small but significant way to assert her independence amidst the chaos.

At school, Emily's resilience is reflected in her commitment to her studies. Despite the distractions and difficulties at home, she remains focused on her education. She listens attentively in class, takes detailed notes, and works diligently on her assignments. Her teachers notice her effort and dedication, even as her grades fluctuate due to the external pressures she faces. Emily's love for learning becomes a source of strength, a beacon of hope that guides her through the darkest times.

Emily also finds solace in her creative pursuits. Writing becomes her refuge, a way to express her emotions and process her experiences. She fills notebooks with poems and stories, pouring her heart onto the pages. This creative outlet provides her with a sense of purpose and accomplishment, allowing her to channel her pain into something meaningful. Her resilience is evident in her ability to find beauty and inspiration in the midst of adversity.

In her interactions with others, Emily's resilience is marked by her kindness and empathy. Despite her own struggles, she remains considerate and compassionate towards her peers. She offers a listening ear to classmates who are going through their own challenges, providing support, and understanding. Her ability to empathize with others, even when she is hurting, is a testament to her strength and character.

Emily's resilience is also evident in her ability to find joy in small moments. She cherishes the rare instances of kindness from neighbours, the warmth of the sun on her face during a walk, and the comfort of a good book. These moments, though fleeting, provide her with a sense of normalcy and happiness. They remind her that there is still beauty in the world, even amidst the difficulties.

Through her resilience, Emily demonstrates an incredible capacity to endure and overcome. She navigates her challenges with a quiet strength, finding ways to maintain a sense of normalcy and hope. Her journey is a testament to the power of the human spirit, a reminder that even in the face of adversity, resilience can light the way forward.

As the signs of neglect become more pronounced, the tension in Emily's life escalates, creating an atmosphere of impending crisis. The once subtle indicators of trouble are now glaringly obvious, and those around her can no longer ignore the severity of her situation.

Emily's physical appearance continues to deteriorate. Her clothes are increasingly tattered, and her once bright eyes are now dull and lifeless. The bruises and cuts on her body, once hidden, are now visible to anyone who looks closely. Her teachers and neighbours exchange worried glances, their concern growing with each passing day. The whispers of "something's not right" become more frequent, and the sense of urgency intensifies.

At school, Emily's academic performance plummets. She struggles to keep up with her assignments, and her grades fall to an all-time low. Her teachers, who have been monitoring her closely, are alarmed by the rapid decline. They hold meetings to discuss Emily's situation, debating the best course of action. The school counsellor, Ms. Johnson, becomes increasingly involved, trying to build a rapport with Emily and gain her trust. Despite her efforts, Emily remains guarded, her fear of revealing too much holding her back.

The neighbours, too, are on edge. Mrs. Thompson, who has always been a source of support for Emily, feels a growing sense of helplessness. She watches Emily from her window, her heart aching as she sees the young girl's condition worsen. The Patels, who live across the street, discuss the situation in hushed tones, wondering if they should contact social services. The fear of making things worse for Emily holds them back, but the signs of trouble are becoming impossible to ignore.

Emily's home life is a powder keg ready to explode. Her father's drinking has reached new heights, and his absences become more frequent and prolonged. Her mother, overwhelmed by her own depression, retreats further into herself, leaving Emily to fend for herself. The house, once a place of refuge, is now a battleground of tension and neglect. Emily's attempts to maintain a sense of normalcy are met with increasing difficulty, and the weight of her responsibilities becomes unbearable.

The tension reaches a breaking point when Emily's health takes a turn for the worse. She collapses at school one day, her body weakened by malnutrition and exhaustion. The incident sends shockwaves through the school, and the teachers and staff realize that immediate action is necessary. The decision to intervene is made, and the wheels are set in motion to ensure Emily's safety and well-being. The sense of impending crisis is palpable, and the signs of trouble are now impossible to ignore. The tension builds to a crescendo, setting the stage for the intervention that will soon take place. Emily's resilience has carried her this far, but the time has come for those around her to step in and provide the support she so desperately needs.

Chapter 3
The Breaking Point

The tension in Emily's home reaches a boiling point one fateful evening. The house, already filled with an air of unease, becomes the stage for a violent argument between her parents that will change everything.

It starts with a seemingly minor disagreement. Emily's father, returning home late and inebriated, stumbles through the door, his eyes bloodshot and his movements unsteady. Emily's mother, already on edge from her own struggles, confronts him about his drinking. Her voice, usually quiet and subdued, is now filled with anger and frustration. The argument quickly escalates, their voices rising to a fever pitch.

Emily, hiding in her room, hears every word. The walls, thin and worn, do little to muffle the sound of their shouting. Her father's slurred accusations and her mother's desperate pleas echo through the house, creating a cacophony of pain and anger. The argument becomes physical, the sound of breaking glass and thudding footsteps adding to the chaos. Emily's heart races as she listens, fear gripping her tightly.

The neighbours, long aware of the tension in the household, are drawn to the commotion. Mrs. Thompson, hearing the escalating argument, decides that enough is enough. She picks up the phone and dials the police, her hands shaking as she explains the situation. The Patels, across the street, also hear the noise and step outside, their concern growing with each passing moment.

The argument reaches its peak when Emily's father, in a fit of rage, throws a chair across the room. The crash is deafening, and Emily's mother screams in fear. Emily, unable to bear it any longer, runs to the front door and flings it open, hoping to escape the turmoil. She is met by the flashing lights of a police car pulling up to the curb.

The police officers, responding to the neighbours' calls, quickly assess the situation. They separate Emily's parents, trying to calm them down and gather information. Emily, standing on the front lawn, watches in a daze as the officers speak to her parents. The reality of the situation sinks in, and she feels a mix of relief and fear. Relief that the argument has been interrupted, but fear of what will happen next.

The officers, seeing the state of the household and the clear signs of neglect, decide that immediate action is necessary. They call for additional support, including social services, to ensure Emily's safety. The neighbours, watching from their windows and doorsteps, feel a mix of emotions—relief that help has arrived, but also concern for what lies ahead for Emily and her family.

The argument marks a turning point in Emily's life. The intervention that follows will bring significant changes, both challenging and hopeful. The breaking point has been reached, and the path to healing and recovery is about to begin.

The arrival of the police marks a pivotal moment in Emily's life, bringing with it a mix of fear, relief, and uncertainty. The flashing blue lights and the sound of sirens pierce the night, drawing the attention of the entire neighbourhood. As the police cars pull up to the curb, the officers quickly exit their vehicles, assessing the situation with practiced efficiency.

The officers approach the house cautiously, their eyes scanning the scene for any immediate threats. They are met by the sight of Emily's father, dishevelled, and clearly intoxicated, shouting incoherently at Emily's mother, who is cowering in a corner, her face streaked with tears. The tension in the air is palpable, and the officers move swiftly to separate the two, ensuring that the situation does not escalate further.

Emily, standing on the front lawn, watches the scene unfold with a mixture of fear and relief. The presence of the police brings a sense of safety, but also a deep-seated anxiety about what will happen next. One of the officers, noticing Emily's distressed state, approaches her gently, kneeling down to her level. He speaks to her in a calm and reassuring tone, asking her name and if she is okay. Emily, her voice barely above a whisper, tells him her name and nods, though the fear in her eyes is unmistakable.

As the officers begin to piece together the events of the evening, they take note of the condition of the house. The living room is in disarray, with broken furniture and scattered belongings indicating the severity of the argument. The officers also notice the state of neglect that permeates the home—the dirty dishes piled high in the sink, the unwashed clothes strewn about, and the general sense of disrepair.

The officer speaking with Emily gently asks her to show him around the house. Emily hesitates but eventually leads him inside, her small frame dwarfed by the chaos around her. As they move through the house, the officer takes note of the signs of neglect that are all too apparent. Emily's bedroom, though tidier than the rest of the house, is sparse and lacks basic necessities. The bed is unmade, and the few toys she has are worn and broken.

The officer's heart aches as he takes in the full extent of Emily's living conditions. He notices the bruises on her arms and legs, the result of untreated injuries, and the hollow look in her eyes that speaks volumes about the emotional toll of her situation. It is clear to him that Emily has been enduring a great deal of hardship, and he knows that immediate action is necessary to ensure her safety and well-being.

The decision is made to involve social services, and the officers begin the process of documenting the scene and gathering information. Emily's parents are questioned separately, and their responses only confirm the severity of the neglect and abuse. The officers work quickly and efficiently, their priority being to protect Emily and provide her with the support she needs.

As the night progresses, arrangements are made for Emily to be taken into protective custody. The officers explain the situation to her as gently as possible, assuring her that she will be safe and cared for. Emily, though scared and uncertain about what the future holds, feels a glimmer of hope. The arrival of the authorities marks the beginning of a new chapter in her life, one where she will finally receive the care and support, she so desperately needs.

The immediate response of the police and social services to Emily's situation is swift and decisive, aimed at ensuring her safety and well-being.

As the police officers separate Emily's parents and assess the scene, they quickly realize the severity of the situation. The signs of neglect and the chaotic state of the household are undeniable. One officer stays with Emily, offering her comfort and reassurance, while the others continue to gather information and document the scene.

The officer with Emily gently explains that they are there to help and that she will be taken to a safe place. Emily, though scared and uncertain, nods in understanding. The officer's calm and kind demeanour helps to ease her anxiety, providing a small measure of comfort amidst the turmoil.

Social services are contacted immediately, and a social worker arrives at the scene within a short time. The social worker, Ms. Harris, is experienced and compassionate, well-versed in handling situations like Emily's. She introduces herself to Emily, speaking in a soothing tone and explaining that she is there to help. Ms. Harris takes the time to listen to Emily, asking gentle questions to understand her situation better.

As Ms. Harris speaks with Emily, the police officers continue their investigation. They take statements from Emily's parents, documenting the details of the argument and the signs of neglect. The officers also take photographs of the house, capturing the disarray and the physical evidence of the neglect. Their thorough documentation will be crucial in ensuring that Emily receives the support she needs.

Ms. Harris, after assessing the situation, decides that it is in Emily's best interest to be removed from the home immediately. She explains to Emily that she will be taken to a safe place where she will be cared for and looked after. Emily, though apprehensive, understands that this is necessary. The thought of leaving her parents and her home is daunting, but the promise of safety and care provides a glimmer of hope.

Arrangements are made for Emily to be placed in temporary foster care. Ms. Harris assures Emily that she will be placed with a kind and caring family who will look after her. She also explains that they will work to ensure that Emily's needs are met and that she will receive the support and care she deserves.

As Emily is escorted to the waiting social services vehicle, she looks back at her house one last time. The flashing lights of the police cars and the presence of the officers and social worker mark a turning point in her life. The immediate response of the authorities and social services sets the stage for the intervention and support that Emily so desperately needs.

The swift and decisive actions of the police and social services provide Emily with a sense of safety and hope. Though the road ahead will be challenging, the immediate response ensures that she is no longer alone in her struggles. Emily's journey towards healing and recovery has begun, and she is now surrounded by people who are dedicated to helping her find a better future.

As the intervention unfolds, Emily's fear and confusion are palpable. The sudden arrival of the police and social services, the flashing lights, and the raised voices create a whirlwind of emotions that she struggles to process.

Emily stands on the front lawn, her small frame trembling as she watches the police officers separate her parents. The sight of her father being restrained and her mother sobbing uncontrollably fills her with a deep sense of dread. She feels a knot tighten in her stomach, her heart pounding in her chest. The familiar surroundings of her home now seem alien and threatening, and she feels an overwhelming urge to run and hide.

The officer who approaches Emily speaks to her in a calm and reassuring tone, but his presence is still intimidating. Emily's mind races with questions and fears. What will happen to her parents? Where will she go? Will she ever see her home again? The uncertainty of the situation amplifies her anxiety, and she feels tears welling up in her eyes.

When the social worker, Ms. Harris, arrives, Emily's fear intensifies. Ms. Harris's kind demeanour and gentle words are meant to comfort, but Emily's trust has been shattered by the neglect and chaos she has endured. She listens to Ms. Harris explain that she will be taken to a safe place, but the words feel distant and unreal. The thought of leaving her parents, despite their flaws, is terrifying. They are the only family she has ever known, and the idea of being separated from them fills her with a profound sense of loss.

As Emily is led to the social services vehicle, she glances back at her house, the place that has been both a source of pain and a semblance of stability. The sight of her parents being questioned by the police is a stark reminder of the reality she is leaving behind. The fear of the unknown looms large, and Emily feels a wave of panic wash over her. She clutches her worn-out teddy bear, Mr. Snuggles, seeking comfort in its familiar presence.

The ride to the temporary foster home is filled with silence, broken only by the occasional reassuring words from Ms. Harris. Emily stares out the window, her mind a whirlwind of thoughts and emotions. The fear of what lies ahead is overwhelming, and she feels a deep sense of confusion about why this is happening to her. She wonders if she did something wrong, if she is to blame for the chaos that has engulfed her life.

Despite the fear and confusion, there is a small glimmer of hope within Emily. The promise of safety and care, though difficult to believe, offers a faint light in the darkness. She clings to this hope, even as her mind is filled with questions and uncertainties. The intervention marks the beginning of a new chapter in her life, one that is fraught with challenges but also holds the potential for healing and recovery.

The intervention at Emily's home does not go unnoticed by the neighbours, who react with a mix of concern, relief, and curiosity. The flashing lights of the police cars and the presence of social services draw the attention of the entire neighbourhood, creating a sense of urgency and unease.

Mrs. Thompson, who had called the police, watches from her window with a heavy heart. She feels a deep sense of relief that help has finally arrived for Emily, but also a pang of guilt for not intervening sooner. As she sees Emily being led to the social services vehicle, she silently prays that the young girl will find the safety and care she so desperately needs. Mrs. Thompson's eyes well up with tears, a mix of sadness and hope for Emily's future.

The Patels, who live across the street, step outside to get a closer look at the unfolding scene. They exchange worried glances, their concern for Emily evident. Mr. Patel shakes his head, muttering about how he had suspected something was wrong but never imagined it was this severe. Mrs. Patel clutches her husband's arm, her eyes fixed on Emily. She feels a maternal instinct to protect the young girl but knows that the authorities are now in charge. The Patels hope that this intervention will lead to a better life for Emily.

Other neighbours gather on their porches and lawns, whispering among themselves. The sight of the police and social services is both alarming and reassuring. They discuss the signs they had noticed over the past months—the dishevelled appearance, the bruises, the isolation—and wonder if they should have done more to help. The intervention serves as a wake-up call, a reminder of the importance of community vigilance and support.

Some neighbours feel a sense of vindication, having long suspected that something was amiss in Emily's home. They had seen the signs but were unsure how to act. The intervention confirms their fears and reinforces the need for collective responsibility in looking out for one another. They resolve to be more proactive in the future, to ensure that no child in their community suffers in silence.

As the police and social services continue their work, the neighbours remain watchful. They are filled with a mix of emotions—relief that Emily is finally receiving help, sadness for the pain she has endured, and hope for her future. The intervention has brought the community together, united in their concern for Emily and their desire to see her safe and cared for.

The reactions of the neighbours highlight the impact of the intervention not just on Emily, but on the entire community. It serves as a powerful reminder of the importance of vigilance, compassion, and collective action in ensuring the well-being of the most vulnerable among us.

The initial investigation by social services into Emily's situation is thorough and meticulous, aimed at understanding the full extent of the neglect and ensuring her immediate safety.

Upon arriving at the scene, Ms. Harris, the social worker, begins by conducting a detailed assessment of the household. She takes note of the physical condition of the home, documenting the disarray and signs of neglect. The broken furniture, dirty dishes, and general state of disrepair are clear indicators of the chaotic environment Emily has been living in. Ms. Harris also observes the lack of basic necessities, such as food and clean clothing, which further highlight the severity of the neglect.

Ms. Harris then speaks with Emily's parents separately to gather more information. Emily's father, still under the influence of alcohol, is uncooperative and defensive. He denies any wrongdoing and blames his behaviour on stress and external factors. Emily's mother, on the other hand, is more forthcoming but clearly overwhelmed by her own struggles with depression. She admits that she has been unable to provide the care and attention Emily needs, citing her own mental health issues as a significant barrier.

The social worker also takes the time to speak with Emily, ensuring that she feels safe and supported. Emily, though hesitant at first, gradually opens up about her experiences. She describes the frequent arguments between her parents, the lack of food, and the emotional neglect she has endured. Her account provides a heartbreaking glimpse into the daily challenges she faces and underscores the urgent need for intervention.

Ms. Harris documents all her findings meticulously, noting the physical and emotional signs of neglect. She takes photographs of the home and records her observations in a detailed report. The evidence gathered during this initial investigation will be crucial in determining the next steps and ensuring that Emily receives the support she needs.

Based on her findings, Ms. Harris concludes that Emily's living conditions are unsafe and that immediate action is necessary. She arranges for Emily to be placed in temporary foster care, where she will be provided with a safe and nurturing environment. The decision is made to initiate a more comprehensive investigation into the family's situation, including assessments of Emily's parents' ability to provide adequate care and support.

The initial investigation by social services is a critical step in ensuring Emily's safety and well-being. It provides a clear and detailed picture of the neglect she has endured and sets the stage for the necessary interventions to support her recovery and future well-being.

From Emily's perspective, the events of that night are a whirlwind of emotions and confusion. The sudden arrival of the police and social services, the flashing lights, and the raised voices create a chaotic scene that she struggles to comprehend.

As she stands on the front lawn, Emily feels a mix of fear and relief. The sight of her father being restrained and her mother's tear-streaked face fills her with dread. She clutches her scruffy teddy bear, Mr. Snuggles, seeking comfort in its familiar presence. The officer who approaches her speaks gently, but his uniform and authoritative demeanour are intimidating. Emily's heart races, and she feels a knot tighten in her stomach.

When the social worker, Ms. Harris, arrives, Emily's anxiety intensifies. Ms. Harris's kind words and gentle tone are meant to reassure her, but Emily's trust has been shattered by the neglect and chaos she has endured. She listens to Ms. Harris explain that she will be taken to a safe place, but the words feel distant and unreal. The thought of leaving her parents, despite their flaws, is terrifying. They are the only family she has ever known, and the idea of being separated from them fills her with a profound sense of loss.

As Emily is led to the social services vehicle, she glances back at her house, the place that has been both a source of pain and a semblance of stability. The flashing lights of the police cars and the presence of the officers and social worker mark a turning point in her life. The fear of the unknown looms large, and Emily feels a wave of panic wash over her. She wonders what will happen to her parents and if she will ever see them again.

During the ride to the temporary foster home, Emily's mind is a whirlwind of thoughts and emotions. She stares out the window, her eyes wide with fear and uncertainty. The fear of what lies ahead is overwhelming, and she feels a deep sense of confusion about why this is happening to her. She wonders if she did something wrong, if she is to blame for the chaos that has engulfed her life.

Despite the fear and confusion, there is a small glimmer of hope within Emily. The promise of safety and care, though difficult to believe, offers a faint light in the darkness. She clings to this hope, even as her mind is filled with questions and uncertainties. The intervention marks the beginning of a new chapter in her life, one that is fraught with challenges but also holds the potential for healing and recovery.

Emily's perspective on the events is a mix of fear, confusion, and a fragile hope. The intervention is a tumultuous experience, but it also represents a chance for a better future. Her journey towards healing and recovery has begun, and she is now surrounded by people who are dedicated to helping her find a brighter path.

The decision to intervene and take Emily into care is made with a heavy heart but with the clear understanding that it is necessary for her safety and well-being. The findings from the initial investigation by social services leave no doubt about the severity of the neglect and the urgent need for action.

Ms. Harris, the social worker, reviews her detailed report, which documents the chaotic state of the household, the lack of basic necessities, and the emotional and physical neglect Emily has endured. The evidence is compelling and paints a stark picture of the environment Emily has been living in. The decision to remove her from this harmful situation is not taken lightly, but it is clear that immediate intervention is essential.

Emily's parents are informed of the decision, and while her mother reacts with a mix of sorrow and resignation, her father's response is one of anger and denial. The police officers present ensure that the situation remains under control, providing support to Ms. Harris as she explains the next steps. Emily's mother, though devastated, acknowledges that she is unable to provide the care Emily needs and reluctantly agrees to the intervention.

Emily, though filled with fear and uncertainty, understands that this decision is meant to protect her. The promise of a safe and nurturing environment offers a glimmer of hope amidst the turmoil. Ms. Harris reassures Emily that she will be placed with a caring foster family who will look after her and provide the support she needs. Emily clings to this hope, even as she grapples with the emotions of leaving her parents and the only home she has ever known.

The neighbours, who have been watching the events unfold, feel a mix of relief and sadness. They understand the necessity of the intervention but are deeply moved by the sight of Emily being taken into care. Their concern for her well-being is palpable, and they silently hope that this marks the beginning of a better future for her.

As Emily is escorted to the social services vehicle, she takes one last look at her house. The flashing lights of the police cars and the presence of the officers and social worker mark a turning point in her life. The decision to intervene sets the stage for the next chapter in Emily's journey—a chapter filled with challenges but also the potential for healing and recovery.

The intervention is a critical step in ensuring Emily's safety and well-being. It marks the beginning of a new path, one where she will receive the care and support, she so desperately needs. The decision to take Emily into care is a difficult but necessary one, setting the stage for her journey towards a brighter and more hopeful future.

Chapter 4
Taken into Care

The decision-making process of social services to remove Emily from her home is a careful and thorough one, driven by the need to ensure her safety and well-being. The process begins with the initial investigation conducted by Ms. Harris, the social worker, who meticulously documents the signs of neglect and the chaotic state of the household.

Ms. Harris's report includes detailed observations of the physical condition of the home, the lack of basic necessities, and the emotional and physical neglect Emily has endured. She notes the disarray in the house, the broken furniture, the dirty dishes, and the general state of disrepair. The evidence of neglect is clear and compelling, painting a stark picture of the environment Emily has been living in.

In addition to her observations, Ms. Harris conducts interviews with Emily's parents to gather more information. Emily's father, still under the influence of alcohol, is uncooperative and defensive, denying any wrongdoing and blaming his behaviour on external factors. Emily's mother, overwhelmed by her own struggles with depression, admits that she has been unable to provide the care and attention Emily needs. These interviews provide further insight into the family's situation and underscore the urgent need for intervention.

Ms. Harris also speaks with Emily, ensuring that she feels safe and supported. Emily's account of her experiences, though hesitant at first, provides a heartbreaking glimpse into the daily challenges she faces. She describes the frequent arguments between her parents, the lack of food, and the emotional neglect she has endured. Emily's testimony is a crucial part of the decision-making process, highlighting the severity of her situation.

Based on the findings from the initial investigation, Ms. Harris concludes that Emily's living conditions are unsafe, and that immediate action is necessary. She consults with her colleagues and supervisors, presenting her report and the evidence she has gathered. The team reviews the information carefully, considering the best course of action to ensure Emily's safety and well-being.

The decision to remove Emily from her home is not taken lightly. The team understands the emotional impact this will have on Emily and her family, but they also recognize that her current environment is harmful and unsustainable. The priority is to provide Emily with a safe and nurturing environment where she can receive the care and support she needs.

Once the decision is made, Ms. Harris arranges for Emily to be placed in temporary foster care. She explains the situation to Emily as gently as possible, assuring her that she will be taken to a safe place where she will be cared for. Emily, though filled with fear and uncertainty, understands that this decision is meant to protect her.

The decision-making process of social services is a critical step in ensuring Emily's safety and well-being. It is a careful and thorough process, driven by the need to provide her with the support and care she so desperately needs. The decision to take Emily into care sets the stage for the next chapter in her journey, one that holds the potential for healing and recovery.

The moment of Emily's departure from her home is filled with a mix of emotions, both for her and her parents. The decision to remove her from the household has been made, and now it is time to put that decision into action.

As the social worker, Ms. Harris, gently explains to Emily that she will be taken to a safe place, Emily feels a wave of fear and uncertainty wash over her. She clutches her worn-out teddy bear, Mr. Snuggles, tightly to her chest, seeking comfort in its familiar presence. The thought of leaving her parents and the only home she has ever known is overwhelming, and tears well up in her eyes.

Emily's mother, though devastated by the situation, tries to maintain her composure. She watches with a mix of sorrow and resignation as Ms. Harris helps Emily gather a few belongings. Her eyes are filled with tears, and she struggles to find the words to reassure her daughter. The weight of her own struggles and the realization that she has been unable to provide the care Emily needs weigh heavily on her heart.

Emily's father, still under the influence of alcohol, reacts with anger and denial. He shouts at the social worker, accusing her of overstepping her bounds and insisting that everything is fine. His words are slurred, and his movements are unsteady, but the anger in his voice is clear. The police officers present step in to ensure that the situation remains under control, keeping a close watch on him to prevent any further escalation.

As Emily is led out of the house, she takes one last look at her parents. Her mother, standing in the doorway, gives her a tearful wave, while her father continues to shout and protest. The sight of her parents in such a state is heart-wrenching, and Emily feels a deep sense of loss and confusion. She wonders if she will ever see them again and what the future holds for her.

The social services vehicle is waiting outside, and Ms. Harris gently guides Emily towards it. The neighbours, who have been watching the events unfold, look on with a mix of concern and relief. They understand the necessity of the intervention but are deeply moved by the sight of Emily being taken into care. Their hearts ache for the young girl, and they silently hope that this marks the beginning of a better future for her.

As the vehicle pulls away from the curb, Emily feels a mix of emotions. The fear of the unknown looms large, but there is also a small glimmer of hope. The promise of safety and care, though difficult to believe, offers a faint light in the darkness. Emily clings to this hope, even as her mind is filled with questions and uncertainties.

The departure from her home marks the beginning of a new chapter in Emily's life. It is a difficult and emotional moment, but it also holds the potential for healing and recovery. Emily's journey towards a brighter and more hopeful future has begun, and she is now surrounded by people who are dedicated to helping her find her way.

Emily's arrival at the social services office is a moment filled with trepidation and uncertainty. The journey from her home to the office is a blur of emotions, and as the vehicle pulls up to the building, Emily's heart races with anxiety.

Ms. Harris, the social worker, gently guides Emily out of the car and into the office. The building is a stark contrast to the chaotic environment she has just left behind. It is clean and orderly, with bright lights and a calm atmosphere. Despite the reassuring surroundings, Emily feels a knot of fear tighten in her stomach. She clutches Mr. Snuggles, her worn-out teddy bear, even tighter, seeking comfort in its familiar presence.

Inside the office, Emily is greeted by a receptionist who offers her a warm smile. The receptionist's kind demeanour helps to ease some of Emily's anxiety, but she remains wary and uncertain. Ms. Harris leads Emily to a small, comfortable room where they can talk privately. The room is furnished with soft chairs and a table, and there are colourful posters on the walls depicting happy children and families. The sight of these images brings a mix of hope and sadness to Emily's heart.

Ms. Harris sits down with Emily and begins to explain what will happen next. She speaks in a calm and soothing tone, reassuring Emily that she is safe and that they are there to help her. Emily listens intently, her eyes wide with a mix of fear and curiosity. She nods occasionally, trying to absorb the information, but her mind is still reeling from the events of the evening.

As they talk, another caseworker enters the room. Her name is Ms. Roberts, and she introduces herself with a gentle smile. Ms. Roberts has a warm and approachable demeanour, and she takes a seat next to Emily. She asks Emily a few questions about her likes and dislikes, trying to get to know her better. Emily answers hesitantly at first, but Ms. Roberts friendly manner helps to put her at ease.

Ms. Roberts explains that they will be finding a temporary foster home for Emily, where she will be cared for and looked after. She reassures Emily that the foster family has been carefully chosen and that they are kind and understanding. Emily listens, her fear slowly giving way to a glimmer of hope. The promise of a safe and nurturing environment is something she has longed for, and she clings to the possibility that things might get better.

The initial interactions with the caseworkers are a crucial step in helping Emily feel safe and supported. Ms. Harris and Ms. Roberts compassionate and understanding approach helps to ease some of her fears and provides her with a sense of stability. Emily's journey towards healing and recovery has begun, and she is now surrounded by people who are dedicated to helping her find a brighter future.

Emily's confusion and fear about being taken away from her parents are overwhelming. The sudden intervention by social services and the police has turned her world upside down, leaving her grappling with a whirlwind of emotions.

As she sits in the social services office, clutching her teddy bear, Mr. Snuggles, Emily's mind races with questions. Why is this happening? What did she do wrong? The explanations given by the social workers, though kind and gentle, feel distant and unreal. The words "safe place" and "care" are hard to grasp when all she can think about is the home she has just left behind.

Emily's fear is palpable. The thought of being separated from her parents, despite their flaws, is terrifying. They are the only family she has ever known, and the idea of being taken away from them fills her with a profound sense of loss. She wonders if she will ever see them again and what will happen to them without her. The uncertainty of the situation amplifies her anxiety, and she feels tears welling up in her eyes.

The unfamiliar surroundings of the social services office add to her confusion. The bright lights, the strange faces, and the unfamiliar sounds create a sense of disorientation. Emily feels like she is in a different world, far removed from the chaotic but familiar environment of her home. The kind words and reassuring smiles of the social workers provide some comfort, but they cannot fully alleviate her fear and confusion.

Emily's thoughts are a jumble of emotions. She feels a deep sense of guilt, wondering if she is to blame for the intervention. Did she do something wrong to cause this? The weight of these thoughts is heavy, and she struggles to make sense of them. The fear of the unknown looms large, and she feels a wave of panic wash over her.

Despite the fear and confusion, there is a small glimmer of hope within Emily. The promise of safety and care, though difficult to believe, offers a faint light in the darkness. She clings to this hope, even as her mind is filled with questions and uncertainties. The intervention marks the beginning of a new chapter in her life, one that is fraught with challenges but also holds the potential for healing and recovery.

Emily's confusion and fear are a natural response to the sudden and dramatic changes in her life. The journey ahead will be difficult, but with the support and care of the social workers and her new foster family, she will begin to find her way towards a brighter and more hopeful future.

Emily's temporary placement in an emergency foster home is a significant step in her journey towards safety and stability. After the initial assessment at the social services office, arrangements are made for her to stay with a foster family who can provide the care and support she needs.

The drive to the foster home is filled with a mix of emotions for Emily. She stares out the window, her mind a whirlwind of thoughts and fears. The unfamiliar surroundings and the uncertainty of what lies ahead weigh heavily on her. Ms. Harris, the social worker, sits beside her, offering gentle reassurances and explaining what to expect. Emily listens, but her anxiety remains palpable.

Upon arriving at the foster home, Emily is greeted by Mrs. Collins, a kind and nurturing woman who has been a foster parent for many years. Mrs. Collins welcomes Emily with a warm smile and a gentle hug, immediately putting her at ease. The house is cozy and inviting, a stark contrast to the chaotic environment Emily has just left behind. The sight of the tidy living room, the soft lighting, and the comforting smells of home-cooked food provide a sense of safety and comfort.

Mrs. Collins shows Emily to her room, a small but cozy space decorated with cheerful colours and soft furnishings. There is a bed with fresh linens, a dresser, and a small desk with a lamp. The room feels warm and inviting, and Emily is touched by the effort that has been made to make her feel welcome. She places Mr. Snuggles, her worn-out teddy bear, on the bed, finding comfort in its familiar presence.

As Emily settles into her new surroundings, Mrs. Collins

explains the house rules and routines in a gentle and understanding manner. She reassures Emily that she is safe and that they are there to support her. Emily listens attentively, her fear slowly giving way to a sense of relief. The promise of a stable and nurturing environment offers a glimmer of hope amidst the uncertainty.

Over the next few days, Emily begins to adjust to her new life in the foster home. Mrs. Collins and her family are kind and patient, providing Emily with the care and attention she has longed for. They include her in family activities, such as meals and outings, helping her to feel like a part of the family. Emily's initial apprehension gradually fades, replaced by a growing sense of belonging and security.

The temporary placement in the foster home is a crucial step in Emily's journey towards healing and recovery. It provides her with a safe and nurturing environment where she can begin to rebuild her sense of self and find hope for the future. The support and care she receives from Mrs. Collins and her family help to ease her fears and provide a foundation for her to thrive.

Emily's adjustment period in the new foster home is a time of significant change and adaptation. The transition from her chaotic home environment to a stable and nurturing setting is both challenging and transformative.

In the first few days, Emily is understandably apprehensive. The unfamiliar surroundings and the presence of new faces make her feel uneasy. Mrs. Collins, her foster mother, is patient and understanding, giving Emily the space she needs to acclimate. She encourages Emily to explore her new room and the house at her own pace, reassuring her that she is safe and welcome.

Emily's interactions with the other children in the foster home are initially tentative. There are two other foster children, Sarah and Jake, who have been with the Collins family for several months. Sarah, a few years older than Emily, is kind and welcoming, while Jake, who is around Emily's age, is more reserved. Emily observes them from a distance, unsure of how to approach them.

Mrs. Collins facilitates gentle introductions, encouraging the children to play together and share their interests. She organizes group activities, such as board games and outdoor play, to help them bond. Emily, though shy at first, gradually begins to open up. She finds comfort in the structured routines and the consistent care provided by Mrs. Collins.

One afternoon, while playing in the backyard, Sarah invites Emily to join her in a game of hopscotch. Emily hesitates but eventually agrees, her curiosity overcoming her shyness. The simple game becomes a turning point, as Emily starts to feel more comfortable interacting with Sarah and Jake. The laughter and camaraderie they share help to ease her anxiety and build her confidence.

As the days go by, Emily's adjustment continues. She begins to participate more actively in family activities, such as mealtimes and outings. Mrs. Collins notices Emily's growing confidence and encourages her to express herself. Emily starts to share her thoughts and feelings, finding solace in the supportive environment.

Emily's adjustment period is not without its challenges. She occasionally experiences moments of sadness and fear, missing her parents and the familiarity of her old life. Mrs. Collins is attentive to these moments, offering comfort and reassurance. She encourages Emily to talk about her feelings and provides a safe space for her to express her emotions.

The interactions with Sarah and Jake also play a crucial role in Emily's adjustment. They become her companions and confidants, helping her to navigate the complexities of her new life. The bond they form is a source of strength and support, providing Emily with a sense of belonging and community.

Emily's adjustment period in the foster home is a journey of healing and growth. The supportive and nurturing environment helps her to rebuild her sense of self and find hope for the future. The interactions with Mrs. Collins and the other children provide her with the stability and care she needs to thrive.

Emily's adjustment to her new environment is closely monitored through regular visits from her caseworker, Ms. Harris. These visits are crucial for assessing Emily's well-being and ensuring that she is receiving the care and support she needs.

Ms. Harris schedules her first visit a few days after Emily's placement in the foster home. She arrives with a warm smile and a gentle demeanour, immediately putting Emily at ease. Mrs. Collins welcomes her into the home, and they sit down together to discuss Emily's progress. Emily, though still a bit apprehensive, feels a sense of comfort in Ms. Harris's presence.

During the visit, Ms. Harris takes the time to speak with Emily privately. They sit in Emily's room, a cozy space that has quickly become her sanctuary. Ms. Harris asks Emily how she is feeling and if she has any concerns or questions. Emily, holding Mr. Snuggles tightly, shares her thoughts and feelings. She talks about her initial fears and how she is slowly adjusting to her new surroundings. Ms. Harris listens attentively, offering reassurance and support.

Ms. Harris also observes Emily's interactions with Mrs. Collins and the other children in the foster home. She notes the positive dynamics and the efforts made by Mrs. Collins to create a nurturing environment. Emily's growing bond with Sarah and Jake is evident, and Ms. Harris is pleased to see Emily participating in family activities and forming connections.

The caseworker visits continue on a regular basis, each one providing an opportunity to assess Emily's progress and address any concerns. Ms. Harris keeps detailed notes on Emily's physical and emotional well-being, her academic performance, and her social interactions. She collaborates closely with Mrs. Collins, ensuring that Emily's needs are being met and that she is
thriving in her new environment.

Emily's adjustment is not without its challenges, and Ms. Harris is there to provide guidance and support. She helps Emily navigate her feelings of loss and confusion, encouraging her to express her emotions and seek comfort in the supportive environment of the foster home. Ms. Harris also works with Emily's teachers to ensure that she receives the necessary academic support and that her educational needs are addressed.

The ongoing assessment of Emily's situation is a collaborative effort, involving regular communication between Ms. Harris, Mrs. Collins, and other professionals involved in Emily's care. This comprehensive approach ensures that Emily's well-being is prioritized and that any issues are promptly addressed.

Through these regular visits and assessments, Emily begins to feel a sense of stability and security. The consistent support from Ms.

Harris and the nurturing environment provided by Mrs. Collins help her to heal and grow. Emily's journey towards a brighter future is marked by the dedication and care of those around her, ensuring that she is never alone in her struggles.

As Emily begins to settle into her temporary foster home, the preparations for her placement in a more permanent foster home are set in motion. The goal is to ensure that Emily finds a stable and nurturing environment where she can continue to heal and thrive.

Ms. Harris, the social worker, works diligently to identify a suitable foster family for Emily. She reviews the profiles of several potential families, considering factors such as their experience, the presence of other children, and their ability to provide the emotional and physical support Emily needs. The process is thorough and meticulous, aimed at finding the best possible match for Emily's long-term well-being.

During this time, Ms. Harris continues her regular visits to the temporary foster home, closely monitoring Emily's progress. She speaks with Mrs. Collins and the other children, gathering insights into Emily's adjustment and overall well-being. Emily's growing confidence and sense of security are encouraging signs, and Ms. Harris is pleased with the positive environment Mrs. Collins has created.

Emily is kept informed about the process, with Ms. Harris explaining each step in a way that is easy for her to understand. She reassures Emily that the goal is to find a family where she can feel safe, loved, and supported. Emily listens attentively, her initial fears gradually giving way to a cautious optimism. The promise of a permanent home offers a glimmer of hope, and she begins to look forward to the possibility of a brighter future.

As the search for a permanent foster family progresses, Ms. Harris arranges for Emily to meet with potential families. These meetings are carefully planned to ensure that Emily feels comfortable and supported. The first few meetings are nerve-wracking for Emily, but Ms. Harris is always by her side, offering reassurance and encouragement. Emily's interactions with the potential families are positive, and she begins to feel a sense of connection with some of them.

After several meetings, Ms. Harris identifies a family that she believes is the perfect match for Emily. The Johnsons, a kind and experienced foster family, have a warm and welcoming home. They have two children of their own and have fostered several children over the years. Their compassionate and understanding nature makes them an ideal choice for Emily's long-term placement.

Ms. Harris arranges for Emily to spend a weekend with the Johnsons, giving her a chance to experience life in their home. The weekend is filled with activities and bonding moments, and Emily feels a sense of belonging for which she has longed. The Johnsons are patient and attentive, making sure that Emily feels comfortable and included. By the end of the weekend, Emily is excited about the prospect of joining their family.

The preparations for Emily's placement in the Johnsons' home are finalized, and a date is set for her move. Ms. Harris ensures that all necessary paperwork is completed, and that Emily's transition is as smooth as possible. She continues to provide support and guidance, helping Emily navigate the emotions and uncertainties of the move.

The day of the move arrives, and Emily is filled with a mix of excitement and nervousness. Mrs. Collins helps her pack her belongings, offering words of encouragement and reassurance. Emily says her goodbyes, grateful for the care and support she has received in the temporary foster home.

As Emily steps into the Johnsons' home, she feels a sense of hope and possibility. The journey has been challenging, but she is now surrounded by people who are dedicated to helping her heal and thrive. The preparations for her placement in a more permanent foster home mark the beginning of a new chapter in Emily's life, one filled with the promise of stability, love, and a brighter future.

Chapter 5
The Foster Home

Emily's introduction to the Johnsons marks the beginning of a new chapter in her life. The Johnson family, known for their warmth and compassion, welcomes Emily with open arms, providing her with the stability and care she so desperately needs.

The Johnsons' home is a cozy, two-story house nestled in a quiet neighbourhood. The front yard is well-maintained, with a garden filled with colourful flowers and a swing hanging from a sturdy oak tree. The house exudes a sense of warmth and comfort, a stark contrast to the chaotic environment Emily has left behind.

Mr. and Mrs. Johnson are experienced foster parents who have dedicated their lives to providing a safe and nurturing environment for children in need. Mr. Johnson, a tall man with a kind smile and a gentle demeanour, works as a high school teacher. He has a passion for education and enjoys helping children reach their full potential. His calm and patient nature makes him a reassuring presence in the household.

Mrs. Johnson, a warm and nurturing woman with a heart of gold, is a stay-at-home mum who dedicates her time to caring for the children. She has a natural ability to make everyone feel welcome and loved. Her gentle voice and comforting hugs provide a sense of security for Emily. Mrs. Johnson is also an excellent cook, and the delicious aromas of home-cooked meals often fill the house, creating a comforting and inviting atmosphere.

The Johnsons have two biological children, Emma and Finn, who are both in their early teens. Emma, a bright and cheerful girl with a love for reading and art, is excited to welcome Emily into their home. She quickly takes Emily under her wing, showing her around the house and introducing her to their daily routines. Finn, a friendly and energetic boy who loves sports and outdoor activities, is equally welcoming. He invites Emily to join him in playing football in the backyard, helping her feel included and part of the family.

The Johnson household is filled with laughter and love. The family enjoys spending time together, whether it's playing board games, watching movies, or going on weekend outings. They have a strong sense of togetherness and support each other through thick and thin. This sense of unity and care is exactly what Emily needs to begin her journey towards healing and recovery.

As Emily settles into her new home, she begins to feel a sense of belonging and security. The Johnsons' warmth and kindness help to ease her fears and provide her with the stability she has longed for. The transition is not without its challenges, but with the support of the Johnson family, Emily starts to find hope and happiness in her new environment.

Emily's first impressions of the Johnsons and their home are a mix of awe, relief, and cautious optimism. As she steps into the cozy, two-story house, she is immediately struck by the warmth and comfort that radiate from every corner. The front yard, with its colourful flowers and inviting swing, sets the tone for the welcoming environment she is about to enter.

The Johnsons greet Emily with open arms. Mr. Johnson, with his kind smile and gentle demeanour, immediately puts her at ease. His calm presence is reassuring, and Emily feels a sense of safety that she hasn't experienced in a long time. Mrs. Johnson's warm hug and soothing voice provide an instant sense of comfort. Her nurturing nature is evident, and Emily is touched by the genuine care and concern she feels from her new foster mother.

The house itself is a stark contrast to the chaotic environment Emily has left behind. The living room is tidy and inviting, with soft lighting and comfortable furniture. The walls are adorned with family photos and artwork, creating a sense of warmth, and belonging. The delicious aroma of home-cooked food wafts through the air, adding to the comforting atmosphere.

Emily's new room is a small but cozy space, decorated with

cheerful colours and soft furnishings. The bed, with its fresh linens and fluffy pillows, looks incredibly inviting. A small desk with a lamp and a dresser complete the room, making it feel like a true sanctuary. Emily places Mr. Snuggles, her worn-out teddy bear, on the bed, finding comfort in its familiar presence.

Emma and Finn, the Johnsons' children, are equally welcoming. Emma's bright and cheerful personality immediately puts Emily at ease. She shows Emily around the house, explaining the daily routines and making her feel included. Finn's friendly and energetic nature helps to break the ice, and he invites Emily to join him in playing football in the backyard. Their genuine kindness and enthusiasm help Emily feel like she is part of the family.

As Emily settles into her new environment, she begins to feel a sense of hope and possibility. The Johnsons' warmth and kindness provide a stark contrast to the neglect and chaos she has experienced. The structured routines and consistent care help to ease her fears and provide a sense of stability. Emily's first impressions of the Johnsons and their home are overwhelmingly positive, and she begins to believe that she might finally have found a place where she can heal and thrive.

Emily's transition to the Johnsons' foster home, while filled with hope and warmth, is not without its initial challenges. Adjusting to a new environment, even one as welcoming as the Johnsons,' brings its own set of difficulties for Emily.

One of the first challenges Emily faces is adapting to the structured routines of the Johnson household. The predictability and order are a stark contrast to the chaotic and unpredictable environment she has left behind. While the routines provide a sense of stability, Emily initially struggles to adjust. Simple tasks like waking up at a set time, following a schedule for meals, and adhering to bedtime routines feel foreign and overwhelming. The Johnsons, understanding her background, are patient and gentle, helping her gradually acclimate to the new structure.

Another significant challenge is building trust and forming connections with the Johnson family. Emily's past experiences have left her wary and guarded, making it difficult for her to open up and trust others. She is hesitant to share her thoughts and feelings, fearing judgment or rejection. The Johnsons, particularly Mrs. Johnson, work hard to create a safe and supportive environment, encouraging Emily to express herself at her own pace. They understand that building trust takes time and are committed to being patient and understanding.

Emily also faces challenges in her interactions with Emma and Finn. While they are welcoming and kind, Emily's initial shyness and fear of rejection make it difficult for her to fully engage with them. She often feels like an outsider, unsure of how to join in their activities or conversations. Emma and Finn, sensing her hesitation, make extra efforts to include her, inviting her to play games, join family outings, and participate in household chores. Their consistent kindness and inclusivity help Emily slowly start to feel more comfortable and accepted.

The emotional toll of her past experiences also presents a significant challenge for Emily. She carries with her the weight of neglect and trauma, which manifests in moments of sadness, anxiety, and fear. Nightmares and flashbacks are common, disrupting her sleep and leaving her feeling exhausted and vulnerable. Mrs. Johnson, with her nurturing nature, provides comfort and reassurance during these difficult times, helping Emily feel safe and supported.

Academically, Emily faces challenges as well. The disruption in her education due to her unstable home life has left her behind in her studies. She struggles to keep up with her schoolwork and feels overwhelmed by the expectations. The Johnsons, recognizing her potential, work closely with her teachers to provide the necessary support and resources. They encourage Emily to take things one step at a time, celebrating her progress and helping her build confidence in her abilities.

Despite these initial challenges, Emily's resilience, and the unwavering support of the Johnson family help her navigate this difficult transition. Each small victory, whether it's adjusting to a routine, forming a new friendship, or overcoming a fear, is a step towards healing and growth. The journey is not easy, but with the love and care of the Johnsons, Emily begins to find her footing and look forward to a brighter future.

The Johnson household operates on a foundation of structure and consistency, which provides a sense of stability and security for all the children in their care. The rules and routines are designed to create a nurturing environment where everyone feels safe and supported.

The day begins with a structured morning routine. The children wake up at 7:00 AM, giving them enough time to get ready for school. Breakfast is a family affair, with everyone gathering around the kitchen table to share a meal. Mrs. Johnson prepares a variety of healthy options, ensuring that everyone starts their day with a nutritious breakfast. This routine helps Emily feel a sense of normalcy and sets a positive tone for the day.

After breakfast, the children head off to school. Emily is enrolled in the local school, where she receives additional support to help her catch up academically. The Johnsons maintain close communication with her teachers to monitor her progress and address any challenges. After school, there is a designated time for homework and study. The Johnsons provide a quiet and supportive environment, helping Emily develop good study habits and stay on track with her assignments.

The Johnson household operates on a system of shared responsibilities. Each child has specific chores to complete, such as setting the table, tidying their rooms, or helping with laundry. These chores are age-appropriate and designed to teach responsibility and teamwork. Emily is initially hesitant about the chores, but with gentle encouragement from Mrs. Johnson, she begins to take pride in her contributions to the household.

Evenings are reserved for family time. The Johnsons believe in the importance of spending quality time together, whether it's playing board games, watching movies, or going for walks. This time helps to strengthen the bonds between family members and provides a sense of belonging for Emily. She gradually becomes more comfortable participating in these activities, finding joy in the shared experiences.

The bedtime routine is another crucial aspect of the Johnson household. The children are encouraged to wind down with calming activities, such as reading or listening to soft music. Bedtime is at 9:00 PM, ensuring that everyone gets enough rest for the next day. Mrs. Johnson often spends a few minutes with each child before bed, offering words of comfort and reassurance. This routine helps Emily feel safe and secure, easing her transition to sleep.

Emily's adaptation to the Johnsons' rules and routines is a gradual process. Initially, she struggles with the structure, finding it difficult to adjust to the predictability and expectations. However, the Johnsons' patience and understanding make a significant difference. They provide gentle reminders and positive reinforcement, helping Emily feel more comfortable and confident in her new environment.

Over time, Emily begins to appreciate the stability and security that the routines provide. The consistent structure helps to alleviate her anxiety and gives her a sense of control over her daily life. She starts to take pride in her responsibilities and looks forward to the family activities that bring joy and connection.

The rules and routines of the Johnson household play a crucial role in Emily's adjustment and healing. They provide a framework of stability and support, helping her to build a sense of normalcy and belonging. With the Johnsons' guidance and care, Emily gradually adapts to her new environment, finding hope and happiness in the structure and consistency of her new home.

Emily's transition to the Johnsons' foster home, while filled with hope and warmth, is also marked by significant emotional struggles. The weight of her past experiences and the sudden changes in her life create a complex web of emotions that she must navigate.

One of the most profound emotional struggles Emily faces is missing her parents. Despite the neglect and chaos, she endured at home, her parents are still a significant part of her life. The separation from them is a source of deep sorrow and confusion. Emily often finds herself thinking about her mother's tearful face and her father's angry outbursts. She wonders if they miss her too and what their lives are like without her. The longing for her parents is a constant ache in her heart, and she struggles to reconcile her feelings of love and loyalty with the reality of their inability to care for her.

Feeling out of place is another significant challenge for Emily. The Johnsons' home, with its structured routines and nurturing environment, is a stark contrast to the chaotic and unpredictable life she left behind. While the stability is comforting, it also feels foreign and overwhelming. Emily often feels like an outsider, unsure of how to fit into this new world. She is hesitant to fully engage with the Johnson family, fearing rejection or judgment. The sense of not belonging is a heavy burden, and Emily struggles to find her place in this new environment.

Emily's emotional struggles are compounded by the trauma of her past experiences. The neglect and chaos she endured have left deep scars, both physical and emotional. She often experiences moments of intense sadness and anxiety, triggered by memories of her past. Nightmares and flashbacks disrupt her sleep, leaving her feeling exhausted and vulnerable. The emotional toll of her trauma is significant, and Emily finds it difficult to express her feelings or seek comfort.

Despite these challenges, Emily's resilience shines through. She begins to form tentative bonds with the Johnson family, finding moments of connection and comfort. Mrs. Johnson's gentle reassurances and the kindness of Emma and Finn help to ease some of her fears. Emily starts to participate more in family activities, finding joy in the shared experiences. The support and understanding of the Johnson family provide a foundation for Emily to begin healing and finding her place in this new world.

Emily's emotional struggles are a testament to her strength and resilience. The journey is not easy, but with the love and care of the Johnson family, she begins to navigate the complexities of her emotions and find hope for the future. The process of healing is gradual, but each small step forward is a victory, bringing Emily closer to a sense of belonging and peace.

Emily's journey in the Johnsons' foster home is marked by small but significant victories that help her feel more comfortable and accepted. These moments, though seemingly minor, play a crucial role in her healing process and her sense of belonging.

One of the first small victories occurs during a family game night. The Johnsons gather around the dining table to play a board game, a regular tradition in their household. Emily, initially hesitant, joins them with some encouragement from Emma and Finn. As the game progresses, Emily finds herself laughing and enjoying the friendly competition. The warmth and camaraderie of the moment help her feel included and valued. It's a simple but powerful experience that begins to break down her walls of apprehension.

Another significant moment comes when Emily receives praise for her efforts in school. With the support of the Johnsons and her teachers, she has been working hard to catch up academically. One day, she brings home a test with a high score, a result of her dedication and perseverance. Mrs. Johnson beams with pride and gives Emily a heartfelt hug, celebrating her achievement. The recognition and encouragement boost Emily's confidence and reinforce her sense of self-worth.

Emily also experiences a small victory in her interactions with Finn. One afternoon, Finn invites Emily to join him in a game of football in the backyard. Emily, who has always been shy about participating in sports, hesitates but eventually agrees. As they play, Finn's patience and encouragement help Emily feel more at ease. She discovers that she enjoys the game and even scores a goal. The shared laughter and sense of accomplishment strengthen her bond with Finn and help her feel more connected to the family.

A particularly touching moment occurs when Emily helps Mrs. Johnson in the kitchen. Mrs. Johnson invites Emily to bake cookies together, a simple activity that becomes a meaningful experience. As they mix ingredients and shape the dough, Mrs. Johnson shares stories and listens to Emily's thoughts and feelings. The act of creating something together fosters a sense of trust and closeness. When the cookies are done, Emily feels a sense of pride and joy in contributing to the family's traditions.

Emily's small victories extend to her social interactions at school as well. With the support of her teachers and the Johnsons, she begins to make friends and participate more actively in class. One day, she is invited to join a group of classmates for lunch. The invitation, though seemingly small, is a significant step for Emily. She accepts and finds herself enjoying the conversation and camaraderie. The experience helps her feel more accepted and less isolated.

These small victories, while modest, are monumental in Emily's journey towards healing and acceptance. Each positive experience builds her confidence and reinforces her sense of belonging. The support and love of the Johnson family provide a nurturing environment where Emily can thrive and find hope for the future. With each step forward, Emily moves closer to a brighter and more fulfilling life.

The development of relationships between Emily and the Johnsons is a gradual and heartwarming process, marked by moments of connection, trust, and mutual understanding. Each member of the Johnson family plays a crucial role in helping Emily feel accepted and loved.

Mr. Johnson's calm and patient nature makes him a reassuring presence in Emily's life. He takes the time to get to know her, often engaging in conversations about her interests and schoolwork. One evening, while helping Emily with her homework, Mr. Johnson shares stories from his own school days, making her laugh and feel more at ease. His consistent support and gentle encouragement help Emily build confidence in her academic abilities and trust in his guidance.

Mrs. Johnson's nurturing and compassionate demeanour creates a safe space for Emily to express her emotions. She notices when Emily is feeling down and offers comfort through kind words and warm hugs. One particularly touching moment occurs when Emily has a nightmare and wakes up in tears. Mrs. Johnson sits with her, holding her hand and reassuring her until she feels calm enough to go back to sleep. This act of kindness strengthens their bond and helps Emily feel secure in her new home.

Emma's bright and cheerful personality is a source of joy for Emily. She takes Emily under her wing, introducing her to new hobbies and activities. One afternoon, Emma invites Emily to join her in painting. They spend hours together, creating colourful masterpieces and sharing stories. Emma's genuine interest in Emily's thoughts and feelings helps her feel valued and understood. Their shared moments of creativity and laughter lay the foundation for a strong and lasting friendship.

Finn's friendly and energetic nature helps Emily feel included and part of the family. He invites her to join him in various outdoor activities, such as playing football and riding bikes. One day, Finn teaches Emily how to ride a bike, patiently guiding her until she gains confidence. The sense of accomplishment and the shared experience bring them closer together. Finn's playful spirit and willingness to include Emily in his adventures help her feel more connected and accepted.

The Johnsons' commitment to spending quality time together as a family further strengthens their relationships. They enjoy activities such as game nights, movie marathons, and weekend outings. During these moments, Emily feels a sense of belonging and joy. The shared experiences and the Johnsons' unwavering support help her build trust and feel more comfortable in her new environment.

Celebrating milestones and achievements is another way the Johnsons foster a sense of connection. When Emily brings home a good grade or accomplishes a personal goal, the family celebrates with her, reinforcing her sense of self-worth and belonging. These moments of recognition and encouragement help Emily feel appreciated and loved.

The development of relationships between Emily and the Johnsons is a testament to the power of love, patience, and understanding. Each small act of kindness and each shared experience contribute to Emily's sense of security and happiness. With the Johnsons' unwavering support, Emily begins to heal and thrive, finding a place where she truly belongs.

Despite the warmth and support of the Johnson family, Emily continues to face ongoing challenges as she adjusts to her new life. These challenges are a testament to the deep emotional scars left by her past experiences, and the Johnsons' unwavering support plays a crucial role in helping her navigate them.

Emily often experiences waves of intense emotions, including sadness, anxiety, and fear. Nightmares and flashbacks of her past trauma disrupt her sleep, leaving her feeling exhausted and vulnerable. Mrs. Johnson, with her nurturing nature, provides comfort during these difficult times. She sits with Emily, offering a listening ear and reassuring words, helping her feel safe and understood. The Johnsons also encourage Emily to express her feelings through creative outlets like drawing and writing, which provide a therapeutic release for her emotions.

Building trust is a significant challenge for Emily. Her past experiences have made her wary of adults, and she struggles to fully trust the Johnsons, despite their kindness. The Johnsons understand that trust takes time and are patient with Emily. They consistently show her that they are reliable and caring, creating a safe environment where she can gradually open up. Mr. Johnson, in particular, spends time with Emily, engaging in activities she enjoys and building a bond of trust through shared experiences.

Emily's disrupted education has left her behind in her studies, and she often feels overwhelmed by the academic expectations. The Johnsons work closely with her teachers to provide the necessary support and resources. They create a structured study routine and offer help with homework, celebrating her progress and encouraging her to persevere. Emily's confidence in her academic abilities slowly grows, and she begins to see her potential.

Feeling out of place and struggling to make friends is another ongoing challenge for Emily. She often feels like an outsider, unsure of how to connect with her peers. Emma and Finn play a crucial role in helping Emily integrate socially. They invite her to join their activities and introduce her to their friends, making her feel included and valued. The Johnsons also encourage Emily to participate in extracurricular activities, helping her find common interests with other children and build new friendships.

The transition to a new environment and the changes in her daily life are overwhelming for Emily. She misses her parents and the familiarity of her old life, despite its challenges. The Johnsons provide a stable and consistent routine, which helps Emily feel more secure. They also encourage her to talk about her feelings and validate her emotions, helping her navigate the complexities of change.

Recognizing the depth of Emily's emotional struggles, the Johnsons arrange for her to see a therapist. The therapy sessions provide Emily with a safe space to explore her feelings and work through her trauma. The therapist helps Emily develop coping strategies and build resilience, supporting her journey towards healing. The Johnsons are actively involved in her therapeutic process, reinforcing the strategies at home and providing continuous support.

The ongoing challenges Emily faces are significant, but with the Johnsons' unwavering support and love, she begins to navigate them with increasing resilience. Each small step forward is a testament to her strength and the positive impact of the nurturing environment provided by the Johnson family. Emily's journey is one of healing and growth, and with the Johnsons by her side, she continues to move towards a brighter and more hopeful future.

Emily's journey in the Johnsons' foster home is filled with moments of connection and bonding that help her feel more accepted and loved. These moments, though sometimes small, are significant in building her sense of belonging and trust within the family.

One of the most cherished moments for Emily is the bedtime routine with Mrs. Johnson. Each night, Mrs. Johnson reads a story to Emily before bed. The soothing sound of her voice and the comforting presence of Mrs. Johnson help Emily feel safe and secure. These bedtime stories become a special time for them to bond, and Emily looks forward to this nightly ritual. It's a moment of peace and connection that helps Emily feel loved and cared for.

Emily finds joy in helping Mrs. Johnson in the kitchen. One afternoon, they decide to bake cookies together. As they mix the ingredients and shape the dough, Mrs. Johnson shares stories and listens to Emily's thoughts and feelings. The act of creating something together fosters a sense of trust and closeness. When the cookies are done, Emily feels a sense of pride and accomplishment, and the shared experience strengthens their bond.

Finn's friendly and energetic nature helps Emily feel included and part of the family. One day, Finn invites Emily to join him in a game of football in the backyard. Emily, who has always been shy about participating in sports, hesitates but eventually agrees. As they play, Finn's patience and encouragement help Emily feel more at ease. She discovers that she enjoys the game and even scores a goal. The shared laughter and sense of accomplishment bring them closer together, and Emily starts to see Finn as a supportive and caring brother.

Emma's bright and cheerful personality is a source of joy for Emily. She introduces Emily to various art projects, such as painting and crafting. One weekend, they decide to create a mural in the backyard. They spend hours together, painting colourful designs and sharing stories. Emma's genuine interest in Emily's thoughts and feelings helps her feel valued and understood. Their shared moments of creativity and laughter lay the foundation for a strong and lasting friendship.

The Johnsons' commitment to spending quality time together as a family further strengthens their relationships. They enjoy activities such as game nights, where they gather around the dining table to play board games. Emily, initially hesitant, joins them with some encouragement from Emma and Finn. As the game progresses, Emily finds herself laughing and enjoying the friendly competition. The warmth and camaraderie of the moment help her feel included and valued, and she begins to see the Johnsons as her family.

Celebrating milestones and achievements is another way the Johnsons foster a sense of connection. When Emily brings home a good grade or accomplishes a personal goal, the family celebrates with her, reinforcing her sense of self-worth and belonging. These moments of recognition and encouragement help Emily feel appreciated and loved.

These moments of connection and bonding are crucial in helping Emily feel more comfortable and accepted in her new home. The Johnsons' unwavering support and love provide a nurturing environment where Emily can heal and thrive. With each shared experience, Emily's sense of belonging and trust within the family grows stronger, bringing her closer to a brighter and more hopeful future.

As Emily continues to settle into the Johnsons' foster home, she begins to look forward to her future with a sense of hope and optimism. The warmth and stability provided by the Johnson family have created a nurturing environment where Emily can heal and grow.

Emily's days are now filled with moments of joy and connection. She looks forward to the family game nights, where laughter and friendly competition bring everyone closer together. The bedtime stories with Mrs. Johnson have become a cherished ritual, providing comfort and a sense of security. Emily's bond with Emma and Finn continues to strengthen, and she finds herself eagerly anticipating their shared activities and adventures.

The support and encouragement from the Johnsons have helped Emily build confidence in her abilities. She is making steady progress in school, and the recognition of her achievements has boosted her self-esteem. Emily now approaches her studies with a sense of determination and pride, knowing that she has the support of her foster family.

Emily's involvement in extracurricular activities has also opened up new opportunities for her. She has joined the school's art club, where she can express herself creatively and make new friends. The sense of belonging she feels in these activities has helped her overcome her initial shyness and embrace new experiences.

Looking forward, Emily envisions a future filled with possibilities. She dreams of pursuing her interests and talents, knowing that she has the love and support of the Johnson family to guide her. The stability and care she has found in her foster home have given her the foundation she needs to build a brighter future.

Emily's journey is one of resilience and hope. With the unwavering support of the Johnsons, she is beginning to see a future where she can thrive and achieve her dreams. The challenges she has faced have made her stronger, and the love and care she receives every day remind her that she is not alone. Emily's story is a testament to the power of family, healing, and the promise of a better tomorrow.

Chapter 6
Adjusting to a New Life

Emily's experiences at her new school are a blend of challenges and triumphs as she navigates this significant aspect of her new life. The transition to a new school environment is daunting, but it also offers Emily opportunities for growth and connection.

Emily's first day at her new school is filled with nervous anticipation. The unfamiliar faces, the new classrooms, and the bustling hallways are overwhelming. She clutches her backpack tightly, feeling a mix of excitement and anxiety. Mrs. Johnson walks her to the school entrance, offering words of encouragement and a reassuring smile. Emily takes a deep breath and steps into the building, determined to make the best of this new beginning.

One of the biggest challenges for Emily is making new friends. Her initial shyness and fear of rejection make it difficult for her to approach her classmates. However, the supportive environment of the school helps ease her transition. Her teacher, Ms. Thompson, is kind and attentive, introducing Emily to the class and encouraging her to participate in group activities. Emily's classmates are curious and welcoming, and she slowly begins to form connections.

During playtime, Emily meets a girl named Lily, who invites her to join a game of hopscotch. Emily hesitates but eventually agrees, finding comfort in Lily's friendly demeanour. The simple game becomes a turning point, as Emily starts to feel more comfortable interacting with her peers. Over time, she forms a small circle of friends who share her interests and make her feel included.

Keeping up with her studies is another significant challenge for Emily. The disruption in her education due to her unstable home life has left her behind in some subjects. She often feels overwhelmed by the academic expectations and worries about falling further behind. However, the school provides additional support to help her catch up.

Ms. Thompson works closely with Emily, offering extra tutoring sessions and personalized assignments to address her specific needs. The Johnsons also play a crucial role in supporting her academic progress. They create a structured study routine at home and provide help with homework, celebrating her achievements and encouraging her to persevere. Emily's confidence in her academic abilities gradually grows, and she begins to see her potential.

Emily's involvement in extracurricular activities also plays a crucial role in her adjustment. She joins the school's art club, where she can express herself creatively and make new friends. The art club becomes a sanctuary for Emily, a place where she feels valued and understood. She enjoys working on various projects, from painting to crafting, and the sense of accomplishment boosts her self-esteem.

Emily also participates in the school's football team, encouraged by her positive experiences playing with Finn. The physical activity and teamwork help her build confidence and resilience. The support and camaraderie of her teammates make her feel like she is part of something bigger, and she begins to look forward to practices and games.

As Emily continues to navigate her new school life, she experiences moments of growth and self-discovery. The supportive environment, the encouragement from her teachers and foster family, and the friendships she forms all contribute to her sense of belonging and confidence. Emily's journey is marked by small victories, each one bringing her closer to a brighter and more hopeful future.

Emily's experiences at her new school are a testament to her resilience and determination. With the support of the Johnsons and the school community, she begins to thrive academically and socially. The challenges she faces are significant, but each step forward is a triumph, bringing her closer to a sense of stability and happiness.

Emily's involvement in extracurricular activities plays a crucial role in her adjustment to her new life with the Johnsons. These activities provide her with opportunities to explore her interests, build new skills, and form meaningful connections with her peers.

One of the first extracurricular activities Emily joins is the school's art club. Encouraged by her positive experiences with Emma, Emily finds solace and joy in expressing herself creatively. The art club becomes a sanctuary for her, a place where she can let her imagination run wild and create beautiful pieces of art. The supportive environment of the club helps Emily feel valued and understood. She enjoys working on various projects, from painting to crafting, and the sense of accomplishment boosts her self-esteem. The friendships she forms with other club members provide her with a sense of belonging and community.

Emily's involvement in the school's football team is another significant step in her adjustment. Encouraged by her positive experiences playing football with Finn, Emily decides to join the team. The physical activity and teamwork help her build confidence and resilience. The support and camaraderie of her teammates make her feel like she is part of something bigger, and she begins to look forward to practices and games. The sense of achievement she feels when she scores a goal or makes a good play reinforces her self-worth and helps her feel more connected to her peers.

Emily also explores her interest in performing arts by joining the school's drama club. The drama club provides her with an outlet to express her emotions and build her confidence. Emily enjoys participating in rehearsals and performances, where she can step into different roles and explore new aspects of her personality. The supportive and encouraging atmosphere of the drama club helps her overcome her initial shyness and embrace her creativity. The friendships she forms with other club members further enhance her sense of belonging and acceptance.

In addition to school-based activities, Emily becomes involved in community service projects organized by the Johnsons. The family regularly participates in volunteer work, such as helping at local shelters and organizing charity events. Emily finds fulfilment in giving back to the community and making a positive impact on others. The sense of purpose and the shared experiences with the Johnson family strengthen her bond with them and help her feel more integrated into her new life.

Emily's academic interests also lead her to join various

academic clubs, such as the science club and the book club. These clubs provide her with opportunities to explore her intellectual curiosity and engage in stimulating discussions with her peers. The sense of achievement she feels when she contributes to a project or shares her insights in a discussion boosts her confidence and reinforces her sense of self-worth.

Through her involvement in extracurricular activities, Emily develops important life skills, such as teamwork, leadership, and time management. These activities help her build confidence and resilience, enabling her to navigate the challenges of her new life. The positive experiences and the sense of accomplishment she gains from these activities contribute to her overall well-being and happiness.

Emily's involvement in extracurricular activities is a testament to her resilience and determination. With the support of the Johnsons and the school community, she begins to thrive and find joy in her new experiences. The friendships she forms and the skills she develops through these activities help her build a brighter and more hopeful future.

Emily's emotional growth is a gradual and profound journey, marked by her increasing ability to process her past trauma and build a more hopeful future. The supportive environment provided by the Johnson family plays a crucial role in this transformation.

One of the first steps in Emily's emotional growth is learning to acknowledge and express her feelings. Initially, she struggles to articulate her emotions, often feeling overwhelmed by sadness, fear, and confusion. Mrs. Johnson, with her nurturing and patient demeanour, encourages Emily to talk about her feelings. She creates a safe space where Emily can share her thoughts without fear of judgment. Through these conversations, Emily begins to understand that it's okay to feel a range of emotions and that expressing them is a healthy part of healing.

Recognizing the depth of Emily's trauma, the Johnsons arrange for her to see a therapist. The therapy sessions provide Emily with a structured and supportive environment to explore her past experiences and develop coping strategies. The therapist helps Emily understand the impact of her trauma and guides her in processing her emotions. Through techniques such as mindfulness, journaling, and creative expression, Emily learns to manage her anxiety and build resilience. The therapeutic support is instrumental in helping Emily navigate her emotional landscape and find a sense of inner peace.

Building trust is a significant aspect of Emily's emotional growth. Her past experiences have left her wary of adults, making it difficult for her to fully trust the Johnsons. However, their consistent kindness and reliability gradually break down her walls of apprehension. Mr. Johnson's calm presence and Mrs. Johnson's nurturing care help Emily feel safe and valued. The bonds she forms with Emma and Finn also play a crucial role in rebuilding her trust in others. As Emily experiences genuine care and support, she begins to open up and trust the people around her.

Emily's emotional growth is also marked by her development of healthy coping mechanisms. The Johnsons and her therapist teach her various strategies to manage stress and anxiety. Emily learns to use deep breathing exercises, grounding techniques, and positive affirmations to calm herself during moments of distress. She also finds solace in creative activities such as drawing and writing, which provide an outlet for her emotions. These coping mechanisms empower Emily to take control of her emotional well-being and navigate challenges with greater resilience.

As Emily continues to heal, she begins to find joy in new experiences and activities. Her involvement in extracurricular activities, such as the art club and football team, provides her with opportunities to explore her interests and build new skills. The sense of accomplishment and the positive interactions with her peers boost her self-esteem and reinforce her sense of self-worth. Emily's growing confidence and resilience are evident in her willingness to try new things and embrace new opportunities.

The relationships Emily builds with the Johnson family are a cornerstone of her emotional growth. The love and support she receives from Mr. and Mrs. Johnson, as well as the friendships she forms with Emma and Finn, provide her with a strong foundation of stability and security. These relationships help Emily feel valued and understood, reinforcing her sense of belonging. The shared moments of connection and the unwavering support of the Johnsons help Emily heal and thrive.

Emily's emotional growth is a testament to her resilience and the power of a supportive environment. With the love and care of the Johnson family, she begins to process her past trauma and build a more hopeful future. Emily's journey is one of healing and self-discovery, marked by her increasing ability to navigate her emotions and find joy in life. As she continues to grow, Emily looks forward to a future filled with possibilities and the promise of a brighter tomorrow.

Emily's journey towards healing and adjustment is supported by a robust network of individuals and resources dedicated to her well-being. These support systems play a crucial role in helping her navigate the challenges of her new life and build a brighter future. The Johnsons are the cornerstone of Emily's support system. Their unwavering love, patience, and understanding provide Emily with a stable and nurturing environment. Mr. Johnson's calm and reassuring presence, Mrs. Johnson's nurturing care, and the friendship of Emma and Finn create a sense of belonging and security for Emily. The Johnsons' commitment to Emily's well-being is evident in their daily interactions, their involvement in her academic and extracurricular activities, and their efforts to create a supportive and loving home.

Emily's teachers play a significant role in her academic and emotional development. Ms. Thompson, her primary teacher, is particularly attentive to Emily's needs. She provides extra tutoring sessions to help Emily catch up academically and offers encouragement and praise to boost her confidence. Ms. Thompson also maintains open communication with the Johnsons, ensuring that Emily's progress is closely monitored and that any challenges are promptly addressed. The supportive and inclusive environment of the school helps Emily feel valued and understood.

The school counsellors are another vital component of Emily's support system. They provide Emily with a safe space to discuss her feelings and experiences. The counsellors work with Emily to develop coping strategies and build resilience. They also collaborate with her teachers and the Johnsons to create a comprehensive support plan that addresses Emily's academic, emotional, and social needs. The counsellors' guidance and support help Emily navigate the complexities of her emotions and build a sense of self-worth.

Emily's therapist is instrumental in helping her process her past trauma and develop healthy coping mechanisms. The therapy sessions provide Emily with a structured and supportive environment to explore her feelings and experiences. The therapist uses various techniques, such as mindfulness, journaling, and creative expression, to help Emily manage her anxiety and build resilience. The therapeutic support is crucial in helping Emily heal and develop a positive outlook on life.

The leaders of Emily's extracurricular activities, such as the art club, football team, and drama club, also play a significant role in her support system. They provide Emily with opportunities to explore her interests, build new skills, and form meaningful connections with her peers. The positive experiences and the sense of accomplishment Emily gains from these activities contribute to her overall well-being and happiness.

The broader community, including neighbours and local organizations, also contributes to Emily's support system. The Johnsons' involvement in community service projects provides Emily with opportunities to give back and feel connected to the community. The sense of purpose and the shared experiences with the Johnson family and other community members strengthen her bond with them and help her feel more integrated into her new life.

Emily's friends and classmates are an essential part of her support network. The friendships she forms at school and in her extracurricular activities provide her with a sense of belonging and acceptance. Her peers offer companionship, understanding, and encouragement, helping Emily feel less isolated and more connected to her new environment.

The comprehensive support system in place for Emily is a testament to the power of community and the importance of a nurturing environment. With the love and care of the Johnson family, the guidance of her teachers and counsellors, and the support of her peers and community, Emily is able to navigate the challenges of her new life and build a brighter and more hopeful future.

Emily's journey in her new school and foster home is significantly enriched by the development of new friendships. These relationships play a crucial role in her emotional growth and adjustment, providing her with a sense of belonging and support.

One of the first friends Emily makes is Lily, a kind and outgoing girl in her class. Their friendship begins during playtime when Lily invites Emily to join a game of hopscotch. Emily, initially hesitant, finds comfort in Lily's friendly demeanour. As they play, Emily starts to feel more at ease, and the simple game becomes a turning point in her social interactions. Lily's genuine kindness and inclusivity help Emily feel accepted and valued. They soon become close friends, sharing lunch together and working on school projects. Lily's friendship provides Emily with a sense of stability and companionship, easing her transition into the new school environment.

Emily's involvement in the art club introduces her to a group of like-minded peers who share her passion for creativity. The supportive environment of the club helps Emily feel valued and understood. She enjoys working on various projects, from painting to crafting, and the sense of accomplishment boosts her self-esteem. The friendships she forms with other club members provide her with a sense of belonging and community. They often collaborate on art projects, share ideas, and encourage each other's creativity. These positive interactions help Emily build confidence and develop her artistic skills.

Joining the school's football team is another significant step in Emily's social development. Encouraged by her positive experiences playing football with Finn, Emily decides to join the team. The physical activity and teamwork help her build confidence and resilience. The support and camaraderie of her teammates make her feel like she is part of something bigger, and she begins to look forward to practices and games. The sense of achievement she feels when she scores a goal or makes a good play reinforces her self worth and helps her feel more connected to her peers.

Emily's interest in performing arts leads her to join the school's drama club. The drama club provides her with an outlet to express her emotions and build her confidence. Emily enjoys participating in rehearsals and performances, where she can step into different roles and explore new aspects of her personality. The supportive and encouraging atmosphere of the drama club helps her overcome her initial shyness and embrace her creativity. The friendships she forms with other club members further enhance her sense of belonging and acceptance.

In the classroom, Emily begins to form connections with her classmates through group projects and class discussions. Her teacher, Ms. Thompson, encourages collaborative learning, which helps Emily interact more with her peers. These interactions provide Emily with opportunities to share her ideas and contribute to group work, boosting her confidence and reinforcing her sense of self-worth. The positive feedback and encouragement from her classmates help Emily feel more integrated into the school community.

The development of new friendships has a profound impact on Emily's emotional well-being and adjustment. These relationships provide her with a sense of belonging and support, helping her navigate the challenges of her new life. The positive interactions and shared experiences with her friends boost her self-esteem and reinforce her sense of self-worth. Emily's growing confidence and resilience are evident in her willingness to try new things and embrace new opportunities. Emily's new friendships are a testament to her resilience and the power of a supportive environment.

With the love and care of the Johnson family and the support of her friends, Emily begins to thrive and find joy in her new experiences. The friendships she forms help her build a brighter and more hopeful future, filled with possibilities and the promise of a better tomorrow.

Emily's journey towards healing involves developing various coping mechanisms to deal with her feelings of abandonment and the emotional scars left by her past. These strategies, supported by the Johnson family and her therapist, help her navigate her complex emotions and build resilience.

Emily's therapist introduces her to several therapeutic techniques that become essential in managing her feelings of abandonment. One of the most effective methods is mindfulness, which helps Emily stay grounded in the present moment and reduce anxiety. Through guided meditation and breathing exercises, Emily learns to calm her mind and focus on the here and now. This practice provides her with a sense of control and peace, helping her manage overwhelming emotions.

Journaling becomes a powerful tool for Emily to process her thoughts and feelings. She starts keeping a diary where she writes about her daily experiences, her fears, and her hopes. This private space allows Emily to express herself freely and reflect on her journey. The act of writing helps her make sense of her emotions and provides a therapeutic release. Over time, Emily's journal entries become a testament to her growth and resilience.

Emily finds solace in creative activities such as drawing, painting, and crafting. These outlets allow her to express her emotions in a non-verbal way, providing a sense of relief and accomplishment. The art club at school becomes a sanctuary where Emily can explore her creativity and connect with others who share her interests. The positive feedback and encouragement from her peers and teachers boost her self-esteem and reinforce her sense of self-worth.

Engaging in physical activities, such as playing football and participating in outdoor games, helps Emily channel her energy and reduce stress. The physical exertion releases endorphins, which improve her mood and overall well-being. The camaraderie and teamwork involved in these activities also provide Emily with a sense of belonging and support. The positive experiences on the football field and during family outings with the Johnsons help Emily build confidence and resilience.

Developing trust in the Johnson family is a gradual but crucial process for Emily. The consistent kindness and reliability of Mr. and Mrs. Johnson, along with the supportive friendships with Emma and Finn, help Emily feel safe and valued. The Johnsons' unwavering support and understanding create a nurturing environment where Emily can open up and share her feelings. This trust-building process is essential in helping Emily overcome her fear of abandonment and develop healthy relationships.

Emily learns to use positive affirmations as a way to combat negative thoughts and build self-confidence. With the guidance of her therapist and the encouragement of the Johnsons, Emily creates a list of affirmations that she repeats daily. Phrases like "I am strong," "I am loved," and "I am capable" help Emily shift her mindset and reinforce her sense of self-worth. These affirmations become a source of strength and motivation, helping Emily navigate challenging moments.

The relationships Emily forms with her friends, teachers, and the Johnson family play a vital role in her coping mechanisms. The sense of belonging and acceptance she feels in these relationships provides her with a strong support network. Emily learns to lean on her friends and family for comfort and encouragement, knowing that she is not alone in her journey. The shared experiences and positive interactions help Emily build resilience and find joy in her new life.

Emily's coping mechanisms are a testament to her strength and determination. With the support of the Johnson family, her therapist, and her friends, Emily develops the tools she needs to manage her feelings of abandonment and build a brighter future. Each coping strategy contributes to her emotional growth and resilience, helping her navigate the complexities of her past and embrace the possibilities of her future.

Emily's academic journey in her new school is marked by both significant progress and ongoing challenges. The supportive environment provided by the Johnson family and her teachers plays a crucial role in helping her navigate these challenges and achieve her academic goals.

When Emily first starts at her new school, she faces several academic challenges. The disruption in her education due to her unstable home life has left her behind in some subjects, particularly in math and science. She often feels overwhelmed by the academic expectations and worries about falling further behind. The unfamiliar curriculum and the pressure to catch up add to her anxiety.

Emily's teachers, particularly Ms. Thompson, are attentive to her needs and provide additional support to help her succeed. Ms. Thompson offers extra tutoring sessions after school, focusing on the areas where Emily needs the most help. She breaks down complex concepts into manageable steps, making it easier for Emily to understand and retain the information. The personalized attention and encouragement from Ms. Thompson boost Emily's confidence and motivate her to keep trying.

The Johnsons create a structured study routine at home to support Emily's academic progress. They set aside specific times for homework and study, ensuring that Emily has a quiet and conducive environment to focus on her assignments. Mr. Johnson, with his background in education, often helps Emily with her homework, providing guidance and explanations when needed. The consistent routine and the Johnsons' involvement in her studies help Emily develop good study habits and stay on track with her schoolwork.

The Johnsons celebrate Emily's academic achievements, no matter how small, reinforcing her sense of self-worth and accomplishment. When Emily brings home a good grade or completes a challenging assignment, the family acknowledges her hard work and dedication. These moments of recognition and encouragement boost Emily's confidence and motivate her to continue striving for success.

Emily's friendships at school also play a significant role in her academic progress. Her friends, particularly Lily, offer support and encouragement, helping Emily feel more comfortable and confident in the classroom. They often study together, share notes, and collaborate on group projects. The positive interactions with her peers provide Emily with a sense of belonging and support, making her academic journey less daunting.

Emily's involvement in extracurricular activities, such as the art club and football team, also contributes to her academic progress. These activities provide her with a balanced and fulfilling school experience, helping her develop time management skills and reduce stress. The sense of accomplishment and the positive feedback she receives in these activities boost her overall confidence and well-being, which in turn positively impacts her academic performance.

Despite her progress, Emily continues to face some academic challenges. There are moments when she feels overwhelmed by the workload and the pressure to catch up. She occasionally struggles with self-doubt and fears of not being able to meet expectations. However, the support systems in place, including her teachers, the Johnsons, and her friends, help her navigate these challenges and stay focused on her goals.

Emily's academic journey is a testament to her resilience and determination. With the unwavering support of the Johnson family, her teachers, and her friends, she continues to make steady progress and build confidence in her abilities. The challenges she faces are significant, but each step forward is a triumph, bringing her closer to a brighter and more hopeful future.

Emily's story is one of growth and perseverance, marked by her ability to overcome obstacles and achieve her academic goals. The supportive environment and the positive reinforcement she receives play a crucial role in her success, helping her build a strong foundation for her future.

The Johnson household is a harmonious blend of warmth, structure, and mutual respect, creating an environment where every member feels valued and supported. The dynamics within the family play a crucial role in helping Emily adjust and find her place.

Mr. Johnson, with his calm and patient demeanour, is the steady anchor of the family. As a high school teacher, he brings a sense of discipline and encouragement to the household. He is always ready to lend a listening ear or offer guidance, whether it's helping with homework or discussing life's challenges. His gentle approach helps Emily feel safe and understood, and she begins to see him as a reliable father figure.

Mrs. Johnson is the nurturing heart of the family. Her warm and compassionate nature creates a comforting atmosphere where everyone feels cared for. She is attentive to the needs of each family member, ensuring that they feel loved and supported. Mrs. Johnson's ability to balance structure with empathy helps Emily feel secure and valued. Her bedtime stories, cooking sessions, and heartfelt conversations become cherished moments for Emily, reinforcing her sense of belonging.

Emma, the Johnsons' bright and cheerful daughter, is a source of joy and companionship for Emily. Her love for reading and art provides common ground for the two girls to bond. Emma's inclusive and friendly nature helps Emily feel welcomed and accepted. She often takes the initiative to involve Emily in various activities, from painting projects to family game nights. Emma's genuine interest in Emily's thoughts and feelings helps her feel valued and understood, fostering a strong sisterly bond.

Finn, the energetic and friendly son, brings a sense of fun and adventure to the household. His love for sports and outdoor activities provides Emily with opportunities to engage in physical play and build her confidence. Finn's patience and encouragement help Emily feel more comfortable participating in activities she once found intimidating. Their shared moments of play and laughter strengthen their bond, and Emily begins to see Finn as a supportive and caring brother.

The Johnsons maintain a structured routine that provides stability and predictability for everyone. Mornings start with a family breakfast, where they share plans for the day and offer words of encouragement. Evenings are reserved for family time, whether it's playing board games, watching movies, or going for walks. These routines help Emily feel a sense of normalcy and security, reinforcing her place within the family.

The Johnson household operates on a system of shared responsibilities, teaching the children the importance of teamwork and cooperation. Each family member has specific chores, such as setting the table, tidying their rooms, or helping with laundry. Emily initially finds the chores challenging, but with gentle encouragement from Mrs. Johnson, she begins to take pride in her contributions. The shared responsibilities help Emily feel like an integral part of the family, fostering a sense of belonging and accomplishment.

The Johnsons celebrate each other's achievements and milestones, reinforcing a sense of self-worth and accomplishment. When Emily brings home a good grade or accomplishes a personal goal, the family acknowledges her hard work and dedication. These moments of recognition and celebration boost Emily's confidence and motivate her to continue striving for success.

The Johnsons provide unwavering emotional support for Emily, helping her navigate the complexities of her past and build a brighter future. They encourage her to express her feelings and validate her emotions, creating a safe space for her to heal and grow. The love and care she receives from the Johnson family help Emily build trust and resilience, reinforcing her sense of self-worth and belonging.

The dynamics within the Johnson household create a nurturing and supportive environment where Emily can thrive. The love, patience, and understanding of each family member help Emily feel accepted and valued, allowing her to build a brighter and more hopeful future.

As Emily settles into her new life with the Johnsons, she begins to explore and develop her personal interests and hobbies. These activities not only provide her with joy and fulfilment but also play a crucial role in her emotional growth and healing.

Emily's love for art becomes a significant part of her life. Encouraged by Emma and the supportive environment of the art club at school, Emily dives into various creative projects. She enjoys painting, drawing, and crafting, finding solace and expression in her artwork. The art club provides her with a space to explore her creativity and connect with others who share her passion. Emily's artistic talents flourish, and she takes pride in her creations, often sharing them with the Johnson family and her friends.

Emily discovers a love for reading, inspired by Emma's enthusiasm for books. The Johnsons have a cozy reading nook in their home, filled with a variety of books. Emily spends hours immersed in diffcrent worlds, finding comfort and escape in the stories. She enjoys discussing her favourite books with Emma and the rest of the family, and they often recommend new titles to each other. Reading becomes a cherished hobby for Emily, helping her expand her imagination and knowledge.

Emily's involvement in the school's football team introduces her to the joys of physical activity and teamwork. Encouraged by Finn and her positive experiences on the field, Emily develops a passion for football. She enjoys the camaraderie of her teammates and the sense of accomplishment that comes with improving her skills. The physical exertion also helps Emily manage stress and anxiety, providing a healthy outlet for her energy. Emily looks forward to practices and games, finding joy in the sport and the friendships she forms.

Emily's interest in performing arts leads her to join the school's drama club. The drama club provides her with an outlet to express her emotions and build her confidence. Emily enjoys participating in rehearsals and performances, where she can step into different roles and explore new aspects of her personality. The supportive and encouraging atmosphere of the drama club helps her overcome her initial shyness and embrace her creativity. The friendships she forms with other club members further enhance her sense of belonging and acceptance.

Inspired by the Johnsons' commitment to giving back, Emily becomes involved in community service projects. She finds fulfilment in helping others and making a positive impact on her community. Whether it's volunteering at local shelters, organizing charity events, or participating in neighbourhood clean-ups, Emily's involvement in community service provides her with a sense of purpose and connection. The shared experiences with the Johnson family and other community members strengthen her bond with them and help her feel more integrated into her new life.

The Johnsons often take family outings to explore nature, whether it's hiking in nearby parks, visiting botanical gardens, or having picnics by the lake. Emily discovers a love for the outdoors, finding peace and inspiration in the natural world. These outings provide her with opportunities to bond with the Johnson family and appreciate the beauty of nature. Emily's growing appreciation for the environment also leads her to participate in eco-friendly initiatives and learn more about conservation.

Emily's exploration of her personal interests and hobbies is a testament to her resilience and determination. With the support of the Johnson family and the opportunities provided by her new environment, Emily begins to thrive and find joy in her new experiences. These activities not only enrich her life but also play a crucial role in her emotional growth and healing, helping her build a brighter and more hopeful future.

As Emily continues to settle into her new life with the Johnsons, she begins to look ahead to her future with a mix of hope and uncertainty. The journey she has embarked on is filled with both challenges and triumphs, and the support of the Johnson family has been instrumental in helping her navigate this path.

Emily's experiences in the Johnson household have given her a renewed sense of hope. The love, care, and stability provided by the Johnsons have helped her heal and grow in ways she never thought possible. She looks forward to continuing her education, exploring her interests, and building on the friendships she has formed. The positive reinforcement and encouragement she receives from the Johnsons and her teachers have boosted her confidence, and she now believes in her ability to achieve her goals.

Emily dreams of pursuing her passion for art and creativity. She envisions herself continuing to develop her artistic skills, perhaps even considering a future career in the arts. The support she receives from the Johnsons and her involvement in the art club have given her the confidence to dream big and work towards her aspirations.

Despite the hope and optimism, Emily is also aware of the uncertainties that lie ahead. The memories of her past and the trauma she has experienced are still present, and she knows that healing is a continuous process. There are moments when she feels overwhelmed by the challenges she faces, and the fear of the unknown can be daunting.

Emily's journey is not without its setbacks, and she understands that there will be difficult days. However, the coping mechanisms she has developed, the therapeutic support she receives, and the unwavering love of the Johnson family provide her with the tools to navigate these challenges. Emily is learning to embrace the uncertainty and face it with resilience and determination.

Looking ahead, Emily is determined to build a brighter future for herself. She is committed to her education and personal growth, and she is excited about the opportunities that lie ahead. The sense of belonging and acceptance she feels in the Johnson household has given her the foundation she needs to thrive.

Emily's journey is a testament to her strength and resilience. With the support of the Johnson family, her teachers, and her friends, she is ready to face the future with hope and courage. The challenges she has overcome and the progress she has made are a source of inspiration, and she is determined to continue moving forward.

As Emily looks ahead, she carries with her the lessons she has learned and the love she has received. Her story is one of healing, growth, and the promise of a brighter tomorrow. With hope in her heart and the support of those around her, Emily is ready to embrace the future and all the possibilities it holds.

Chapter 7
The Court Hearing

The preparations for Emily's court hearing are a meticulous and emotionally charged process, involving multiple meetings with lawyers, caseworkers, and the Johnson family. The goal is to ensure that Emily's best interests are represented and that she feels supported throughout the proceedings.

Emily's legal representation is crucial in preparing for the court hearing. The Johnsons arrange for Emily to meet with her lawyer, Ms. Parker, a compassionate and experienced attorney specializing in family law. During their initial meetings, Ms. Parker explains the legal process to Emily in a way that is easy for her to understand. She reassures Emily that her voice will be heard and that her well-being is the top priority.

Ms. Parker gathers detailed information about Emily's background, her experiences in her previous home, and her current situation with the Johnsons. She reviews all relevant documents, including reports from social services and school records, to build a comprehensive case. Ms. Parker also prepares Emily for the types of questions she might be asked in court, helping her feel more confident and less anxious about the upcoming hearing.

Ms. Harris, Emily's caseworker, plays a pivotal role in the preparations. She coordinates with Ms. Parker and the Johnsons to ensure that all necessary information is gathered and presented accurately. Ms. Harris conducts regular visits to the Johnson household to monitor Emily's progress and well-being. She documents her observations and compiles reports that will be presented in court.

Ms. Harris also spends time with Emily, discussing the court process and addressing any concerns or fears she might have. She reassures Emily that she will be there to support her throughout the hearing. The bond of trust that has developed between Emily and Ms. Harris provides a source of comfort and stability during this challenging time.

The Johnsons are deeply involved in the preparations for the court hearing. They provide emotional support and reassurance to Emily, helping her feel secure and loved. Mr. and Mrs. Johnson explain the importance of the hearing and encourage Emily to be honest and open about her experiences. They emphasize that the goal is to ensure her safety and well-being.

The Johnsons also work closely with Ms. Parker and Ms. Harris, providing any additional information or documentation needed for the case. They attend meetings and discussions, offering their insights and perspectives on Emily's progress and adjustment. Their active involvement demonstrates their commitment to Emily's future and reinforces her sense of belonging and security.

Preparing for the court hearing is not just about gathering information: it's also about ensuring that Emily feels emotionally ready. The Johnsons, Ms. Parker, and Ms. Harris all play a role in helping Emily manage her emotions and build confidence. They encourage her to express her feelings and validate her concerns, creating a supportive environment where she feels heard and understood.

Emily's therapist also provides additional support, helping her develop coping strategies to manage anxiety and stress. Through mindfulness exercises, positive affirmations, and therapeutic conversations, Emily learns to navigate her emotions and build resilience. The combined efforts of her support network help Emily feel more prepared and empowered as the court hearing approaches.

The preparations for the court hearing are a collaborative effort, involving the dedication and care of everyone involved in Emily's life. The goal is to ensure that Emily's voice is heard and that her best interests are represented. With the support of her lawyer, caseworker, and the Johnson family, Emily faces the upcoming hearing with a sense of hope and determination, ready to take the next step towards a brighter future.

As the court hearing approaches, Emily's anxiety and fears intensify. The uncertainty of the outcome and the weight of her past experiences create a complex web of emotions that she struggles to navigate.

One of Emily's primary sources of anxiety is the fear of the unknown. The court hearing represents a significant and unfamiliar event in her life, and she is unsure of what to expect. Despite the reassurances from Ms. Parker, her lawyer, and Ms. Harris, her caseworker, the thought of standing before a judge and discussing her past is daunting. Emily worries about the questions she might be asked and whether she will be able to articulate her feelings and experiences clearly.

Emily is deeply concerned about the outcome of the court hearing. She fears that the decision might not be in her favour and that she could be separated from the Johnson family, who have become her source of stability and love. The possibility of returning to her previous home or being placed in another unfamiliar environment fills her with dread. Emily's anxiety is heightened by the uncertainty of her future and the potential for further upheaval in her life.

The court hearing requires Emily to revisit and discuss her past experiences, which are filled with trauma and pain. The thought of reliving these memories in a formal setting is overwhelming. Emily fears that she might break down or become too emotional during the hearing, which could affect her ability to communicate effectively. The anticipation of facing her past in such a public and structured environment adds to her anxiety.

Emily feels a significant amount of pressure to perform well during the court hearing. She understands the importance of her testimony and the impact it could have on the judge's decision. This pressure to present herself in a certain way and to convey her experiences accurately adds to her stress. Emily worries about making mistakes or saying something that could be misinterpreted, which could potentially affect the outcome of the hearing.

Despite her anxiety, Emily finds solace in the support and reassurance provided by the Johnson family, Ms. Parker, and Ms. Harris. They remind her that she is not alone and that they will be there to support her throughout the process. Mrs. Johnson, in particular, offers comforting words and gentle hugs, helping Emily feel more secure. The consistent presence and encouragement from her support network provide Emily with a sense of stability and hope.

To manage her anxiety, Emily relies on the coping strategies, she has developed with the help of her therapist. She practices mindfulness exercises and deep breathing techniques to calm her mind and body. Journaling becomes a therapeutic outlet for her to express her fears and emotions. Emily also finds comfort in creative activities, such as drawing and painting, which help her process her feelings in a non-verbal way.

Ms. Parker and Ms. Harris work closely with Emily to build her confidence and prepare her for the hearing. They conduct mock sessions, where Emily practices answering questions and expressing her thoughts. These sessions help Emily feel more prepared and less anxious about the actual hearing. The positive reinforcement and encouragement she receives from her support network boost her confidence and help her feel more empowered.

Emily's anxiety and fears about the court hearing are significant, but with the unwavering support of the Johnson family, her lawyer, and her caseworker, she begins to navigate these emotions with increasing resilience. The journey is challenging, but Emily's strength and determination, coupled with the love and care of those around her, help her face the upcoming hearing with hope and courage.

The day of the court hearing arrives, and the atmosphere is charged with a mix of anticipation and anxiety. Emily, accompanied by the Johnson family, Ms. Parker, and Ms. Harris, enters the courthouse with a sense of determination and hope.

As they step into the courtroom, Emily takes in the formal setting. The room is filled with rows of benches, a judge's bench at the front, and tables for the lawyers and their clients. The air is thick with the gravity of the proceedings. Emily feels a surge of nervousness but is reassured by the presence of her support network. Mrs. Johnson gives her a comforting smile, and Ms. Parker places a reassuring hand on her shoulder.

The hearing begins with the opening statements from both sides. Ms. Parker, representing Emily, presents a compelling case for why Emily should remain with the Johnson family. She outlines the positive impact the Johnsons have had on Emily's well-being, highlighting her academic progress, emotional growth, and the supportive environment they provide. Ms. Parker emphasizes that Emily's best interests are at the heart of their argument.

The opposing side, representing Emily's biological parents, presents their case, arguing for the possibility of reunification. They acknowledge the past issues but argue that the parents have made efforts to improve their situation. The judge listens attentively, taking notes and considering the arguments presented.

The presentation of evidence is a critical part of the hearing. Ms. Parker begins by submitting detailed reports from Ms. Harris, the caseworker, documenting Emily's progress and the positive changes observed since she has been with the Johnsons. These reports include observations of Emily's emotional and academic development, her interactions with the Johnson family, and her overall well-being.

Ms. Parker also presents statements from Emily's teachers, highlighting her academic achievements and the support she has received from the Johnsons. The teachers' testimonies emphasize the stability and encouragement Emily has experienced, which have contributed to her academic success.

Next, Ms. Parker calls Mrs. Johnson to the stand. Mrs. Johnson speaks with heartfelt sincerity about Emily's journey since joining their family. She describes the initial challenges Emily faced, the small victories she has achieved, and the strong bonds she has formed with each family member. Mrs. Johnson's testimony paints a vivid picture of the loving and nurturing environment they have created for Emily.

Emily's therapist is also called to testify. The therapist provides professional insights into Emily's emotional growth and the therapeutic progress, she has made. She discusses the coping mechanisms Emily has developed, and the positive impact of the stable and supportive environment provided by the Johnsons. The therapist's testimony underscores the importance of continuity and stability in Emily's healing process.

One of the most poignant moments of the hearing is Emily's testimony. With Ms. Parker by her side, Emily takes the stand. She feels a mix of fear and determination as she faces the judge. Ms. Parker gently guides her through the process, asking questions that allow Emily to share her experiences and feelings.

Emily speaks about her life with the Johnsons, describing the love and support she has received. She talks about her progress in school, her involvement in extracurricular activities, and the sense of belonging she feels. Emily's voice trembles at times, but she finds strength in the presence of her support network. Her testimony is heartfelt and sincere, providing a powerful insight into her journey and her hopes for the future.

As the first day of the hearing concludes, the judge thanks everyone for their testimonies and adjourns the court. Emily feels a sense of relief and exhaustion. The day has been emotionally draining, but she is grateful for the support she has received. The Johnsons, Ms. Parker, and Ms. Harris offer words of encouragement, reminding Emily that they are with her every step of the way.

The beginning of the court hearing is a crucial step in determining Emily's future. The presentation of evidence and the heartfelt testimonies provide a comprehensive view of Emily's journey and the positive impact of the Johnson family. With the support of her legal team and the unwavering love of the Johnsons, Emily faces the hearing with hope and determination, ready to take the next step towards a brighter future.

The court hearing continues with the testimonies of Emily's biological parents, who are attempting to regain custody. Their statements are a mix of remorse, hope, and determination, as they try to convince the court of their ability to provide a stable and loving environment for Emily.

Emily's mother, Mrs. Smith, takes the stand first. She appears nervous but determined to make her case. With a trembling voice, she begins by acknowledging the mistakes she has made in the past. She admits to the neglect and instability that Emily experienced while living with them, expressing deep regret for the pain and hardship it caused.

Mrs. Smith explains that she has been working hard to turn her life around. She describes the steps she has taken to improve her situation, including attending parenting classes, seeking counselling, and securing stable employment. She emphasizes her commitment to providing a better life for Emily and her desire to be a responsible and loving mother.

Throughout her testimony, Mrs. Smith speaks about the bond she shares with Emily and her hope for reunification. She acknowledges the positive impact the Johnsons have had on Emily but insists that she is now capable of providing the care and support her daughter needs. Mrs. Smith's testimony is heartfelt and emotional, reflecting her deep love for Emily and her determination to make amends.

Next, Emily's father, Mr. Smith, takes the stand. He appears more composed but equally determined to regain custody of his daughter. Mr. Smith begins by acknowledging the challenges and mistakes of the past. He admits to the instability and neglect that Emily faced and expresses sincere remorse for his actions.

Mr. Smith outlines the steps he has taken to address his issues, including attending anger management classes, seeking therapy, and maintaining steady employment. He emphasizes his commitment to creating a stable and nurturing environment for Emily. Mr. Smith speaks about the changes he has made in his life and his desire to be a better father.

During his testimony, Mr. Smith also acknowledges the positive role the Johnsons have played in Emily's life. He expresses gratitude for their care and support but insists that he and Mrs. Smith are now capable of providing a loving and stable home for Emily. Mr. Smith's testimony is earnest and sincere, reflecting his determination to rebuild his relationship with his daughter.

Following their testimonies, both parents are cross-examined by Ms. Parker. She asks probing questions about their past behaviour, the steps they have taken to improve their situation, and their plans for Emily's future. Ms. Parker's questions are designed to assess the credibility of their claims and their ability to provide a stable and supportive environment for Emily.

The cross-examination is challenging for both parents, as they are forced to confront their past mistakes and provide detailed explanations of their efforts to change. Despite the difficult questions, they remain composed and reiterate their commitment to Emily's well-being.

Emily listens to her parents' testimonies with a mix of emotions. She feels a deep sense of love and loyalty towards them but is also aware of the pain and instability she experienced in their care. The conflicting emotions are overwhelming, and Emily struggles to process her feelings.

The support of the Johnson family, Ms. Parker, and Ms. Harris provides Emily with a sense of stability and reassurance. They remind her that her well-being is the top priority and that the court's decision will be based on what is best for her future.

The testimonies of Emily's parents add a complex layer to the court hearing. Their attempts to regain custody are sincere and heartfelt, reflecting their desire to make amends and provide a better life for Emily. The court must now weigh their testimonies against the evidence presented by the Johnsons and other witnesses to determine the best outcome for Emily's future.

The case presented by social services is a critical component of the court hearing, providing a detailed account of the neglect Emily experienced and its profound impact on her well-being. Ms. Harris, the caseworker, takes the stand to present the findings and evidence gathered during her involvement with Emily and her family.

Ms. Harris begins by outlining the history of neglect that led to Emily's removal from her biological parents' home. She presents detailed reports documenting the conditions Emily was subjected to, including instances of inadequate supervision, lack of basic necessities, and emotional neglect. These reports are based on home visits, interviews with Emily and her parents, and observations made by social services.

Ms. Harris describes the chaotic and unstable environment in which Emily lived. She highlights the frequent absences of her parents, leaving Emily to fend for herself for extended periods. The lack of proper nutrition, hygiene, and medical care are also emphasized, painting a stark picture of the neglect Emily endured. Ms. Harris provides specific examples, such as Emily missing school due to lack of proper clothing and the absence of a stable routine, which further impacted her development.

The testimony then shifts to the impact of this neglect on Emily's physical, emotional, and psychological well-being. Ms. Harris explains that the prolonged exposure to neglect had significant consequences for Emily's health and development. She presents evidence of Emily's malnourishment, frequent illnesses, and developmental delays observed during her initial assessments.

Ms. Harris also discusses the emotional and psychological toll the neglect took on Emily. She describes Emily's initial presentation as withdrawn, anxious, and fearful. The lack of a stable and nurturing environment left Emily with deep-seated feelings of insecurity and abandonment. Ms. Harris provides examples of Emily's behavioural issues, such as difficulty trusting adults, trouble forming relationships, and signs of anxiety and depression.

Ms. Harris then details the intervention measures taken by social services to address Emily's needs and ensure her safety. She describes the decision to place Emily in the Johnsons' foster home, highlighting the positive changes observed since the placement. Ms. Harris presents reports documenting Emily's progress in the Johnson household, including improvements in her physical health, emotional stability, and academic performance.

The testimony includes specific examples of Emily's growth and development. Ms. Harris describes how Emily has gained weight, her health has stabilized, and she is now thriving in a structured and supportive environment. She also highlights Emily's emotional growth, noting her increased confidence, ability to form trusting relationships, and participation in school and extracurricular activities.

Based on the evidence presented, Ms. Harris makes a strong recommendation for Emily to remain with the Johnson family. She emphasizes the importance of stability and continuity in Emily's life, arguing that the positive environment provided by the Johnsons is crucial for her ongoing development and well-being. Ms. Harris stresses that any disruption to Emily's current placement could have detrimental effects on her progress and emotional health.

Ms. Harris concludes her testimony by reiterating the primary goal of social services: to ensure the best interests of the child. She firmly believes that Emily's best interests are served by remaining with the Johnson family, where she has found the love, care, and stability she needs to heal and thrive.

The case presented by social services is a compelling and comprehensive account of the neglect Emily experienced and the positive impact of her placement with the Johnsons. The detailed evidence and heartfelt testimony from Ms. Harris provide a clear picture of Emily's journey and the critical importance of maintaining her current placement for her future well-being.

From Emily's perspective, the court hearing is a whirlwind of emotions, filled with anxiety, hope, and a deep longing for stability. As she sits in the courtroom, surrounded by the Johnson family, her lawyer Ms. Parker, and her caseworker Ms. Harris, Emily reflects on her journey and her hopes for the future.

Emily's anxiety is palpable as she listens to the proceedings. The formal setting of the courtroom, the presence of the judge, and the gravity of the situation weigh heavily on her. She worries about the outcome and the possibility of being separated from the Johnson family, who have become her source of love and security. The thought of returning to her previous life or facing further uncertainty fills her with dread.

Despite her fears, Emily holds onto a sense of hope and determination. She knows that the Johnsons, Ms. Parker, and Ms. Harris are all fighting for her best interests. Their unwavering support gives her the strength to face the hearing with courage. Emily hopes that the judge will see the positive changes she has experienced since living with the Johnsons and recognize the stability and care they provide.

As the hearing progresses, Emily reflects on her journey and the significant progress she has made. She thinks about the initial challenges she faced when she first arrived at the Johnsons' home, the small victories she has achieved, and the strong bonds she has formed with each family member. Emily recalls the love and support she has received, which have helped her heal and grow.

Emily's deepest desire is for stability and a sense of belonging. She longs to continue living with the Johnsons, where she feels safe, loved, and valued. The thought of being uprooted again and facing further disruption is overwhelming. Emily hopes that the court will recognize the importance of maintaining her current placement and allow her to stay with the Johnson family.

Looking ahead, Emily dreams of a future filled with possibilities. She envisions herself continuing to thrive academically, exploring her interests, and building on the friendships she has formed. Emily hopes to pursue her passion for art and creativity, perhaps even considering a future career in the arts. The support she receives from the Johnsons and her involvement in extracurricular activities have given her the confidence to dream big and work towards her aspirations.

Emily feels a deep sense of gratitude for the support she has received from the Johnson family, Ms. Parker, and Ms. Harris. Their dedication and care have made a significant difference in her life, helping her navigate the challenges and find hope for the future. Emily is thankful for their presence in the courtroom, providing her with the reassurance and strength she needs to face the hearing.

While the uncertainty of the outcome is daunting, Emily is determined to face it with resilience and courage. She knows that whatever happens, she has the support of the Johnson family and her legal team. Emily is ready to share her story and hopes that her voice will be heard, and her best interests will be considered.

Emily's perspective on the court hearing is a mix of anxiety, hope, and determination. Her journey is a testament to her strength and resilience, and she faces the hearing with the support of those who care deeply for her. Emily's hopes for the future are rooted in the stability and love she has found with the Johnson family, and she dreams of a brighter and more hopeful tomorrow.

The day of the court's verdict arrives, and the atmosphere in the courtroom is tense with anticipation. Emily sits with the Johnson family, Ms. Parker, and Ms. Harris, feeling a mix of anxiety and hope. The judge enters the courtroom, and everyone rises, then takes their seats as the judge begins to speak.

The judge starts by summarizing the evidence and testimonies presented during the hearing. The judge acknowledges the efforts made by Emily's biological parents to improve their situation and their sincere desire to regain custody. However, the judge also emphasizes the importance of considering Emily's best interests and the impact of her past experiences on her well-being. The judge outlines several key factors that influenced the decision.

The judge highlights the significant progress Emily has made since being placed with the Johnson family. The reports from Ms. Harris, the caseworker, and the testimonies from Emily's teachers and therapist provide compelling evidence of her improved physical health, emotional stability, and academic performance. The judge notes that Emily has thrived in the structured and supportive environment provided by the Johnsons.

The judge emphasizes the importance of stability and continuity in Emily's life. The evidence presented by social services and the Johnsons demonstrates that Emily has found a sense of security and belonging in her current placement. The judge acknowledges that any disruption to this stability could have detrimental effects on Emily's progress and emotional health.

The judge takes into account Emily's own wishes and feelings, as expressed during her testimony. Emily's heartfelt statements about her experiences with the Johnsons and her desire to remain with them carry significant weight in the decision-making process. The judge recognizes the importance of honouring Emily's voice and ensuring that her best interests are prioritized.

While acknowledging the efforts made by Emily's biological parents to address their issues and improve their situation, the judge also considers the limitations and challenges they still face. The judge expresses concern about the potential for relapse and the ability of the parents to provide a stable and nurturing environment consistently.

After carefully considering all the evidence and testimonies, the judge delivers the verdict: Emily will remain in the foster care of the Johnson family. The judge explains that this decision is based on the overwhelming evidence of Emily's well-being and progress in her current placement, the importance of stability and continuity, and Emily's own wishes.

The judge commends the Johnson family for their dedication and care, acknowledging the positive impact they have had on Emily's life. The judge also encourages Emily's biological parents to continue their efforts to improve their situation and maintain a positive relationship with Emily through supervised visits and ongoing support.

As the verdict is announced, Emily feels a wave of relief and gratitude. The anxiety and uncertainty that had weighed heavily on her are replaced by a sense of hope and security. She looks at the Johnson family, who are beaming with pride and joy, and feels a deep sense of belonging and love.

The judge's decision marks a new chapter in Emily's life. With the support of the Johnson family, her teachers, and her therapist, Emily is ready to continue her journey of healing and growth. The stability and care provided by the Johnsons will allow her to build a brighter and more hopeful future.

Emily's story is a testament to the power of love, resilience, and the importance of prioritizing the best interests of the child. The court's verdict ensures that Emily can continue to thrive in a nurturing and supportive environment, surrounded by people who care deeply for her well-being.

The court's verdict to keep Emily in the foster care of the Johnson family brings a wave of emotions for everyone involved. The decision marks a significant turning point in Emily's life, filled with both relief and lingering uncertainties.

For Emily, the verdict brings an overwhelming sense of relief. The anxiety and fear that had weighed heavily on her throughout the hearing are replaced by a profound sense of security. Knowing that she can continue living with the Johnson family, where she feels loved and supported, fills her with gratitude. Emily feels a deep sense of belonging and looks forward to building a brighter future with the Johnsons.

Despite her relief, Emily also experiences a mix of emotions. She feels a lingering sadness and guilt about her biological parents. The court's decision, while in her best interest, means that her parents' efforts to regain custody were not enough. Emily struggles with feelings of loyalty and love towards her parents, coupled with the recognition that the stability and care provided by the Johnsons are crucial for her well-being. These conflicting emotions are challenging for Emily to navigate, but the support of the Johnson family helps her process her feelings.

Emily's biological parents, Mr. and Mrs. Smith, are deeply

disappointed by the court's verdict. The decision to keep Emily in foster care is a painful reminder of their past mistakes and the challenges they still face. They feel a profound sense of loss and regret, knowing that their efforts to improve their situation were not enough to regain custody of their daughter.

Despite their disappointment, Mr. and Mrs. Smith are determined to continue working towards a better future. They recognize the importance of maintaining a positive relationship with Emily and commit to participating in supervised visits and ongoing support. The court's decision serves as a catalyst for further self-improvement and a renewed commitment to being the best parents they can be.

The Johnson family is overjoyed by the court's decision. The verdict affirms their dedication and love for Emily, and they are grateful for the opportunity to continue providing her with a stable and nurturing home. Mr. and Mrs. Johnson, along with Emma and Finn, celebrate the decision with Emily, reinforcing their commitment to her well-being and happiness.

The Johnsons understand that the journey ahead will still have its challenges, but they are ready to face them together as a family. They continue to support Emily's emotional growth, academic progress, and personal interests, ensuring that she has the foundation she needs to thrive.

In the aftermath of the verdict, Emily begins to look forward to her future with renewed hope and optimism. The stability and love provided by the Johnson family give her the confidence to pursue her dreams and build a brighter future. Emily's journey is one of resilience and determination, and she is ready to embrace the possibilities that lie ahead.

The emotional aftermath of the court's decision is complex, filled with relief, gratitude, disappointment, and determination. Emily's story is a testament to the power of love, support, and the importance of prioritizing the best interests of the child. With the unwavering support of the Johnson family, Emily continues to heal and grow, looking forward to a future filled with hope and promise.

Throughout the emotionally charged court hearing and its aftermath, the Johnson family provides unwavering support to Emily, ensuring she feels loved, secure, and valued. Their dedication and care play a crucial role in helping Emily navigate this challenging period.

Mrs. Johnson is a constant source of emotional reassurance for Emily. She offers comforting words and gentle hugs, reminding Emily that she is not alone. Mrs. Johnson listens attentively to Emily's fears and anxieties, validating her feelings and providing a safe space for her to express herself. This nurturing presence helps Emily feel understood and supported, easing her emotional burden.

Mr. Johnson's calm and steady presence provides a sense of stability for Emily. He takes the time to explain the court process to her, helping her understand what to expect and alleviating some of her fears. Mr. Johnson's patience and reliability reinforce Emily's sense of security, making her feel more confident and less anxious about the outcome.

Emma and Finn play a significant role in supporting Emily through this difficult time. They engage her in fun activities and family bonding moments, helping to distract her from the stress of the court hearing. Whether it's playing board games, going for walks, or working on art projects together, Emma and Finn's companionship provides Emily with a sense of normalcy and joy.

The Johnsons consistently offer encouragement and praise to boost Emily's confidence. They celebrate her small victories and acknowledge her efforts, reinforcing her sense of self-worth. This positive reinforcement helps Emily build resilience and maintain a hopeful outlook, even in the face of uncertainty.

Recognizing the emotional toll of the court hearing, the Johnsons ensure that Emily continues to receive therapeutic support. They coordinate with her therapist to provide additional sessions and coping strategies tailored to her needs. The therapist helps Emily manage her anxiety and process her emotions, providing her with tools to navigate this challenging period.

The Johnsons create a safe and nurturing environment where Emily feels secure and valued. They maintain a structured routine that provides stability and predictability, helping Emily feel more grounded. The family's unwavering support and love create a sense of belonging that is crucial for Emily's emotional well-being.

The Johnsons prioritize open communication, encouraging

Emily to share her thoughts and feelings. They listen without judgment and offer guidance and reassurance. This open dialogue helps Emily feel heard and understood, reinforcing her trust in the Johnson family.

The Johnsons celebrate each milestone and achievement, no matter how small, reinforcing Emily's sense of accomplishment. These moments of recognition and celebration boost Emily's confidence and motivate her to continue striving for success.

The support Emily receives from the Johnsons during this difficult time is a testament to their love and dedication. Their unwavering presence, emotional reassurance, and open communication provide Emily with the foundation she needs to navigate the challenges and build a brighter future. With the Johnson family by her side, Emily feels empowered and hopeful, ready to face whatever comes next.

In the days following the court's decision, Emily begins to come to terms with the outcome and looks forward to her future with a mix of hope and determination. The support of the Johnson family and her broader network plays a crucial role in helping her navigate this transition.

Emily starts to accept the court's decision, recognizing that it is in her best interest. The stability and love she has found with the Johnsons provide a strong foundation for her to heal and grow. Emily reflects on her journey and acknowledges the progress she has made, both emotionally and academically. This acceptance is a significant step in her healing process, allowing her to focus on the positive aspects of her new life.

With the court's decision providing a sense of security, Emily begins to look ahead with optimism. She is excited about continuing her education and exploring her interests. The support she receives from the Johnsons, her teachers, and her friends gives her the confidence to pursue her dreams. Emily envisions a future where she can thrive, both personally and academically, and she is determined to make the most of the opportunities before her.

The bonds Emily has formed with the Johnson family continue to grow stronger. She feels a deep sense of belonging and is grateful for their unwavering support. Emily also maintains a positive relationship with her biological parents through supervised visits, which helps her reconcile her feelings of love and loyalty towards them. These relationships provide her with a sense of stability and connection, reinforcing her emotional well-being.

Emily is eager to embrace new opportunities and experiences. She continues to participate in extracurricular activities, such as the art club and football team, which bring her joy and fulfilment. Emily also explores new hobbies and interests, finding creative outlets that help her express herself and build confidence. The encouragement and praise she receives from the Johnsons and her peers motivate her to keep pushing forward.

Emily's journey is marked by personal growth and resilience. She has developed coping mechanisms to manage her anxiety and stress, and she continues to work with her therapist to build emotional strength. Emily's ability to navigate challenges and embrace change is a testament to her determination and inner strength. She is proud of the progress she has made and looks forward to continuing her journey of self-discovery and growth.

As Emily looks ahead, she feels a sense of hope and excitement for the future. The stability and love provided by the Johnson family have given her the foundation she needs to build a brighter and more hopeful tomorrow. Emily is ready to face whatever challenges come her way, knowing that she has the support and encouragement of those who care deeply for her.

Emily's story is one of resilience, hope, and the power of a supportive environment. With the unwavering support of the Johnson family, her teachers, and her friends, Emily is ready to embrace the future and all the possibilities it holds. Her journey is a testament to the strength of the human spirit and the importance of love and stability in fostering growth and healing.

Chapter 8
Building Trust

Emily's initial attempts to open up to the Johnsons about her past are tentative and filled with a mix of fear and hope. The process of sharing her experiences is challenging, but the Johnsons' unwavering support and patience help her take the first steps towards building trust.

At first, Emily is hesitant to talk about her past. The memories of neglect and instability are painful, and she fears that sharing them might change the way the Johnsons see her. She often feels a lump in her throat when she thinks about opening up, and the words seem to get stuck. However, the Johnsons' consistent kindness and understanding create a safe environment where Emily begins to feel more comfortable.

Emily's initial attempts to open up come in small, cautious steps. One evening, while helping Mrs. Johnson bake cookies, Emily mentions a memory from her previous home. It's a simple recollection, but it's a significant moment for Emily. Mrs. Johnson listens attentively, offering gentle encouragement without pressing for more details. This response reassures Emily that she can share her thoughts without fear of judgment.

Bedtime becomes a special time for Emily to open up. Mrs. Johnson's bedtime stories and soothing presence create a comforting atmosphere where Emily feels safe. One night, after a particularly vivid nightmare, Emily finds the courage to talk about her fears. Mrs. Johnson holds her hand and listens patiently, offering words of comfort and reassurance. These bedtime conversations become a crucial part of Emily's healing process, helping her feel understood and supported.

Emily also uses art as a way to express her feelings and share her past. During an art club session, she creates a painting that reflects her emotions. The colours and shapes convey a sense of turmoil and hope. When Emma asks about the painting, Emily hesitates but then decides to share the story behind it. Emma's genuine interest and empathy make Emily feel valued and understood. This creative outlet allows Emily to communicate her experiences in a non-verbal way, providing a sense of relief and connection.

The Johnsons' unwavering support plays a crucial role in helping Emily open up. They create a nurturing environment where Emily feels safe to share her thoughts and feelings. Mr. Johnson's calm presence and Mrs. Johnson's nurturing care provide a sense of stability and security. Emma and Finn's friendship and inclusivity help Emily feel accepted and valued. The family's consistent encouragement and understanding reinforce Emily's trust in them.

Emily's therapist also provides guidance and support in helping her open up about her past. Through therapeutic conversations and exercises, Emily learns to articulate her feelings and process her experiences. The therapist helps Emily develop coping strategies to manage her anxiety and build resilience. These sessions provide Emily with the tools she needs to navigate her emotions and share her story.

As Emily continues to take small steps towards opening up, she begins to build trust with the Johnsons. Each shared memory and conversation strengthens their bond and reinforces Emily's sense of belonging. The Johnsons' unwavering support and patience help Emily feel more secure and confident in sharing her past. This process of building trust is a crucial part of Emily's healing journey, allowing her to move forward with hope and resilience.

Emily's initial attempts to open up to the Johnsons are marked by courage and determination. With the love and support of the Johnson family, she begins to navigate the complexities of her past and build a brighter future. The process of sharing her experiences helps Emily feel understood and valued, reinforcing her sense of self-worth, and belonging.

Building trust between Emily and the Johnsons is a gradual

process, nurtured through various activities and shared moments that foster connection and understanding. These experiences help Emily feel more secure and valued, reinforcing her sense of belonging within the family.

One of the most effective trust-building activities is the Johnsons' regular family game nights. These evenings are filled with laughter, friendly competition, and bonding. Emily initially feels hesitant to join in, but the Johnsons' enthusiasm and inclusivity soon make her feel comfortable. Whether it's playing board games, card games, or charades, these moments of shared fun help Emily relax and connect with each family member. The positive interactions and the sense of camaraderie strengthen her trust in the Johnsons.

Cooking together becomes a cherished activity for Emily and Mrs. Johnson. They spend time in the kitchen, preparing meals and baking treats. Mrs. Johnson patiently teaches Emily new recipes and techniques, creating a warm and supportive environment. The act of creating something together fosters a sense of accomplishment and teamwork. These cooking sessions provide Emily with opportunities to share stories and open up about her feelings, deepening her bond with Mrs. Johnson.

Finn's love for outdoor activities provides Emily with opportunities to build trust through shared adventures. Finn invites Emily to join him in various outdoor pursuits, such as hiking, biking, and playing football. These activities help Emily build confidence and resilience, as she learns new skills and overcomes challenges. The shared experiences and the encouragement from Finn help Emily feel more connected and supported, reinforcing her trust in him as a caring brother.

Emma's passion for art becomes a bridge for building trust with Emily. They spend hours together working on art projects, from painting to crafting. Emma's genuine interest in Emily's creativity and her encouraging words help Emily feel valued and understood. The shared moments of creativity and collaboration foster a sense of trust and friendship between the two girls. Emily begins to see Emma as a supportive and caring sister, someone on whom she can rely.

Bedtime stories with Mrs. Johnson become a special ritual that helps Emily feel safe and secure. Each night, Mrs. Johnson reads a story to Emily, creating a comforting and calming atmosphere. These moments of closeness provide Emily with a sense of stability and reassurance. The bedtime routine becomes a time for Emily to share her thoughts and feelings, knowing that Mrs. Johnson is there to listen and support her. This nightly ritual strengthens their bond and reinforces Emily's trust in Mrs. Johnson.

The Johnsons make a point of celebrating Emily's milestones and achievements, no matter how small. Whether it's a good grade, a successful art project, or a personal goal, the family acknowledges and celebrates her accomplishments. These moments of recognition and praise boost Emily's confidence and reinforce her sense of self-worth. The positive reinforcement helps Emily feel appreciated and valued, deepening her trust in the Johnsons.

The Johnsons' commitment to Emily's emotional well-being is evident in their support for her therapeutic sessions. They work closely with her therapist to ensure that Emily receives the care and guidance she needs. The Johnsons' involvement in her therapeutic process demonstrates their dedication to her healing and growth. This consistent support helps Emily feel more secure and trusting, knowing that the Johnsons are committed to her well-being.

The Johnsons prioritize open communication, encouraging Emily to share her thoughts and feelings. They create a safe and non-judgmental environment where Emily feels comfortable expressing herself. The family's willingness to listen and understand helps Emily feel heard and valued. This open dialogue fosters a sense of trust and connection, reinforcing Emily's belief that she is an integral part of the Johnson family.

These trust-building activities and moments play a crucial role in helping Emily feel secure and valued within the Johnson household. The shared experiences, positive interactions, and unwavering support from the Johnsons create a nurturing environment where Emily can heal, grow, and build a brighter future.

Emily's journey towards emotional security is marked by several significant breakthroughs. These moments are pivotal in helping her feel more secure and connected with the Johnson family, reinforcing her sense of belonging and self-worth.

One of the most profound emotional breakthroughs occurs

when Emily finally shares her full story with the Johnsons. One evening, after a particularly challenging day, Emily feels a surge of courage and decides to open up about her past. She sits down with Mr. and Mrs. Johnson and begins to recount her experiences of neglect and instability. The Johnsons listen with empathy and compassion, offering words of comfort and reassurance. This moment of vulnerability is a turning point for Emily, as she feels a weight lifted off her shoulders. The Johnsons' unwavering support and understanding help Emily feel more secure and valued.

Another significant breakthrough happens during an art club session. Emily creates a powerful painting that reflects her inner turmoil and hope for the future. When she shares the painting with Emma and the art club members, she explains the emotions behind it. The positive feedback and encouragement she receives make Emily feel understood and appreciated. This experience helps Emily realize that she can express her feelings in creative ways and that her voice matters. The sense of accomplishment and connection she feels through her art boosts her confidence and emotional security.

Emily's recurring nightmares are a source of anxiety and fear. One night, after waking up from a particularly distressing dream, she decides to talk to Mrs. Johnson about it. Mrs. Johnson listens patiently and helps Emily understand that her nightmares are a way for her mind to process past trauma. Together, they come up with strategies to manage the nightmares, such as creating a calming bedtime routine and using positive affirmations. Over time, Emily's nightmares become less frequent, and she feels more in control of her emotions. This breakthrough helps Emily feel safer and more secure in her new home.

Emily's relationship with Finn also experiences a significant breakthrough. During a family outing to a nearby park, Finn invites Emily to join him in a game of football. Initially hesitant, Emily decides to give it a try. Finn's patience and encouragement help her feel more comfortable, and she starts to enjoy the game. When Emily scores her first goal, the entire family cheers for her, and she feels a surge of pride and accomplishment. This moment strengthens her bond with Finn and reinforces her sense of belonging within the family. Emily begins to see Finn as a supportive and caring brother, which helps her feel more secure.

Emily's sessions with her therapist also lead to significant emotional breakthroughs. Through guided conversations and exercises, Emily learns to articulate her feelings and develop healthy coping mechanisms. One breakthrough occurs when Emily successfully uses mindfulness techniques to manage her anxiety during a particularly stressful day. The therapist praises her progress, and Emily feels a sense of empowerment and control over her emotions. These therapeutic breakthroughs help Emily build resilience and emotional strength, contributing to her overall sense of security.

The Johnsons' practice of celebrating Emily's achievements, no matter how small, plays a crucial role in her emotional growth. When Emily receives a good grade on a challenging assignment, the family throws a small celebration to acknowledge her hard work. These moments of recognition and praise boost Emily's confidence and reinforce her sense of self-worth. The positive reinforcement helps Emily feel appreciated and valued, contributing to her emotional security.

These significant emotional breakthroughs are pivotal in helping Emily feel more secure and connected with the Johnson family. The shared experiences, positive interactions, and unwavering support from the Johnsons create a nurturing environment where Emily can heal, grow, and build a brighter future.

Emily's academic journey is marked by significant achievements that play a crucial role in boosting her confidence and reinforcing her sense of self-worth. The support from the Johnson family and her teachers helps her overcome initial challenges and thrive in her new school environment.

When Emily first starts at her new school, she faces several academic challenges. The disruption in her education due to her unstable home life has left her behind in some subjects. However, with the help of her teachers and the Johnsons, Emily begins to catch up. Ms. Thompson, her primary teacher, provides extra tutoring sessions and personalized assignments to address her specific needs. The Johnsons create a structured study routine at home, ensuring that Emily has a quiet and conducive environment to focus on her studies.

Emily's hard work and determination soon start to pay off. Her grades begin to improve, and she receives positive feedback from her teachers. The first time Emily brings home a report card with significantly better grades, the Johnsons celebrate her achievement with a small family gathering. They praise her efforts and dedication, reinforcing her sense of accomplishment. This recognition boosts Emily's confidence and motivates her to continue striving for academic success.

As Emily becomes more comfortable in her new school, she starts to participate more actively in class. She raises her hand to answer questions, contributes to group discussions, and collaborates with her classmates on projects. Ms. Thompson notices Emily's increased engagement and praises her for her contributions. This positive reinforcement helps Emily feel more confident in her abilities and encourages her to take on new challenges.

Emily's academic success is further highlighted when she receives awards and recognition for her achievements. During a school assembly, Emily is presented with a certificate for her outstanding performance in a science project. The applause from her peers and teachers fills her with pride and joy. The Johnsons attend the assembly and cheer for Emily, making her feel valued and supported. This public recognition reinforces Emily's belief in her capabilities and inspires her to set higher goals.

Emily's academic success also strengthens her relationships with her peers. Her classmates begin to see her as a capable and hardworking student, and they seek her help with assignments and projects. Emily's willingness to assist her peers and share her knowledge fosters a sense of camaraderie and mutual respect. These positive interactions help Emily feel more integrated into the school community and boost her self-esteem.

Emily's involvement in extracurricular activities, such as the art club and football team, also contributes to her academic success. The skills she develops in these activities, such as teamwork, time management, and creative thinking, enhance her overall performance in school. The sense of accomplishment she feels in these activities translates into increased confidence in her academic pursuits.

With her newfound confidence and academic success, Emily

begins to dream about her future. She sets her sights on higher education and explores potential career paths that align with her interests and talents. The support and encouragement from the Johnsons and her teachers give her the confidence to pursue her aspirations and believe in her potential.

Emily's academic success is a testament to her resilience and determination. The support from the Johnson family and her teachers plays a crucial role in helping her overcome challenges and achieve her goals. Each achievement boosts Emily's confidence and reinforces her sense of self-worth, paving the way for a brighter and more hopeful future.

Emily's discovery of art becomes a transformative and therapeutic outlet for her emotions, providing her with a means to express herself and process her feelings in a creative and non-verbal way. This newfound passion plays a crucial role in her healing journey and personal growth.

Emily's initial exposure to art comes through Emma, who is an avid artist. Emma often spends her free time drawing and painting, and she invites Emily to join her. At first, Emily is hesitant, unsure of her abilities and feeling self-conscious about her work. However, Emma's enthusiasm and encouragement help Emily feel more comfortable. She begins to experiment with different mediums, from coloured pencils to watercolours, and discovers a sense of joy and freedom in the creative process.

Encouraged by her positive experiences with Emma, Emily decides to join the school's art club. The club provides a supportive and inclusive environment where Emily can explore her creativity and connect with other students who share her passion. The art club becomes a sanctuary for Emily, a place where she feels valued and understood. The club's activities, such as collaborative projects and art exhibitions, give Emily a sense of accomplishment and pride in her work.

Art becomes a powerful tool for Emily to express her emotions and process her past experiences. Through her drawings and paintings, she is able to convey feelings that are difficult to articulate with words. Emily's artwork often reflects her inner turmoil, as well as her hopes and dreams for the future. The act of creating art provides her with a therapeutic release, helping her manage anxiety and stress. Emily finds solace in the creative process, and her art becomes a means of self-discovery and healing.

The positive feedback and encouragement Emily receives from her peers, teachers, and the Johnson family further boost her confidence. Her art teacher, Ms. Rivera, recognizes Emily's talent and provides guidance and support to help her develop her skills. The Johnsons proudly display Emily's artwork around the house, reinforcing her sense of accomplishment and self-worth. These affirmations help Emily feel more confident in her abilities and motivate her to continue exploring her artistic talents.

Emily's involvement in art becomes an essential coping mechanism for managing her emotions. Whenever she feels overwhelmed or anxious, she turns to her sketchbook or easel. The act of creating art helps her focus her mind and channel her energy into something positive. Emily's therapist also encourages her to use art as a form of expression, incorporating it into their sessions as a way to explore her feelings and experiences. This creative outlet provides Emily with a sense of control and empowerment, helping her navigate the complexities of her emotions.

Through her art, Emily builds meaningful connections with others. She forms friendships with fellow art club members, who share her passion and provide a supportive community. These relationships help Emily feel more integrated into the school environment and reinforce her sense of belonging. Emily also bonds with the Johnson family through shared creative activities, such as family art projects and visits to local galleries. These experiences strengthen her relationships and create lasting memories.

Emily's discovery of art opens up new possibilities for her future. She begins to dream about pursuing a career in the arts, whether as an artist, illustrator, or art therapist. The support and encouragement she receives from the Johnsons and her teachers give her the confidence to explore these aspirations. Emily sets goals for herself, such as participating in art competitions and applying to art schools, and she works diligently to achieve them.

Emily's journey with art is a testament to the healing power of creativity. Through her artistic expression, she finds a therapeutic outlet for her emotions, builds confidence, and discovers new possibilities for her future. The support and encouragement from the Johnson family and her school community play a crucial role in helping Emily thrive and embrace her passion for art.

The Johnson family creates a nurturing and supportive environment that plays a crucial role in helping Emily thrive. Their unwavering love, patience, and understanding provide Emily with the stability and security she needs to heal and grow.

The Johnsons prioritize Emily's emotional wellbeing, offering consistent reassurance and encouragement. Mrs. Johnson's nurturing care and Mr. Johnson's calm presence create a safe space where Emily feels valued and understood. They listen attentively to her concerns, validate her feelings, and provide comforting words and gentle hugs. This emotional support helps Emily feel secure and boosts her confidence.

The Johnsons establish a structured routine that provides Emily with a sense of predictability and stability. Mornings start with a family breakfast, where they share plans for the day and offer words of encouragement. Evenings are reserved for family time, whether it's playing board games, watching movies, or going for walks. This routine helps Emily feel grounded and reduces her anxiety, allowing her to focus on her studies and personal growth.

The Johnsons are deeply involved in Emily's academic journey. They create a quiet and conducive environment for her to study and complete her homework. Mr. Johnson, with his background in education, often helps Emily with her assignments, providing guidance and explanations when needed. The Johnsons celebrate Emily's academic achievements, reinforcing her sense of accomplishment and motivating her to continue striving for success.

The Johnsons encourage Emily to explore her interests and hobbies, providing her with opportunities to discover her passions. They support her involvement in extracurricular activities, such as the art club and football team, and celebrate her achievements in these areas. The Johnsons' encouragement helps Emily build confidence and develop new skills, contributing to her overall well-being and happiness.

The Johnsons prioritize open communication, encouraging

Emily to share her thoughts and feelings. They create a non-judgmental environment where Emily feels comfortable expressing herself. The family's willingness to listen and understand helps Emily feel heard and valued, reinforcing her trust in the Johnsons.

Recognizing the importance of professional support, the Johnsons ensure that Emily continues to receive therapeutic care. They coordinate with her therapist to provide additional sessions and coping strategies tailored to her needs. The Johnsons' involvement in her therapeutic process demonstrates their commitment to her healing and growth, helping Emily build resilience and emotional strength.

The Johnsons celebrate each milestone and achievement, no matter how small, reinforcing Emily's sense of self-worth and accomplishment. Whether it's a good grade, a successful art project, or a personal goal, the family acknowledges and celebrates her efforts. These moments of recognition boost Emily's confidence and motivate her to continue striving for success.

The Johnsons' consistent kindness and reliability help Emily build trust in them. They create a nurturing environment where Emily feels safe to share her thoughts and feelings. The family's unwavering support and patience reinforce Emily's sense of security and belonging, allowing her to open up and build deeper connections with each family member.

The supportive environment provided by the Johnsons plays a crucial role in helping Emily thrive. Their love, patience, and understanding create a nurturing space where Emily can heal, grow, and build a brighter future. With the Johnson family by her side, Emily feels empowered and hopeful, ready to embrace the possibilities that lie ahead.

Emily's journey is marked by numerous challenges, but with the unwavering support of the Johnson family, she learns to navigate these obstacles and emerge stronger. The Johnsons' love, patience, and guidance play a crucial role in helping Emily overcome her difficulties and build resilience.

One of the first challenges Emily faces is catching up academically. The disruption in her education due to her unstable home life has left her behind in several subjects. Emily often feels overwhelmed by the workload and fears she won't be able to meet the expectations. However, with the help of her teachers and the Johnsons, she begins to make progress. Mr. Johnson provides extra tutoring sessions, breaking down complex concepts into manageable steps. The structured study routine at home ensures that Emily has a quiet and conducive environment to focus on her studies. The Johnsons celebrate each academic achievement, no matter how small, boosting Emily's confidence and motivating her to keep trying.

Emily's past experiences have left her with deep seated feelings of insecurity and abandonment. She often struggles with anxiety and fear, especially when faced with new situations or challenges. The Johnsons provide a nurturing and supportive environment where Emily feels safe to express her emotions. Mrs. Johnson's comforting presence and Mr. Johnson's calm reassurance help Emily feel understood and valued. The family's consistent kindness and reliability gradually break down Emily's walls of apprehension, allowing her to build trust and feel more secure.

Emily's recurring nightmares are a source of significant anxiety. The memories of her past trauma often resurface in her dreams, leaving her feeling scared and vulnerable. The Johnsons work closely with Emily's therapist to develop strategies to manage her nightmares. They create a calming bedtime routine, incorporating mindfulness exercises and positive affirmations. Mrs. Johnson stays with Emily until she falls asleep, providing a sense of security. Over time, Emily's nightmares become less frequent, and she learns to manage her anxiety more effectively.

Initially, Emily finds it challenging to integrate socially at her new school. She feels self-conscious and fears rejection from her peers. The Johnsons encourage Emily to participate in extracurricular activities, such as the art club and football team, where she can connect with others who share her interests. These activities provide Emily with opportunities to build friendships and develop social skills. The positive interactions and the sense of belonging she experiences help Emily feel more confident and accepted.

Emily's past experiences have made it difficult for her to trust adults. She often feels wary and guarded, fearing that she might be let down again. The Johnsons' consistent support and understanding help Emily gradually build trust. They create a nurturing environment where Emily feels safe to share her thoughts and feelings. The family's unwavering presence and encouragement reinforce Emily's sense of security and belonging, allowing her to open up and build deeper connections.

Emily often struggles with self-doubt, questioning her abilities and worth. The Johnsons provide constant encouragement and positive reinforcement, helping Emily build confidence in herself. They celebrate her achievements and remind her of her strengths, reinforcing her sense of self-worth. The family's belief in Emily's potential motivates her to set higher goals and work towards them with determination.

The Johnsons ensure that Emily continues to receive therapeutic support to address her emotional and psychological needs. Her therapist helps her develop coping mechanisms to manage stress and anxiety. Through guided conversations and exercises, Emily learns to articulate her feelings and process her past experiences. The therapeutic support, combined with the Johnsons' love and care, helps Emily build resilience and emotional strength.

Emily's journey is a testament to her resilience and determination. With the unwavering support of the Johnson family, she learns to navigate her challenges and build a brighter future. The love, patience, and guidance provided by the Johnsons play a crucial role in helping Emily overcome her difficulties and thrive.

The development of strong friendships plays a pivotal role in Emily's journey, providing her with a sense of belonging, support, and joy. These relationships help Emily build confidence and navigate the challenges of her new life.

One of the first friends Emily makes is Lily, a kind and outgoing girl in her class. Their friendship begins during playtime when Lily invites Emily to join a game of hopscotch. Emily, initially hesitant, finds comfort in Lily's friendly demeanour. As they play, Emily starts to feel more at ease, and the simple game becomes a turning point in her social interactions. Lily's genuine kindness and inclusivity help Emily feel accepted and valued. They soon become close friends, sharing lunch together and working on school projects. Lily's friendship provides Emily with a sense of stability and companionship, easing her transition into the new school environment.

      Emily's involvement in the art club introduces her to a group of like-minded peers who share her passion for creativity. The supportive environment of the club helps Emily feel valued and understood. She enjoys working on various projects, from painting to crafting, and the sense of accomplishment boosts her self-esteem. The friendships she forms with other club members provide her with a sense of belonging and community. They often collaborate on art projects, share ideas, and encourage each other's creativity. These positive interactions help Emily build confidence and develop her artistic skills.

      Joining the school's football team is another significant step in Emily's social development. Encouraged by her positive experiences playing football with Finn, Emily decides to join the team. The physical activity and teamwork help her build confidence and resilience. The support and camaraderie of her teammates make her feel like she is part of something bigger, and she begins to look forward to practices and games. The sense of achievement she feels when she scores a goal or makes a good play reinforces her self-worth and helps her feel more connected to her peers.

      Emily's interest in performing arts leads her to join the school's drama club. The drama club provides her with an outlet to express her emotions and build her confidence. Emily enjoys participating in rehearsals and performances, where she can step into different roles and explore new aspects of her personality. The supportive and encouraging atmosphere of the drama club helps her overcome her initial shyness and embrace her creativity. The friendships she forms with other club members further enhance her sense of belonging and acceptance.

      In the classroom, Emily begins to form connections with her classmates through group projects and class discussions. Her teacher, Ms. Thompson, encourages collaborative learning, which helps Emily interact more with her peers. These interactions provide Emily with opportunities to share her ideas and contribute to group work, boosting her confidence and reinforcing her sense of self-worth. The positive feedback and encouragement from her classmates help Emily feel more integrated into the school community.

The development of new friendships has a profound impact on Emily's emotional well-being and adjustment. These relationships provide her with a sense of belonging and support, helping her navigate the challenges of her new life. The positive interactions and shared experiences with her friends boost her self-esteem and reinforce her sense of self-worth. Emily's growing confidence and resilience are evident in her willingness to try new things and embrace new opportunities.

Emily's new friendships are a testament to her resilience and the power of a supportive environment. With the love and care of the Johnson family and the support of her friends, Emily begins to thrive and find joy in her new experiences. The friendships she forms help her build a brighter and more hopeful future, filled with possibilities and the promise of a better tomorrow.

Emily's journey with the Johnson family is marked by significant personal growth and increasing self-confidence. The supportive environment and the love she receives play a crucial role in helping her develop a strong sense of self-worth and resilience.

Emily's academic success is a testament to her hard work and determination. With the support of her teachers and the Johnsons, she overcomes initial challenges and begins to excel in her studies. Her improved grades and positive feedback from her teachers boost her confidence and motivate her to set higher goals. Emily's participation in class discussions and group projects further enhances her self-esteem, as she realizes the value of her contributions.

Emily's discovery of art becomes a powerful outlet for her emotions and a source of personal growth. Through her involvement in the art club, she develops her artistic skills and gains recognition for her talent. The positive feedback and encouragement she receives from her peers and teachers help Emily build confidence in her abilities. Her artwork becomes a means of self-expression, allowing her to process her feelings and experiences in a creative and therapeutic way.

The strong friendships Emily forms at school and in her extracurricular activities play a significant role in her personal growth. These relationships provide her with a sense of belonging and support, helping her navigate the challenges of her new life. The positive interactions and shared experiences with her friends boost Emily's self-esteem and reinforce her sense of self-worth. She learns to trust others and build meaningful connections, which contribute to her overall well-being.

Emily's ability to overcome challenges is a testament to her resilience and determination. With the unwavering support of the Johnson family, she learns to navigate her fears and anxieties. The coping mechanisms she develops, such as mindfulness exercises and positive affirmations, help her manage stress and build emotional strength. Each challenge she faces and overcomes reinforces her confidence and resilience, empowering her to tackle new obstacles with courage.

The Johnsons encourage Emily to explore her interests and hobbies, providing her with opportunities to discover her passions. Whether it's participating in the art club, joining the football team, or exploring new activities, Emily's involvement in these pursuits helps her build confidence and develop new skills. The sense of accomplishment she feels in these activities contributes to her overall personal growth and happiness.

Emily's sessions with her therapist play a crucial role in her personal growth. Through guided conversations and exercises, she learns to articulate her feelings and develop healthy coping mechanisms. The therapeutic support helps Emily build resilience and emotional strength, allowing her to navigate the complexities of her past and embrace the possibilities of her future. The progress she makes in therapy reinforces her sense of self-worth and empowers her to continue her journey of healing and growth.

The Johnsons' consistent encouragement and positive reinforcement play a significant role in Emily's personal growth. They celebrate her achievements, no matter how small, and remind her of her strengths and capabilities. This positive reinforcement helps Emily build confidence in herself and motivates her to strive for success. The love and support she receives from the Johnsons create a nurturing environment where Emily can thrive and reach her full potential.

Emily's personal growth and increasing self-confidence are a testament to her resilience and determination. With the unwavering support of the Johnson family, she learns to navigate challenges, build meaningful connections, and embrace her passions. Emily's journey is marked by significant achievements and a growing sense of self-worth, paving the way for a brighter and more hopeful future.

As Emily continues to settle into her new life with the Johnsons, she begins to look ahead with a sense of hope and optimism. The journey she has embarked on is filled with both challenges and triumphs, and the support of the Johnson family has been instrumental in helping her navigate this path.

Emily's experiences in the Johnson household have given her a renewed sense of hope. The love, care, and stability provided by the Johnsons have helped her heal and grow in ways she never thought possible. She looks forward to continuing her education, exploring her interests, and building on the friendships she has formed. The positive reinforcement and encouragement she receives from the Johnsons and her teachers have boosted her confidence, and she now believes in her ability to achieve her goals.

Emily dreams of pursuing her passion for art and creativity. She envisions herself continuing to develop her artistic skills, perhaps even considering a future career in the arts. The support she receives from the Johnsons and her involvement in the art club have given her the confidence to dream big and work towards her aspirations.

With the court's decision providing a sense of security, Emily begins to look ahead with optimism. She is excited about continuing her education and exploring her interests. The support she receives from the Johnsons, her teachers, and her friends gives her the confidence to pursue her dreams. Emily envisions a future where she can thrive, both personally and academically, and she is determined to make the most of the opportunities before her.

The bonds Emily has formed with the Johnson family continue to grow stronger. She feels a deep sense of belonging and is grateful for their unwavering support. Emily also maintains a positive relationship with her biological parents through supervised visits, which helps her reconcile her feelings of love and loyalty towards them. These relationships provide her with a sense of stability and connection, reinforcing her emotional well-being.

Looking ahead, Emily is determined to build a brighter future for herself. She is committed to her education and personal growth, and she is excited about the opportunities that lie ahead. The sense of belonging and acceptance she feels in the Johnson household has given her the foundation she needs to thrive.

Emily's journey is a testament to her strength and resilience. With the support of the Johnson family, her teachers, and her friends, she is ready to face the future with hope and courage. The challenges she has overcome and the progress she has made are a source of inspiration, and she is determined to continue moving forward.

As Emily looks ahead, she carries with her the lessons she has learned and the love she has received. Her story is one of healing, growth, and the promise of a brighter tomorrow. With hope in her heart and the support of those around her, Emily is ready to embrace the future and all the possibilities it holds.

Chapter 9
A New Family

The Johnsons' decision to adopt Emily is a heartfelt and deliberate choice, born out of their deep love and commitment to her well-being. The process of adoption is both emotional and procedural, requiring careful consideration and dedication from everyone involved.

The idea of adopting Emily begins to take shape as the Johnsons witness her remarkable progress and the strong bonds she has formed with each family member. Mr. and Mrs. Johnson have numerous discussions about the possibility of adoption, considering the impact it would have on Emily and their family. They reflect on the love and stability they have provided for Emily and the positive changes they have seen in her. The Johnsons are deeply moved by Emily's resilience and determination, and they feel a strong desire to make her a permanent part of their family.

Before making any decisions, the Johnsons have a heartfelt conversation with Emily about the possibility of adoption. They want to ensure that Emily feels comfortable and supported throughout the process. During a quiet evening at home, Mr. and Mrs. Johnson sit down with Emily and gently introduce the idea. They explain what adoption would mean and emphasize that they love her and want her to be a permanent part of their family. Emily is initially overwhelmed by the idea, but as she processes her emotions, she feels a deep sense of gratitude and belonging. The thought of having a forever family fills her with hope and joy.

Once Emily expresses her desire to be adopted, the Johnsons begin the legal and procedural steps required for adoption. They consult with their lawyer, Ms. Parker, who guides them through the process. The first step involves filing a petition for adoption with the family court. This petition includes detailed information about the Johnsons, their relationship with Emily, and their reasons for wanting to adopt her. Ms. Parker ensures that all necessary documents are prepared and submitted accurately.

As part of the adoption process, a home study is conducted to evaluate the Johnsons' suitability as adoptive parents. A social worker visits the Johnson household to assess the living environment and the family dynamics. The social worker conducts interviews with Mr. and Mrs. Johnson, Emily, and other family members to gather information about their relationships and interactions. The Johnsons are open and honest during the evaluation, sharing their experiences and their commitment to Emily's well-being. The social worker's report highlights the loving and supportive environment provided by the Johnsons, reinforcing their suitability as adoptive parents.

The final step in the adoption process is a court hearing, where a judge reviews the petition and the home study report. The Johnsons, accompanied by Ms. Parker and Emily, attend the hearing. The judge asks questions to ensure that the adoption is in Emily's best interest and that she understands the implications of being adopted. Emily, with the support of the Johnsons, confidently expresses her desire to be adopted and her love for her new family. The judge, moved by the heartfelt testimonies and the positive evidence presented, grants the adoption petition.

The day the adoption is finalized is a joyous occasion for the Johnson family. They celebrate with a small gathering of close friends and family, marking the beginning of a new chapter in their lives. Emily feels an overwhelming sense of happiness and security, knowing that she is now a permanent part of the Johnson family. The love and support she receives from the Johnsons give her the confidence to embrace her future with hope and optimism.

The Johnsons' decision to adopt Emily is a testament to their love and dedication. The process, though challenging, is filled with moments of joy and hope. With the adoption finalized, Emily feels more secure and confident in her new life, ready to face the future with the unwavering support of her forever family.

Emily's initial hesitation and fears about being adopted are deeply rooted in her past experiences and the uncertainty of the future. The thought of adoption brings a mix of emotions, including anxiety, fear, and hope.

One of Emily's primary fears is the possibility of rejection. Her past experiences with neglect and instability have left her with deep-seated feelings of insecurity. Emily worries that if she opens her heart to the Johnsons and they decide not to adopt her, she will be left feeling abandoned and unloved once again. This fear of rejection makes her hesitant to fully embrace the idea of adoption.

The uncertainty of the future also contributes to Emily's hesitation. While she feels a strong sense of belonging with the Johnsons, the thought of making it permanent through adoption is overwhelming. Emily is unsure about what the future holds and whether she will be able to meet the expectations of being a permanent member of the Johnson family. The unknown aspects of adoption create anxiety and make her hesitant to take the next step.

Emily's loyalty to her biological parents adds another layer of complexity to her feelings about adoption. Despite the neglect and instability, she experienced, Emily still feels a deep sense of love and loyalty towards her parents. The thought of being adopted by the Johnsons makes her feel conflicted, as if she is betraying her biological parents. This internal struggle creates hesitation and uncertainty about the adoption process.

Change is always challenging, and the prospect of adoption represents a significant change in Emily's life. While she has found stability and love with the Johnsons, the formalization of this relationship through adoption is a major step. Emily fears that this change might bring new challenges and uncertainties. The fear of the unknown and the potential for disruption make her hesitant to fully embrace the idea of adoption.

Emily's hesitation is also driven by a need for reassurance. She wants to be certain that the Johnsons truly want her to be a permanent part of their family and that their love and commitment are unwavering. Emily seeks reassurance that she will be accepted and valued, regardless of her past experiences and the challenges she may face in the future. This need for reassurance makes her cautious about moving forward with the adoption process.

The Johnsons play a crucial role in addressing Emily's fears and hesitation. They provide consistent reassurance and support, emphasizing their love and commitment to her. Mr. and Mrs. Johnson have open and honest conversations with Emily, addressing her concerns and validating her feelings. They emphasize that their desire to adopt her is driven by their deep love and belief in her potential. The Johnsons' patience and understanding help Emily feel more secure and confident in their intentions.

Emily's therapist also provides valuable support in helping her navigate her fears and hesitation. Through guided conversations and exercises, Emily learns to articulate her feelings and process her emotions. The therapist helps Emily understand that her fears are valid and that it's okay to feel uncertain. Together, they work on building coping mechanisms and strategies to manage anxiety and build confidence. The therapeutic support helps Emily feel more empowered and ready to embrace the possibility of adoption.

Emily's initial hesitation and fears about being adopted are complex and multifaceted. However, with the unwavering support of the Johnson family and her therapist, she begins to navigate these emotions and build the confidence to move forward. The journey is challenging, but Emily's resilience and determination, coupled with the love and care of those around her, help her face the future with hope and optimism.

The Johnsons provide Emily with unwavering reassurance and support, helping her navigate her fears and uncertainties about being adopted. Their consistent love and understanding play a crucial role in making Emily feel secure and valued.

The Johnsons prioritize open and honest conversations with Emily. They create a safe space where she feels comfortable expressing her fears and concerns. Mr. and Mrs. Johnson take the time to listen to Emily's worries about adoption, validating her feelings and providing gentle reassurance. They emphasize that their desire to adopt her comes from a place of deep love and commitment, and they assure her that she will always be a cherished member of their family.

Throughout the adoption process, the Johnsons offer consistent encouragement to Emily. They celebrate her achievements, no matter how small, and remind her of her strengths and capabilities.

This positive reinforcement helps Emily build confidence in herself and feel more secure in her place within the family. The Johnsons' unwavering belief in Emily's potential motivates her to embrace the future with hope and optimism.

Mrs. Johnson's nurturing care provides Emily with a sense of emotional security. She offers comforting words and gentle hugs, helping Emily feel understood and valued. Mrs. Johnson's presence is a constant source of reassurance, especially during moments of doubt and anxiety. Her ability to create a warm and loving environment helps Emily feel safe and supported.

Mr. Johnson's calm and steady presence helps Emily build trust in the Johnson family. He takes the time to explain the adoption process to her, alleviating some of her fears and uncertainties. Mr. Johnson's reliability and patience reinforce Emily's sense of security, making her feel more confident in their intentions. His consistent support helps Emily feel more comfortable opening up and sharing her thoughts and feelings.

The Johnsons engage in various family bonding activities that help Emily feel more connected and secure. Whether it's playing board games, going for walks, or working on art projects together, these shared experiences create lasting memories and strengthen their bond. The sense of belonging and togetherness that Emily feels during these activities reinforces her confidence in the Johnsons' love and commitment.

The Johnsons ensure that Emily continues to receive therapeutic support to address her emotional and psychological needs. They work closely with her therapist to provide additional sessions and coping strategies tailored to her needs. The Johnsons' involvement in her therapeutic process demonstrates their commitment to her healing and growth, helping Emily build resilience and emotional strength.

The Johnsons emphasize the permanence of their commitment to Emily. They reassure her that their love and support are unwavering, regardless of the challenges they may face. This reassurance helps Emily feel more secure in her place within the family and more confident in the future. The Johnsons' consistent presence and dedication provide Emily with a sense of stability and belonging.

The reassurance and support Emily receives from the Johnsons play a crucial role in helping her navigate her fears and uncertainties about being adopted. Their unwavering love and understanding create a nurturing environment where Emily feels secure and valued, allowing her to embrace the future with hope and optimism.

The legal process of adoption involves several steps designed to ensure that the adoption is in the best interest of the child and that all legal requirements are met. Here's a detailed look at the steps involved in the adoption process.

The process begins with an initial consultation with an adoption attorney or an adoption agency. The Johnsons meet with their lawyer, Ms. Parker, to discuss their desire to adopt Emily and to understand the legal requirements and procedures involved. This consultation helps them prepare for the steps ahead and ensures they are fully informed about the process.

The next step is to file a petition for adoption with the family court. This petition includes detailed information about the Johnsons, their relationship with Emily, and their reasons for wanting to adopt her. The petition also includes background information about Emily and her biological parents. Ms. Parker ensures that all necessary documents are prepared and submitted accurately.

A home study is conducted to evaluate the Johnsons' suitability as adoptive parents. A social worker visits the Johnson household to assess the living environment and the family dynamics. The social worker conducts interviews with Mr. and Mrs. Johnson, Emily, and other family members to gather information about their relationships and interactions. The home study report includes observations about the family's ability to provide a stable and nurturing environment for Emily.

As part of the home study, background checks are conducted on the Johnsons to ensure they have no criminal history or other issues that could affect their ability to provide a safe and stable home for Emily. These checks include criminal records, child abuse registry checks, and sometimes financial assessments to ensure the family can support the child.

Pre-adoption counselling is often required to help the

prospective adoptive parents and the child prepare for the adoption. This counselling provides guidance on the emotional and psychological aspects of adoption, helping the family navigate any challenges that may arise. The Johnsons participate in counselling sessions to ensure they are fully prepared for the adoption process and to address any concerns Emily may have.

Before the adoption can be finalized, the parental rights of Emily's biological parents must be legally terminated. This step involves a court hearing where the judge reviews the circumstances and determines whether terminating the parental rights is in the best interest of the child. In Emily's case, her biological parents voluntarily relinquish their rights, recognizing that the Johnsons can provide a better future for her.

The final step in the adoption process is a court hearing, where a judge reviews the petition for adoption and the home study report. The Johnsons, accompanied by Ms. Parker and Emily, attend the hearing. The judge asks questions to ensure that the adoption is in Emily's best interest and that she understands the implications of being adopted. Emily, with the support of the Johnsons, confidently expresses her desire to be adopted and her love for her new family. The judge, moved by the heartfelt testimonies and the positive evidence presented, grants the adoption petition.

Once the judge approves the adoption, the adoption is finalized, and a final decree of adoption is issued. This legal document confirms that Emily is now a permanent member of the Johnson family and that the Johnsons have all the legal rights and responsibilities of her parents. The finalization of the adoption is a joyous occasion, marking the beginning of a new chapter in their lives.

After the adoption is finalized, the Johnsons continue to receive post-adoption support to help them navigate any challenges that may arise. This support includes counselling, support groups, and resources to ensure that Emily's transition into her new family is smooth and successful. The Johnsons remain committed to providing Emily with the love, care, and stability she needs to thrive.

The legal process of adoption is thorough and designed to ensure that the best interests of the child are prioritized. With the support of their lawyer, Ms. Parker, and the dedication of the Johnson family, Emily's adoption process is completed successfully, providing her with a loving and permanent home.

Emily's emotional journey as she comes to terms with being adopted is a profound and transformative experience. It is marked by moments of fear, hope, and ultimately, acceptance and joy.

At the beginning of the adoption process, Emily is overwhelmed by a mix of emotions. The fear of the unknown and the possibility of rejection weigh heavily on her mind. She worries about whether she will truly be accepted as a permanent member of the Johnson family and whether she can live up to their expectations. The thought of making such a significant change in her life fills her with anxiety and uncertainty.

Emily also grapples with conflicting emotions about her biological parents. Despite the neglect and instability, she experienced, she still feels a deep sense of love and loyalty towards them. The idea of being adopted by the Johnsons makes her feel as though she is betraying her biological parents. This internal struggle creates a sense of guilt and hesitation, making it difficult for her to fully embrace the idea of adoption.

The unwavering support and reassurance from the Johnsons play a crucial role in helping Emily navigate her emotions. They provide a safe and nurturing environment where she feels comfortable expressing her fears and concerns. Mr. and Mrs. Johnson have open and honest conversations with Emily, addressing her worries and validating her feelings. Their consistent encouragement and love help Emily feel more secure and valued.

Emily's therapist provides valuable guidance in helping her process her emotions and come to terms with the adoption. Through therapeutic conversations and exercises, Emily learns to articulate her feelings and develop healthy coping mechanisms. The therapist helps Emily understand that her fears and conflicting emotions are valid and that it's okay to feel uncertain. This therapeutic support empowers Emily to navigate her emotional journey with resilience and confidence.

As Emily begins to feel more secure in the Johnson household, moments of hope and optimism start to emerge. She experiences small victories and achievements that boost her confidence and reinforce her sense of self-worth. The positive reinforcement and encouragement from the Johnsons and her teachers help Emily believe in her ability to thrive and succeed. These moments of hope provide a glimpse of the bright future that lies ahead.

The turning point in Emily's emotional journey comes when she finally accepts the idea of being adopted. The consistent love and support from the Johnsons, combined with the therapeutic guidance she receives, help her overcome her fears and uncertainties. Emily realizes that being adopted does not mean she is betraying her biological parents; rather, it means she is gaining a loving and supportive family who will always be there for her. This realization fills her with a sense of joy and relief.

The day the adoption is finalized is a momentous occasion for Emily. As the judge grants the adoption petition, Emily feels an overwhelming sense of happiness and security. The fear and uncertainty that once clouded her mind are replaced by a deep sense of belonging and acceptance. Emily knows that she is now a permanent member of the Johnson family, and this knowledge fills her with hope and optimism for the future.

With the adoption finalized, Emily looks ahead with renewed hope and determination. She is excited about continuing her education, exploring her interests, and building on the friendships she has formed. The love and support she receives from the Johnsons give her the confidence to pursue her dreams and embrace the possibilities that lie ahead. Emily's emotional journey is a testament to her resilience and strength, and she is ready to face the future with courage and optimism.

Emily's emotional journey as she comes to terms with being adopted is marked by moments of fear, hope, and ultimately, acceptance and joy. With the unwavering support of the Johnson family and her therapist, Emily navigates her emotions and builds a brighter and more hopeful future.

As Emily settles into her new life with the Johnsons, she begins to build a new identity and a strong sense of belonging. This transformative process is marked by moments of self-discovery, acceptance, and the unwavering support of her new family.

Emily starts to embrace her new role as a member of the Johnson family. She takes pride in being part of a loving and supportive household, and this sense of belonging helps her build a positive self-identity. Emily begins to see herself not just as a foster child, but as a valued and integral part of the Johnson family. This shift in perspective boosts her confidence and reinforces her sense of self-worth.

The Johnsons involve Emily in creating new family traditions, which helps her feel more connected and integrated into the family. Whether it's celebrating holidays, participating in family game nights, or going on weekend outings, these shared experiences create lasting memories and strengthen their bond. Emily's active participation in these traditions helps her feel more secure and valued, reinforcing her sense of belonging.

Emily's exploration of her personal interests plays a significant role in building her new identity. The Johnsons encourage her to pursue her passions, whether it's art, sports, or other hobbies. Emily's involvement in the art club and football team allows her to develop her skills and gain recognition for her talents. These activities provide her with a sense of accomplishment and help her build a positive self-image.

The strong friendships Emily forms at school and in her extracurricular activities contribute to her sense of belonging. These relationships provide her with a supportive network of peers who share her interests and values. The positive interactions and shared experiences with her friends help Emily feel more integrated into her new community. These friendships reinforce her sense of identity and help her build confidence in her social interactions.

Emily's sessions with her therapist continue to play a crucial role in her journey of self-discovery. Through guided conversations and exercises, Emily learns to articulate her feelings and develop a deeper understanding of herself. The therapeutic support helps her process her past experiences and build a positive self-identity. Emily's growing self-awareness and emotional resilience contribute to her overall sense of well-being.

The Johnsons' consistent encouragement and positive reinforcement help Emily build confidence in herself. They celebrate her achievements, no matter how small, and remind her of her strengths and capabilities. This positive reinforcement helps Emily develop a strong sense of self-worth and motivates her to continue striving for success. The love and support she receives from the Johnsons create a nurturing environment where Emily can thrive.

As part of the adoption process, Emily decides to take on the Johnson family name. This symbolic gesture represents her acceptance of her new identity and her commitment to being a permanent member of the family. The Johnsons celebrate this milestone with a small family gathering, reinforcing Emily's sense of belonging and pride in her new identity.

With her new identity and sense of belonging, Emily looks to the future with hope and optimism. She is excited about continuing her education, exploring her interests, and building on the friendships she has formed. The support and encouragement she receives from the Johnsons give her the confidence to pursue her dreams and embrace the possibilities that lie ahead. Emily's journey of self-discovery and acceptance is a testament to her resilience and strength, and she is ready to face the future with courage and optimism.

Emily's process of building a new identity and sense of belonging with the Johnsons is marked by moments of self-discovery, acceptance, and the unwavering support of her new family. With the love and encouragement of the Johnsons, Emily is able to embrace her new identity and build a brighter and more hopeful future.

Celebrating milestones is a cherished tradition in the Johnson household, and these moments play a significant role in reinforcing Emily's sense of belonging and self-worth. Each milestone is an opportunity to acknowledge Emily's achievements and create lasting memories with her new family.

Emily's first birthday with the Johnsons is a joyous occasion. The family goes all out to make her feel special, decorating the house with balloons and streamers. Mrs. Johnson bakes a beautiful cake, and Emily's friends from school and the art club are invited to join the celebration. The day is filled with laughter, games, and heartfelt moments. Emily is overwhelmed with gratitude and happiness, feeling truly loved and appreciated. This celebration marks a significant milestone in her journey, reinforcing her sense of belonging and acceptance.

Emily's academic achievements are celebrated with enthusiasm and pride. When she receives her first report card with improved grades, the Johnsons throw a small family party to acknowledge her hard work and dedication. They present her with a certificate of achievement and a special gift, reinforcing her sense of accomplishment. These celebrations boost Emily's confidence and motivate her to continue striving for success. The positive reinforcement helps her build a strong sense of self-worth and pride in her abilities.

Emily's involvement in the art club leads to several opportunities to showcase her talent. When her artwork is selected for a school exhibition, the Johnsons are there to support her. They attend the exhibition, taking photos and praising her creativity. Emily's art teacher, Ms. Rivera, also acknowledges her talent, further boosting her confidence. These moments of recognition and celebration help Emily feel valued and appreciated, reinforcing her passion for art.

Emily's participation in the school's football team is another source of pride and celebration. When she scores her first goal in a match, the Johnsons cheer for her from the sidelines, capturing the moment on camera. They celebrate her achievement with a special dinner and words of encouragement. These celebrations help Emily feel more confident in her abilities and reinforce her sense of belonging within the team and her family.

The Johnsons create new holiday traditions that include Emily, making her feel like an integral part of the family. Whether it's decorating the Christmas tree, carving pumpkins for Halloween, or participating in an Easter egg hunt, these shared experiences create lasting memories and strengthen their bond. Emily looks forward to these traditions, knowing that she is part of a loving and supportive family.

As Emily progresses through school, her graduation and awards ceremonies become significant milestones. The Johnsons attend these events with pride, celebrating her achievements and capturing the moments on camera. They present her with flowers and gifts, acknowledging her hard work and dedication. These celebrations reinforce Emily's sense of accomplishment and motivate her to continue pursuing her goals.

The day the adoption is finalized is one of the most significant milestones in Emily's life. The Johnsons celebrate this momentous occasion with a special family gathering. They present Emily with a personalized adoption certificate and a heartfelt letter expressing their love and commitment. The celebration is filled with joy and gratitude, marking the beginning of a new chapter in their lives. Emily feels an overwhelming sense of happiness and security, knowing that she is now a permanent member of the Johnson family.

Celebrating milestones is an important tradition in the Johnson household, and these moments play a crucial role in reinforcing Emily's sense of belonging and self-worth. Each celebration is an opportunity to acknowledge her achievements and create lasting memories, helping Emily build a brighter and more hopeful future.

Emily's journey towards adoption is filled with moments of doubt and fear, but with the unwavering support of the Johnson family, she learns to overcome these challenges and embrace her new life.

One of Emily's primary doubts is the fear of rejection. Her past experiences with neglect and instability have left her with deep-seated feelings of insecurity. She worries that if she opens her heart to the Johnsons and they decide not to adopt her, she will be left feeling abandoned and unloved once again. This fear of rejection makes her hesitant to fully embrace the idea of adoption.

The uncertainty of the future also contributes to Emily's doubts. While she feels a strong sense of belonging with the Johnsons, the thought of making it permanent through adoption is overwhelming. Emily is unsure about what the future holds and whether she will be able to meet the expectations of being a permanent member of the Johnson family. The unknown aspects of adoption create anxiety and make her hesitant to take the next step.

Emily's loyalty to her biological parents adds another layer of complexity to her feelings about adoption. Despite the neglect and instability, she experienced, Emily still feels a deep sense of love and loyalty towards her parents. The thought of being adopted by the Johnsons makes her feel conflicted, as if she is betraying her biological parents. This internal struggle creates hesitation and uncertainty about the adoption process.

Change is always challenging, and the prospect of adoption represents a significant change in Emily's life. While she has found stability and love with the Johnsons, the formalization of this relationship through adoption is a major step. Emily fears that this change might bring new challenges and uncertainties. The fear of the unknown and the potential for disruption make her hesitant to fully embrace the idea of adoption.

Emily's doubts are also driven by a need for reassurance. She wants to be certain that the Johnsons truly want her to be a permanent part of their family and that their love and commitment are unwavering. Emily seeks reassurance that she will be accepted and valued, regardless of her past experiences and the challenges she may face in the future. This need for reassurance makes her cautious about moving forward with the adoption process.

The Johnsons play a crucial role in addressing Emily's doubts and fears. They provide consistent reassurance and support, emphasizing their love and commitment to her. Mr. and Mrs. Johnson have open and honest conversations with Emily, addressing her concerns and validating her feelings. They emphasize that their desire to adopt her is driven by their deep love and belief in her potential. The Johnsons' patience and understanding help Emily feel more secure and confident in their intentions.

Emily's therapist also provides valuable support in helping her navigate her doubts and fears. Through guided conversations and exercises, Emily learns to articulate her feelings and process her emotions. The therapist helps Emily understand that her fears are valid and that it's okay to feel uncertain. Together, they work on building coping mechanisms and strategies to manage anxiety and build confidence. The therapeutic support helps Emily feel more empowered and ready to embrace the possibility of adoption.

Throughout the adoption process, there are several moments that provide Emily with reassurance and help her overcome her doubts. The Johnsons celebrate her achievements, no matter how small, and remind her of her strengths and capabilities. These moments of positive reinforcement help Emily build confidence in herself and feel more secure in her place within the family.

As Emily continues to receive love and support from the Johnsons, she begins to overcome her doubts and fears. She realizes that being adopted does not mean she is betraying her biological parents; rather, it means she is gaining a loving and supportive family who will always be there for her. This realization fills her with a sense of joy and relief. Emily feels an overwhelming sense of happiness and security, knowing that she is now a permanent member of the Johnson family.

Emily's journey towards overcoming her doubts and fears about adoption is marked by moments of reassurance, support, and self-discovery. With the unwavering support of the Johnson family and her therapist, Emily learns to navigate her emotions and build a brighter and more hopeful future.

The bonds between Emily and the Johnson family grow stronger over time, nurtured by shared experiences, mutual support, and unwavering love. These moments of connection and understanding help Emily feel more secure and valued as a member of the family.

The Johnsons establish daily routines and rituals that create a sense of stability and predictability for Emily. Morning breakfasts together, evening family dinners, and bedtime stories become cherished moments of connection. These routines provide Emily with a sense of security and belonging, reinforcing her place within the family.

Engaging in shared activities helps strengthen the bonds between Emily and the Johnsons. Whether it's cooking together, playing board games, or going for family walks, these activities create opportunities for laughter, teamwork, and meaningful conversations. Emily feels more connected to each family member as they share these experiences and create lasting memories.

The Johnsons' unwavering support during challenging times plays a crucial role in strengthening their bond with Emily. When Emily faces academic struggles or emotional difficulties, the Johnsons are there to provide guidance, encouragement, and reassurance. Their consistent presence and understanding help Emily feel more secure and valued, knowing that she can rely on them for support.

Celebrating Emily's achievements, no matter how small,

reinforces her sense of self-worth and strengthens her bond with the Johnsons. Whether it's a good grade, a successful art project, or a personal milestone, the family acknowledges and celebrates her efforts. These moments of recognition and praise boost Emily's confidence and reinforce her sense of belonging.

The Johnsons prioritize open communication, encouraging Emily to share her thoughts and feelings. They create a safe and non-judgmental environment where Emily feels comfortable expressing herself. The family's willingness to listen and understand helps Emily feel heard and valued, reinforcing her trust in the Johnsons.

The Johnsons' commitment to Emily's emotional well-being is evident in their support for her therapeutic sessions. They work closely with her therapist to ensure that Emily receives the care and guidance she needs. The Johnsons' involvement in her therapeutic process demonstrates their dedication to her healing and growth, helping Emily build resilience and emotional strength.

Trust is built through consistent actions and reliability. The Johnsons' consistent kindness, patience, and understanding help Emily build trust in them. They create a nurturing environment where Emily feels safe to share her thoughts and feelings. The family's unwavering support and encouragement reinforce Emily's sense of security and belonging, allowing her to open up and build deeper connections.

The Johnsons involve Emily in creating new family traditions, which helps her feel more connected and integrated into the family. Whether it's celebrating holidays, participating in family game nights, or going on weekend outings, these shared experiences create lasting memories and strengthen their bond. Emily's active participation in these traditions helps her feel more secure and valued, reinforcing her sense of belonging.

The Johnsons' consistent encouragement and positive reinforcement help Emily build confidence in herself. They celebrate her achievements and remind her of her strengths and capabilities. This positive reinforcement helps Emily develop a strong sense of self-worth and motivates her to strive for success. The love and support she receives from the Johnsons create a nurturing environment where Emily can thrive.

The strengthening of bonds between Emily and the Johnsons over time is marked by moments of connection, support, and mutual understanding. With the unwavering love and encouragement of the Johnson family, Emily feels more secure and valued, ready to embrace the future with hope and optimism.

As Emily settles into her new life with the Johnsons, she begins to embrace her new family and look forward to a brighter future with hope and optimism. The journey she has embarked on is filled with both challenges and triumphs, and the support of the Johnson family has been instrumental in helping her navigate this path.

Emily feels a deep sense of belonging with the Johnsons. The love, care, and stability they provide have given her the foundation she needs to heal and grow. She no longer feels like an outsider; instead, she is an integral part of the family. This sense of belonging fills her with confidence and security, allowing her to embrace her new identity with pride.

With the support of the Johnsons, Emily begins to dream about her future. She is excited about continuing her education and exploring her interests. The encouragement she receives from her family and teachers gives her the confidence to set ambitious goals and work towards achieving them. Emily envisions a future where she can thrive, both personally and academically, and she is determined to make the most of the opportunities before her.

The bonds Emily has formed with the Johnson family continue to grow stronger. She feels a deep sense of love and gratitude towards Mr. and Mrs. Johnson, who have provided her with unwavering support and guidance. Emily also cherishes her relationships with Emma and Finn, who have become her closest friends and confidants. These strong relationships provide her with a sense of stability and connection, reinforcing her emotional well-being.

Emily is eager to embrace new opportunities and experiences. She continues to participate in extracurricular activities, such as the art club and football team, which bring her joy and fulfilment. Emily also explores new hobbies and interests, finding creative outlets that help her express herself and build confidence. The encouragement and praise she receives from the Johnsons and her peers motivate her to keep pushing forward.

Emily's journey is marked by personal growth and resilience. She has developed coping mechanisms to manage her anxiety and stress, and she continues to work with her therapist to build emotional strength. Emily's ability to navigate challenges and embrace change is a testament to her determination and inner strength. She is proud of the progress she has made and looks forward to continuing her journey of self-discovery and growth.

As Emily looks ahead, she feels a sense of hope and excitement for the future. The stability and love provided by the Johnson family have given her the foundation she needs to build a brighter and more hopeful tomorrow. Emily is ready to face whatever challenges come her way, knowing that she has the support and encouragement of those who care deeply for her.

Emily's story is one of resilience, hope, and the power of a supportive environment. With the unwavering support of the Johnson family, her teachers, and her friends, Emily is ready to embrace the future and all the possibilities it holds. Her journey is a testament to the strength of the human spirit and the importance of love and stability in fostering growth and healing.

Chapter 10
Healing and Growth

Emily's journey of healing and growth is sustained by the continued support she receives from the Johnsons and other key support systems. This unwavering network of care plays a crucial role in helping her navigate challenges and build a brighter future.

The Johnsons remain a constant source of love and encouragement for Emily. They continue to provide a nurturing and stable environment where she feels safe and valued. Mr. and Mrs. Johnson are always there to listen to her concerns, offer guidance, and celebrate her achievements. Their consistent presence and understanding help Emily feel secure and confident in her place within the family.

Mrs. Johnson's nurturing care provides Emily with emotional reassurance. She offers comforting words and gentle hugs, helping Emily feel understood and valued. Mrs. Johnson's presence is a constant source of support, especially during moments of doubt and anxiety. Her ability to create a warm and loving environment helps Emily feel safe and supported.

The Johnsons continue to support Emily's academic journey. They create a quiet and conducive environment for her to study and complete her homework. Mr. Johnson, with his background in education, often helps Emily with her assignments, providing guidance and explanations when needed. The Johnsons celebrate Emily's academic achievements, reinforcing her sense of accomplishment and motivating her to continue striving for success.

Emily's therapist remains an integral part of her support system. Through regular sessions, Emily continues to work on developing healthy coping mechanisms and processing her emotions. The therapist provides a safe space for Emily to articulate her feelings and navigate the complexities of her past experiences. This therapeutic support helps Emily build resilience and emotional strength, empowering her to face challenges with confidence.

Emily's teachers and school counsellors also play a significant role in her continued growth. They provide additional academic support and encouragement, helping Emily stay on track with her studies. The positive feedback and recognition she receives from her teachers boost her confidence and reinforce her sense of self-worth. The school's supportive environment helps Emily feel more integrated and valued as a student.

The friendships Emily has formed at school and in her extracurricular activities continue to provide her with a sense of belonging and support. Her friends offer companionship, encouragement, and a sense of normalcy. These positive interactions help Emily build confidence in her social skills and reinforce her sense of self-worth. The support of her peers plays a crucial role in her overall well-being and happiness.

Emily's involvement in extracurricular activities, such as the art club and football team, continues to be a source of joy and fulfilment. These activities provide her with opportunities to explore her interests, develop new skills, and build meaningful connections. The encouragement and praise she receives from her peers and mentors in these activities help Emily feel more confident and motivated.

The Johnsons ensure that Emily has access to community resources that can support her growth and development. This includes participation in local support groups, workshops, and recreational programs. These resources provide Emily with additional opportunities to learn, grow, and connect with others who share similar experiences. The sense of community and belonging she gains from these resources reinforces her overall well-being.

The Johnsons' consistent encouragement and positive reinforcement help Emily build confidence in herself. They celebrate her achievements and remind her of her strengths and capabilities. This positive reinforcement helps Emily develop a strong sense of self-worth and motivates her to strive for success. The love and support she receives from the Johnsons create a nurturing environment where Emily can thrive.

The continued support Emily receives from the Johnsons and other key support systems plays a crucial role in her healing and growth. With the unwavering love and encouragement of her family, therapist, teachers, and friends, Emily is able to navigate challenges, build resilience, and embrace a brighter and more hopeful future.

Emily's journey with the Johnson family is marked by significant academic and personal achievements. These milestones reflect her hard work, determination, and the unwavering support she receives from her new family.

Emily's dedication to her studies pays off as her grades steadily improve. With the support of her teachers and the Johnsons, she catches up on subjects where she was previously struggling. Her report cards begin to reflect her hard work, and she consistently receives positive feedback from her teachers. The Johnsons celebrate each academic milestone, reinforcing Emily's sense of accomplishment and motivating her to continue striving for success.

Emily's academic achievements are further highlighted when she receives awards and recognition for her efforts. She is presented with certificates for outstanding performance in subjects like science and art. During school assemblies, Emily is called up to receive her awards, and the applause from her peers and teachers fills her with pride and joy. These moments of recognition boost her confidence and reinforce her belief in her abilities.

Emily becomes more actively involved in her classes, participating in discussions and group projects. Her teachers notice her increased engagement and praise her for her contributions. Emily's willingness to share her ideas and collaborate with her classmates helps her build confidence and develop important social skills. Her active participation in class discussions also enhances her learning experience and academic performance.

Emily's passion for art flourishes as she explores her creativity through various mediums. Her involvement in the art club allows her to develop her skills and gain recognition for her talent. Emily's artwork is selected for school exhibitions, and she receives praise from her peers and teachers. The positive feedback and encouragement she receives help Emily build confidence in her artistic abilities and reinforce her sense of self-worth.

Emily's participation in the school's football team is another source of personal growth and achievement. She works hard during practices and games, and her dedication pays off when she scores her first goal. The support and encouragement from her teammates and the Johnsons boost her confidence and motivate her to continue improving. Emily's involvement in sports helps her develop teamwork skills, resilience, and a sense of accomplishment.

Emily's ability to form strong friendships is a significant personal achievement. Her positive interactions with her peers help her build a supportive network of friends who share her interests and values. These friendships provide Emily with a sense of belonging and companionship, helping her navigate the challenges of her new life. The bonds she forms with her friends reinforce her social skills and contribute to her overall well-being.

Emily's journey is marked by significant personal growth and resilience. She develops healthy coping mechanisms to manage her anxiety and stress, and she continues to work with her therapist to build emotional strength. Emily's ability to navigate challenges and embrace change is a testament to her determination and inner strength. She is proud of the progress she has made and looks forward to continuing her journey of self-discovery and growth.

Emily's academic and personal achievements are a testament to her resilience and determination. With the unwavering support of the Johnson family, she is able to overcome challenges, build confidence, and embrace a brighter and more hopeful future. Each milestone she reaches reinforces her sense of self-worth and motivates her to continue striving for success.

Emily's journey of healing and growth inspires her to become an advocate for raising awareness about child neglect. Her personal experiences and the support she receives from the Johnsons motivate her to make a difference in the lives of other children facing similar challenges.

Emily's involvement in advocacy begins with finding her voice and sharing her story. Encouraged by the Johnsons and her therapist, she starts to speak openly about her experiences with neglect and the impact it had on her life. Emily's willingness to share her story helps her process her emotions and empowers her to take an active role in raising awareness. She realizes that by speaking out, she can help others understand the importance of providing support and stability to children in need.

Emily's first step in advocacy is giving presentations at her school. With the support of her teachers and the Johnsons, she prepares a presentation about child neglect and the importance of fostering a supportive environment for all children. Emily's presentations are heartfelt and informative, drawing from her personal experiences to highlight the challenges faced by neglected children. Her classmates and teachers are moved by her story, and Emily's courage inspires others to take action and support their peers.

Emily's advocacy efforts extend beyond her school. She becomes involved in community organizations that focus on child welfare and support services. Emily volunteers at local shelters and participates in awareness campaigns, using her story to educate others about the signs of neglect and the importance of early intervention. Her involvement in these organizations provides her with a sense of purpose and fulfilment, knowing that she is making a positive impact in her community.

As Emily gains confidence in her advocacy work, she is invited to speak at public events and conferences. She shares her journey of overcoming neglect and finding a loving and supportive family with the Johnsons. Emily's speeches are powerful and inspiring, resonating with audiences and encouraging them to take action. Her ability to connect with others through her story helps raise awareness about the importance of providing safe and nurturing environments for all children.

Emily collaborates with advocacy groups that focus on child welfare and protection. She participates in workshops and training sessions, learning more about the issues faced by neglected children and the resources available to support them. Emily's involvement in these groups allows her to contribute to policy discussions and initiatives aimed at improving the lives of vulnerable children. Her insights and experiences provide valuable perspectives that help shape advocacy efforts.

Emily takes an active role in creating awareness campaigns to educate the public about child neglect. She works with her school and community organizations to develop informational materials, such as brochures, posters, and social media content. Emily's creative talents shine as she designs visually engaging materials that effectively communicate the importance of supporting neglected children. These campaigns reach a wide audience, helping to raise awareness and promote positive change.

Emily's advocacy work also includes mentoring and supporting other children who have experienced neglect. She volunteers as a peer mentor, offering guidance and encouragement to younger children facing similar challenges. Emily's empathy and understanding make her a trusted and supportive figure, helping these children feel less alone and more hopeful about their future. Her mentorship provides a sense of connection and community, reinforcing the importance of support networks.

Emily's advocacy efforts have a lasting impact on her community and beyond. Her courage and determination inspire others to take action and support vulnerable children. Emily's story serves as a powerful reminder of the resilience of the human spirit and the importance of providing love and stability to those in need. Her legacy of advocacy and awareness continues to make a difference, helping to create a brighter and more hopeful future for all children.

Emily's involvement in advocacy and raising awareness about child neglect is a testament to her strength and determination. With the support of the Johnson family and her community, she uses her voice and experiences to make a positive impact and inspire change. Emily's journey of healing and growth is marked by her commitment to helping others and creating a better world for all children.

Emily's journey in overcoming her past trauma is a testament to her resilience and the power of a supportive environment. With the help of therapy and the unwavering support of the Johnson family, Emily learns to navigate her emotions and build a brighter future.

Emily's healing journey begins with regular sessions with her therapist, Dr. Collins. Through guided conversations and exercises, Emily learns to articulate her feelings and process her past experiences. Dr. Collins provides a safe and non-judgmental space where Emily can explore her emotions and develop healthy coping mechanisms. The therapeutic support helps Emily build resilience and emotional strength, empowering her to face challenges with confidence.

One of the key aspects of Emily's therapy is developing coping mechanisms to manage her anxiety and stress. Dr. Collins introduces Emily to mindfulness exercises, such as deep breathing and meditation, which help her stay grounded and calm during moments of distress. Emily also learns to use positive affirmations to counter negative thoughts and build self-confidence. These coping mechanisms become essential tools in Emily's journey of healing and growth.

Emily's recurring nightmares are a significant source of anxiety. Dr. Collins works with Emily to understand the underlying causes of her nightmares and develop strategies to manage them. Together, they create a calming bedtime routine that includes reading, listening to soothing music, and practicing relaxation techniques. Over time, Emily's nightmares become less frequent, and she feels more in control of her emotions.

The Johnsons play a crucial role in helping Emily build trust and feel secure. Their consistent kindness, patience, and understanding create a nurturing environment where Emily feels safe to share her thoughts and feelings. The family's unwavering support and encouragement reinforce Emily's sense of security and belonging, allowing her to open up and build deeper connections.

Art becomes a powerful tool for Emily to express her emotions and process her trauma. Through her involvement in the art club, Emily discovers the therapeutic benefits of creative expression. She uses her artwork to convey feelings that are difficult to articulate with words, finding solace and relief in the creative process. The positive feedback and encouragement she receives from her peers and teachers help Emily build confidence in her artistic abilities and reinforce her sense of self-worth.

The strong relationships Emily forms with the Johnson family and her friends provide her with a sense of stability and support. These relationships help Emily feel less alone and more connected to those around her. The love and care she receives from the Johnsons, combined with the companionship of her friends, create a supportive network that reinforces her emotional well-being.

The Johnsons celebrate each milestone in Emily's healing journey, no matter how small. Whether it's a good grade, a successful art project, or a personal achievement, the family acknowledges and celebrates her efforts. These moments of recognition boost Emily's confidence and reinforce her sense of self-worth. The positive reinforcement helps Emily feel appreciated and valued, contributing to her overall sense of well-being.

As Emily continues to heal and grow, she begins to look to the future with hope and optimism. The stability and love provided by the Johnson family give her the foundation she needs to build a brighter and more hopeful tomorrow. Emily is ready to face whatever challenges come her way, knowing that she has the support and encouragement of those who care deeply for her.

Emily's journey in overcoming her past trauma is marked by moments of resilience, growth, and the unwavering support of her therapist and the Johnson family. With their help, Emily learns to navigate her emotions, build confidence, and embrace a brighter future.

Emily's journey of healing is enriched by her discovery of new passions and interests. These activities provide her with a sense of joy, fulfilment, and a therapeutic outlet for her emotions.

Emily's involvement in the art club becomes a significant source of healing and self-expression. She discovers a passion for painting and drawing, finding solace in the creative process. Art allows Emily to convey her emotions in a non-verbal way, helping her process her past experiences and express her hopes for the future. The positive feedback and encouragement she receives from her peers and teachers boost her confidence and reinforce her sense of self-worth. Emily's artwork becomes a powerful tool for self-discovery and healing.

Joining the school's football team introduces Emily to the world of team sports. She quickly develops a passion for football, enjoying the physical activity and the camaraderie of her teammates. The support and encouragement from her coach and teammates help

Emily build confidence and resilience. Playing football provides her with a sense of accomplishment and belonging, reinforcing her sense of self-worth. The physical activity also helps Emily manage stress and anxiety, contributing to her overall well-being.

Emily's interest in performing arts leads her to join the school's drama club. She discovers a love for acting and performing, finding joy in stepping into different roles and exploring new aspects of her personality. The supportive and encouraging atmosphere of the drama club helps Emily overcome her initial shyness and embrace her creativity. Participating in rehearsals and performances provides her with a sense of accomplishment and boosts her confidence. The friendships she forms with other club members further enhance her sense of belonging and acceptance.

Emily's passion for writing and storytelling becomes another therapeutic outlet for her emotions. She starts keeping a journal, where she writes about her thoughts, feelings, and experiences. Writing allows Emily to process her emotions and reflect on her journey of healing and growth. She also enjoys writing short stories and poems, using her creativity to explore different themes and ideas. The positive feedback she receives from her teachers and peers encourages her to continue developing her writing skills.

Emily's interest in music and dance provides her with another avenue for self-expression and healing. She takes up playing the piano and enjoys learning new pieces and practicing regularly. Music becomes a source of comfort and relaxation, helping Emily manage stress and anxiety. She also joins a dance class, where she discovers the joy of movement and rhythm. Dancing allows Emily to express herself physically and emotionally, contributing to her overall sense of well-being.

Emily's love for nature and the outdoors becomes a significant part of her healing journey. The Johnsons often take her on hikes, nature walks, and camping trips, providing her with opportunities to connect with the natural world. Emily finds peace and tranquillity in nature, enjoying the beauty and serenity of the outdoors. These experiences help her feel grounded and connected, reinforcing her sense of well-being and happiness.

Emily's involvement in volunteering and community service

provides her with a sense of purpose and fulfilment. She volunteers at local shelters and participates in community clean-up events, using her time and energy to make a positive impact. The act of helping others reinforces Emily's sense of self-worth and contributes to her overall sense of well-being. Volunteering also provides her with opportunities to build meaningful connections and develop a sense of community.

Emily's discovery of new passions and interests plays a crucial role in her healing journey. These activities provide her with joy, fulfilment, and therapeutic outlets for her emotions. With the support and encouragement of the Johnson family, Emily is able to explore her interests, build confidence, and embrace a brighter and more hopeful future.

Emily's journey with the Johnson family has given her the confidence and support she needs to dream big and work towards a bright future. Her plans are a testament to her resilience, determination, and the unwavering encouragement she receives from her new family.

Emily is determined to continue her education and pursue higher studies. She dreams of attending a prestigious university where she can further develop her skills and knowledge. With the support of the Johnsons, Emily begins to explore different universities and programs that align with her interests. She attends college fairs, meets with academic advisors, and researches scholarship opportunities. The Johnsons help her prepare for entrance exams and college applications, providing guidance and encouragement every step of the way.

Emily's passion for art continues to flourish, and she dreams of pursuing a career in the arts. She sets her sights on attending an art school where she can hone her skills and explore various artistic disciplines. Emily participates in art competitions and exhibitions, building a portfolio of her work. The Johnsons support her by providing art supplies, attending her exhibitions, and encouraging her to take art classes and workshops. Emily's dedication to her craft and the positive feedback she receives motivate her to pursue her artistic dreams with confidence.

Emily is also interested in exploring different career options that align with her passions and strengths. She takes advantage of career counselling services at her school, where she learns about various professions and the educational paths required to achieve them. Emily participates in internships and job shadowing programs, gaining hands-on experience in fields that interest her. The Johnsons encourage her to explore her options and support her in making informed decisions about her future career.

Emily understands the importance of having a strong support network as she works towards her goals. She continues to build meaningful relationships with her teachers, mentors, and peers, seeking guidance and advice from those who have experience in her areas of interest. Emily also stays connected with her therapist, who provides ongoing support and helps her navigate any challenges she may face. The Johnsons remain her biggest supporters, offering love, encouragement, and practical assistance as she pursues her dreams.

In addition to her academic and career aspirations, Emily sets personal goals that contribute to her overall well-being and happiness. She continues to participate in extracurricular activities, such as the art club and football team, which bring her joy and fulfilment. Emily also prioritizes self-care, incorporating mindfulness exercises and relaxation techniques into her daily routine. She sets goals for her physical health, such as maintaining a balanced diet and staying active, and works towards achieving them with the support of the Johnsons.

Emily's experiences have inspired her to give back to the community and help others who are facing similar challenges. She volunteers at local shelters and participates in awareness campaigns, using her story to educate others about the importance of providing support and stability to vulnerable children. Emily's involvement in community service provides her with a sense of purpose and fulfilment, reinforcing her commitment to making a positive impact in the world.

As Emily looks to the future, she feels a sense of hope and excitement for the possibilities that lie ahead. The stability and love provided by the Johnson family have given her the foundation she needs to build a brighter and more hopeful tomorrow. Emily is ready to face whatever challenges come her way, knowing that she has the support and encouragement of those who care deeply for her.

Emily's plans for the future are a testament to her resilience, determination, and the unwavering support of the Johnson family. With their love and encouragement, she is able to dream big, set ambitious goals, and work towards achieving them with confidence and optimism.

Emily's journey of healing and growth inspires her to give back to the community and help other children who are facing similar challenges. Her personal experiences and the support she receives from the Johnsons motivate her to make a positive impact in the lives of others.

Emily begins her efforts to give back by volunteering at local shelters that provide support to children and families in need. She helps organize activities, assists with meal preparation, and offers a listening ear to children who are going through difficult times. Emily's empathy and understanding make her a comforting presence for these children, and her willingness to share her story provides them with hope and encouragement.

Emily takes an active role in raising awareness about child neglect and the importance of providing support and stability to vulnerable children. She participates in awareness campaigns organized by community organizations and schools. Emily gives presentations, creates informational materials, and uses social media to spread the message. Her efforts help educate the public about the signs of neglect and the resources available to support affected children.

Emily becomes a mentor to younger children who have experienced neglect or trauma. She volunteers as a peer mentor at her school and in community programs, offering guidance and support to those who need it. Emily's ability to relate to these children on a personal level makes her a trusted and supportive figure. Her mentorship helps these children feel less alone and more hopeful about their future.

Emily organizes fundraising events to support organizations that provide services to neglected and abused children. She plans bake sales, charity runs, and art auctions, using her creativity and organizational skills to raise funds. The money raised goes towards providing essential resources, such as clothing, school supplies, and counselling services, to children in need. Emily's efforts make a tangible difference in the lives of these children and their families.

Emily collaborates with advocacy groups to work on policy initiatives aimed at improving the lives of vulnerable children. She participates in workshops and training sessions, learning about the issues faced by neglected children and the legislative processes involved in creating change. Emily's insights and experiences provide valuable perspectives that help shape advocacy efforts. Her involvement in policy work helps raise awareness and promote positive change at a systemic level.

Emily helps create support networks for children and families affected by neglect. She works with community organizations to establish support groups, where children and their caregivers can share their experiences and receive guidance. These support networks provide a sense of community and belonging, helping families navigate the challenges they face. Emily's efforts help strengthen these networks and ensure that children and families have access to the resources they need.

Emily uses her voice to inspire others and advocate for change. She is invited to speak at public events, conferences, and schools, where she shares her journey of overcoming neglect and finding a loving and supportive family. Emily's speeches are powerful and moving, resonating with audiences, and encouraging them to take action. Her storytelling helps raise awareness and inspire others to support vulnerable children.

Emily's efforts to give back to the community have a lasting impact. Her dedication to helping others and raising awareness about child neglect inspires those around her to get involved and make a difference. Emily's story serves as a powerful reminder of the resilience of the human spirit and the importance of providing love and stability to those in need. Her legacy of advocacy and support continues to make a positive impact, helping to create a brighter and more hopeful future for all children.

Emily's commitment to giving back to the community and helping other children in similar situations is a testament to her strength and determination. With the support of the Johnson family and her community, she uses her experiences to make a positive impact and inspire change. Emily's journey of healing and growth is marked by her dedication to helping others and creating a better world for all children.

The relationships Emily builds with her adoptive family and friends grow stronger over time, nurtured by shared experiences, mutual support, and unwavering love. These bonds play a crucial role in her healing journey and personal growth.

The Johnsons establish daily routines and rituals that create a sense of stability and predictability for Emily. Morning breakfasts together, evening family dinners, and bedtime stories become cherished moments of connection. These routines provide Emily with a sense of security and belonging, reinforcing her place within the family.

Engaging in shared activities helps strengthen the bonds between Emily and the Johnsons. Whether it's cooking together, playing board games, or going for family walks, these activities create opportunities for laughter, teamwork, and meaningful conversations. Emily feels more connected to each family member as they share these experiences and create lasting memories.

The Johnsons' unwavering support during challenging times plays a crucial role in strengthening their bond with Emily. When Emily faces academic struggles or emotional difficulties, the Johnsons are there to provide guidance, encouragement, and reassurance. Their consistent presence and understanding help Emily feel more secure and valued, knowing that she can rely on them for support.

Celebrating Emily's achievements, no matter how small, reinforces her sense of self-worth and strengthens her bond with the Johnsons. Whether it's a good grade, a successful art project, or a personal milestone, the family acknowledges and celebrates her efforts. These moments of recognition and praise boost Emily's confidence and reinforce her sense of belonging.

The Johnsons prioritize open communication, encouraging Emily to share her thoughts and feelings. They create a safe and non-judgmental environment where Emily feels comfortable expressing herself. The family's willingness to listen and understand helps Emily feel heard and valued, reinforcing her trust in the Johnsons.

Emily's friendships at school continue to grow stronger as she becomes more involved in class activities and group projects. Her classmates appreciate her contributions and enjoy spending time with her. These positive interactions help Emily build confidence in her social skills and reinforce her sense of belonging within the school community.

Emily's involvement in the art club and football team provides her with opportunities to build meaningful connections with her peers. The shared passion for art and sports creates a sense of camaraderie and mutual support. Emily's friendships with her club and team members deepen as they collaborate on projects, practice together, and celebrate each other's achievements.

Emily's participation in the drama club introduces her to a new group of friends who share her interest in performing arts. The supportive and encouraging atmosphere of the drama club helps Emily overcome her initial shyness and embrace her creativity. The friendships she forms with other club members further enhance her sense of belonging and acceptance.

Emily's role as a peer mentor allows her to build supportive relationships with younger students who look up to her for guidance and encouragement. These mentoring relationships provide Emily with a sense of purpose and fulfilment, reinforcing her commitment to helping others. The positive impact she has on her mentees strengthens her own sense of self-worth and confidence.

The Johnsons engage in various family bonding activities that help Emily feel more connected and secure. Whether it's playing board games, going for walks, or working on art projects together, these shared experiences create lasting memories and strengthen their bond. The sense of belonging and togetherness that Emily feels during these activities reinforces her confidence in the Johnsons' love and commitment.

The Johnsons' commitment to Emily's emotional well-being is evident in their support for her therapeutic sessions. They work closely with her therapist to ensure that Emily receives the care and guidance she needs. The Johnsons' involvement in her therapeutic process demonstrates their dedication to her healing and growth, helping Emily build resilience and emotional strength.

The Johnsons' consistent encouragement and positive reinforcement help Emily build confidence in herself. They celebrate her achievements and remind her of her strengths and capabilities. This positive reinforcement helps Emily develop a strong sense of self-worth and motivates her to strive for success. The love and support she receives from the Johnsons create a nurturing environment where Emily can thrive.

The strengthening of relationships with her adoptive family and friends over time is marked by moments of connection, support, and mutual understanding. With the unwavering love and encouragement of the Johnson family and her friends, Emily feels more secure and valued, ready to embrace the future with hope and optimism.

Emily's journey with the Johnson family has been transformative, filled with moments of growth, healing, and self-discovery. As she reflects on her experiences, she recognizes the valuable lessons she has learned along the way.

Emily reflects on how embracing change has been a significant part of her journey. Moving in with the Johnsons and adapting to a new environment was initially daunting, but it taught her the importance of being open to new experiences. Emily learned that change, while challenging, can lead to positive outcomes and personal growth. She now approaches new situations with a sense of curiosity and optimism, knowing that they can bring about meaningful transformations.

Emily's journey has shown her the power of resilience. Overcoming the challenges of her past and navigating the complexities of her emotions required strength and determination. Emily learned that resilience is not about avoiding difficulties but about facing them head-on and finding ways to move forward. This lesson has empowered her to tackle obstacles with confidence and to view setbacks as opportunities for growth.

One of the most profound lessons Emily has learned is the importance of having a strong support system. The unwavering love and encouragement from the Johnsons, her friends, and her therapist have been instrumental in her healing journey. Emily realizes that it's okay to seek help and lean on others during difficult times. She understands that support from loved ones can provide the strength and reassurance needed to overcome challenges and achieve personal goals.

Emily's discovery of art and other creative outlets has taught her the value of self-expression. Through painting, writing, and performing, she found ways to process her emotions and communicate her experiences. Emily learned that creativity can be a powerful tool for healing and self-discovery. It has allowed her to explore different aspects of her identity and to express herself in ways that words alone cannot capture.

Emily's involvement in advocacy and raising awareness about child neglect has shown her the impact one person can make. By sharing her story and working to support others, she learned that her experiences could inspire change and provide hope to those in similar situations. Emily understands the importance of using her voice to advocate for vulnerable children and to promote positive change in her community.

Emily's journey has taught her the importance of setting goals and working towards her dreams. With the support of the Johnsons, she learned to believe in her abilities and to strive for success. Emily understands that achieving her goals requires dedication, hard work, and perseverance. She is now more confident in her ability to pursue her passions and to create a bright future for herself.

Reflecting on her journey, Emily feels a deep sense of gratitude for the love and support she has received. She appreciates the Johnsons for providing her with a stable and nurturing environment, her friends for their companionship, and her therapist for guiding her through her healing process. Emily has learned to cherish the positive relationships in her life and to express her gratitude to those who have helped her along the way.

As Emily looks to the future, she feels a sense of hope and excitement for the possibilities that lie ahead. She is proud of the progress she has made and is determined to continue her journey of growth and self-discovery. Emily understands that while challenges may arise, she has the strength, resilience, and support to overcome them. She is ready to embrace the future with confidence and optimism, knowing that she has the tools and resources to build a bright and fulfilling life.

Emily's personal reflections on her journey highlight the valuable lessons she has learned and the growth she has experienced. With the support of the Johnson family and her community, she is ready to face the future with hope and determination, embracing the possibilities that lie ahead.

As Emily reflects on her journey and the incredible support she has received from the Johnson family, she feels a profound sense of empowerment and resilience. Her experiences have shaped her into a strong, confident, and hopeful individual, ready to embrace the future with open arms.

Emily is excited about the endless possibilities that lie ahead. She looks forward to continuing her education, exploring her passions, and pursuing her dreams. The support and encouragement she receives from the Johnsons give her the confidence to set ambitious goals and work towards achieving them. Emily is determined to make the most of the opportunities before her, knowing that she has the strength and resilience to overcome any challenges that come her way.

With a clear vision of her future, Emily is committed to building a life filled with purpose and fulfilment. She dreams of attending a prestigious university, developing her artistic talents, and making a positive impact in her community. Emily's dedication to her goals and her unwavering determination drive her to strive for excellence in everything she does. She is ready to face the future with optimism and enthusiasm, confident in her ability to create a bright and successful life.

The bonds Emily has formed with the Johnson family and her friends continue to grow stronger. She cherishes the love and support she receives from her adoptive family, knowing that they will always be there for her. Emily also values the friendships she has built, which provide her with a sense of belonging and companionship. These relationships are a source of strength and comfort, reinforcing her sense of self-worth and happiness.

Emily's experiences have inspired her to give back to the community and help others who are facing similar challenges. She is passionate about raising awareness about child neglect and advocating for vulnerable children. Emily's involvement in community service and advocacy work provides her with a sense of purpose and fulfilment. She is determined to use her voice and experiences to make a positive impact and inspire change.

Emily's journey has taught her the importance of resilience and personal growth. She has developed healthy coping mechanisms to manage stress and anxiety, and she continues to work on building emotional strength. Emily's ability to navigate challenges and embrace change is a testament to her inner strength and determination. She is proud of the progress she has made and is committed to continuing her journey of self-discovery and growth.

As Emily looks to the future, she feels a sense of hope and excitement for the possibilities that lie ahead. The stability and love provided by the Johnson family have given her the foundation she needs to build a brighter and more hopeful tomorrow. Emily is ready to face whatever challenges come her way, knowing that she has the support and encouragement of those who care deeply for her.

Emily's story is one of resilience, hope, and the power of a supportive environment. With the unwavering support of the Johnson family, her teachers, and her friends, Emily is ready to embrace the future and all the possibilities it holds. Her journey is a testament to the strength of the human spirit and the importance of love and stability in fostering growth and healing.

Chapter 11
Looking Back

As Emily looks back on her early years, she reflects on the challenges she faced and the journey that brought her to where she is today. Her reflections are filled with a mix of emotions, including sadness, gratitude, and a deep sense of resilience.

Emily's early years were marked by instability and uncertainty. She recalls moving from place to place, never staying in one home for long. The lack of a stable environment made it difficult for her to form lasting relationships and feel secure. Emily often felt like she was living in a state of constant upheaval, unsure of what the future held.

Emily remembers the feelings of neglect and abandonment that permeated her early childhood. She often felt invisible and unimportant, as if her needs and emotions didn't matter. The absence of consistent care and attention left her feeling isolated and alone. These experiences shaped her perception of herself and the world around her, making it difficult for her to trust others and believe in her own worth.

The instability and neglect Emily experienced contributed to her struggles with anxiety. She often felt overwhelmed by fear and uncertainty, especially when faced with new situations or challenges. Emily's anxiety manifested in various ways, including nightmares, panic attacks, and a constant sense of unease. These struggles made it difficult for her to focus on her studies and engage with her peers.

Emily's academic journey was fraught with difficulties. The frequent moves and lack of support made it challenging for her to keep up with her schoolwork. She often felt behind in her studies and struggled to catch up. Emily's academic performance suffered, and she began to doubt her abilities and potential. The lack of stability and support in her early years left her feeling discouraged and defeated.

Despite the challenges she faced, Emily also reflects on moments of resilience and strength. She recalls times when she found solace in her creativity, using art and writing as outlets for her emotions. Emily's ability to find joy in small moments and her determination to keep going, even when things were tough, are testaments to her inner strength. These moments of resilience helped her navigate the difficulties of her early years and laid the foundation for her future growth.

As Emily reflects on her journey, she feels a deep sense of gratitude for the support she has received along the way. The love and care of the Johnson family, the guidance of her teachers and therapist, and the companionship of her friends have all played crucial roles in her healing and growth. Emily recognizes that she would not be where she is today without the unwavering support of those who believed in her and helped her overcome her challenges.

Emily's reflections on her past are filled with valuable lessons. She has learned the importance of resilience, the power of support, and the value of self-expression. Emily understands that her experiences, while difficult, have shaped her into the strong and determined individual she is today. She is proud of her journey and the progress she has made, and she looks forward to continuing her path of growth and self-discovery.

Emily's reflections on her early years and the challenges she faced highlight her resilience and determination. With the support of the Johnson family and her community, she has overcome significant obstacles and built a brighter and more hopeful future. Emily's journey is a testament to the strength of the human spirit and the importance of love and stability in fostering growth and healing.

Emily's journey of healing involves acknowledging the pain of her past while also recognizing the strength she has developed along the way. This process is both challenging and empowering, allowing her to embrace her experiences and grow from them.

Emily understands that in order to heal, she must confront the painful memories of her past. With the support of her therapist, Dr. Collins, she begins to explore the feelings of neglect, abandonment, and insecurity that have shaped her early years. Emily learns to articulate her emotions, expressing the hurt and sadness she felt during those difficult times. This process is not easy, but it is a crucial step in her healing journey.

Through therapeutic conversations, Emily gains a deeper understanding of how her past experiences have impacted her. Dr. Collins helps her identify the patterns of thought and behaviour that stem from her early trauma. Emily learns to recognize the triggers that cause her anxiety and fear, and she develops strategies to manage these emotions. The therapeutic support provides Emily with a safe space to process her pain and begin to heal.

Emily finds solace in journaling, using it as a tool to reflect on her past and her journey of healing. Writing about her experiences allows her to process her emotions and gain clarity. Emily's journal becomes a place where she can express her thoughts and feelings without judgment. Through reflection, she begins to see how far she has come and the strength she has developed along the way.

As Emily acknowledges the pain of her past, she also recognizes the resilience that has carried her through difficult times. She reflects on the moments of strength and determination that have helped her overcome challenges. Emily realizes that despite the hardships she faced, she has always found a way to keep going. This recognition of her resilience empowers her and reinforces her belief in her ability to navigate future challenges.

The unwavering support of the Johnson family plays a crucial role in helping Emily acknowledge her pain and recognize her strength. They provide a nurturing and stable environment where she feels safe to express her emotions. The Johnsons celebrate her achievements and remind her of her capabilities, reinforcing her sense of self-worth. Their love and encouragement help Emily see herself as a strong and resilient individual.

Emily's journey of acknowledging her pain and recognizing her strength helps her build confidence in herself. She learns to trust her abilities and believe in her potential. Emily's academic and personal achievements become sources of pride, reinforcing her sense of self-worth. The positive reinforcement she receives from the Johnsons and her teachers boosts her confidence and motivates her to continue striving for success.

Emily understands that her journey of healing is ongoing, and that growth comes from embracing both the pain and the strength within her. She is committed to continuing her therapeutic work, exploring new interests, and building meaningful relationships. Emily's ability to acknowledge her pain and recognize her strength allows her to move forward with hope and optimism.

As Emily looks to the future, she feels a sense of empowerment and resilience. She knows that her past experiences have shaped her, but they do not define her. Emily is ready to embrace new opportunities and challenges, confident in her ability to overcome them. She is determined to build a bright and fulfilling future, supported by the love and encouragement of the Johnson family and her community.

Emily's journey of acknowledging the pain of her past and recognizing her strength is a testament to her resilience and determination. With the support of her therapist and the Johnson family, she is able to embrace her experiences, heal, and grow into a confident and empowered individual.

Emily's journey of healing and growth is deeply intertwined with the support she received from social services and her adoptive family, the Johnsons. Her reflections are filled with gratitude for the people and systems that have played a crucial role in her transformation.

Emily is profoundly grateful for the initial intervention by social services that brought her to the Johnsons. The social workers who recognized her situation and took action to ensure her safety made a significant impact on her life. Emily understands that without their intervention, she might not have found the stability and love she now enjoys.

Throughout her journey, social services provided continuous support to Emily and the Johnsons. Regular check-ins, counselling services, and resources helped ensure that Emily's needs were met. Emily appreciates the dedication and care of the social workers who were always there to offer guidance and assistance. Their commitment to her well-being played a crucial role in her healing process.

Social services connected Emily with various resources that supported her growth and development. From educational programs to therapeutic services, these resources helped Emily build resilience and confidence. She is thankful for the opportunities provided by social services, which enabled her to explore her interests and pursue her goals.

Emily's gratitude for the Johnson family knows no bounds. From the moment she arrived at their home, the Johnsons welcomed her with open arms and hearts. Their unwavering love and support created a nurturing environment where Emily felt safe and valued. She is deeply thankful for their patience, understanding, and encouragement, which have been instrumental in her healing journey.

The Johnsons provided Emily with the stability she had longed for. Their consistent routines, family traditions, and daily acts of kindness helped Emily feel secure and grounded. Emily appreciates the sense of belonging and normalcy that the Johnsons brought into her life, allowing her to thrive and grow.

The Johnsons encouraged Emily to explore her passions and interests, providing her with the tools and opportunities to develop her talents. Whether it was supporting her involvement in the art club, attending her football games, or celebrating her academic achievements, the Johnsons were always there to cheer her on. Emily is grateful for their belief in her potential and their commitment to helping her succeed.

Mrs. Johnson's nurturing care and Mr. Johnson's steady presence provided Emily with emotional reassurance. Their ability to listen, offer comfort, and provide guidance helped Emily navigate her fears and anxieties. Emily is thankful for the emotional support they provided, which helped her build confidence and resilience.

The Johnsons celebrated every milestone in Emily's journey, no matter how small. Their recognition of her achievements and their constant encouragement reinforced Emily's sense of self-worth. Emily is grateful for the joy and pride they brought into her life, making her feel valued and appreciated.

As Emily looks to the future, she carries with her a deep sense of gratitude for the support, she has received. The intervention of social services and the unwavering love of the Johnson family have been pivotal in her transformation. Emily's journey is a testament to the power of support and the importance of providing love and stability to those in need. She is determined to honour the support she has received by giving back to the community and helping others who are facing similar challenges.

Emily's reflections on her gratitude highlight the profound impact that social services and the Johnson family have had on her life. With their support, she has been able to heal, grow, and build a brighter and more hopeful future.

Emily's journey has been filled with valuable lessons that have shaped her into the resilient and hopeful individual she is today. Reflecting on her experiences, she recognizes the profound impact these lessons have had on her personal growth and outlook on life.

One of the most important lessons Emily has learned is the power of resilience. Despite the challenges and hardships, she faced, Emily discovered an inner strength that helped her persevere. She learned that resilience is not about avoiding difficulties but about facing them head-on and finding ways to overcome them. This lesson has empowered Emily to tackle obstacles with confidence and to view setbacks as opportunities for growth.

Emily's journey has taught her the significance of having a strong support system. The unwavering love and encouragement from the Johnsons, her friends, and her therapist have been instrumental in her healing process. Emily understands that it's okay to seek help and lean on others during difficult times. She has learned that support from loved ones can provide the strength and reassurance needed to overcome challenges and achieve personal goals.

Through her experiences, Emily has learned to recognize her own worth and build confidence in herself. The positive reinforcement and encouragement she received from the Johnsons and her teachers helped her believe in her abilities and potential. Emily learned that her past does not define her and that she is capable of achieving great things. This newfound confidence has motivated her to pursue her dreams and embrace new opportunities.

Emily discovered the therapeutic benefits of self-expression through art, writing, and other creative outlets. These activities allowed her to process her emotions and communicate her experiences in a meaningful way. Emily learned that creativity can be a powerful tool for healing and self-discovery. It has helped her explore different aspects of her identity and express herself in ways that words alone cannot capture.

Emily's journey has instilled in her a deep sense of empathy and compassion for others. Her experiences have made her more understanding and sensitive to the struggles of those around her. Emily has learned the importance of kindness and the impact it can have on someone's life. She is committed to using her experiences to help others and make a positive difference in her community.

Emily's involvement in advocacy and raising awareness about child neglect has shown her the impact one person can make. By sharing her story and working to support others, she learned that her experiences could inspire change and provide hope to those in similar situations. Emily understands the importance of using her voice to advocate for vulnerable children and to promote positive change in her community.

Emily's journey has taught her the importance of setting goals and working towards her dreams. With the support of the Johnsons, she learned to believe in her abilities and to strive for success. Emily understands that achieving her goals requires dedication, hard work, and perseverance. She is now more confident in her ability to pursue her passions and to create a bright future for herself.

Reflecting on her journey, Emily feels a deep sense of gratitude for the love and support she has received. She appreciates the Johnsons for providing her with a stable and nurturing environment, her friends for their companionship, and her therapist for guiding her through her healing process. Emily has learned to cherish the positive relationships in her life and to express her gratitude to those who have helped her along the way.

As Emily looks to the future, she feels a sense of hope and excitement for the possibilities that lie ahead. She is proud of the progress she has made and is determined to continue her journey of growth and self-discovery. Emily understands that while challenges may arise, she has the strength, resilience, and support to overcome them. She is ready to embrace the future with confidence and optimism, knowing that she has the tools and resources to build a bright and fulfilling life.

Emily's reflections on the lessons she has learned highlight the profound impact her experiences have had on her personal growth. With the support of the Johnson family and her community, she is ready to face the future with hope and determination, embracing the possibilities that lie ahead.

Emily's journey with the Johnson family has been transformative, marked by significant personal growth and the development of inner strength. Her experiences have shaped her into a resilient and confident individual, ready to face the future with hope and determination.

Emily's emotional resilience has grown immensely since she joined the Johnson family. Through therapy and the unwavering support of her adoptive family, she has learned to navigate her emotions and develop healthy coping mechanisms. Emily's ability to manage stress and anxiety has improved, allowing her to face challenges with a calm and composed demeanour. Her resilience is evident in her ability to bounce back from setbacks and continue moving forward with determination.

Emily's confidence and sense of self-worth have flourished. The positive reinforcement and encouragement she receives from the Johnsons and her teachers have helped her believe in her abilities and potential. Emily no longer doubts her worth; instead, she embraces her strengths and accomplishments with pride. This newfound confidence motivates her to pursue her dreams and take on new challenges with enthusiasm.

Emily's academic performance has improved significantly, reflecting her dedication and hard work. She has received awards and recognition for her achievements, boosting her confidence and reinforcing her belief in her capabilities. Emily's involvement in extracurricular activities, such as the art club and football team, has also contributed to her personal growth. These activities provide her with opportunities to develop new skills, build meaningful relationships, and gain a sense of accomplishment.

Emily's experiences have inspired her to take on leadership roles and advocate for others. She has become a mentor to younger students, offering guidance and support to those who need it. Emily's involvement in advocacy work, raising awareness about child neglect, has given her a sense of purpose and fulfilment. Her ability to use her voice to inspire change and support vulnerable children is a testament to her growth and strength.

Emily's journey has instilled in her a deep sense of empathy and compassion for others. Her experiences have made her more understanding and sensitive to the struggles of those around her. Emily's ability to connect with others on an emotional level and offer support and encouragement is a reflection of her personal growth. She is committed to using her experiences to help others and make a positive impact in her community.

Emily's personal growth is also evident in her future aspirations. She has set ambitious goals for herself, including pursuing higher education and developing her artistic talents. Emily's determination to achieve her dreams and her willingness to work hard to reach her goals reflect her inner strength and resilience. She is excited about the possibilities that lie ahead and is ready to embrace the future with confidence and optimism.

As Emily reflects on her journey, she feels a deep sense of gratitude for the support she has received. The love and encouragement of the Johnson family, her friends, and her therapist have been instrumental in her growth. Emily's ability to acknowledge her past, embrace her present, and look forward to the future with hope is a testament to her personal growth and strength.

Emily's journey of personal growth and the development of inner strength is a testament to her resilience and determination. With the support of the Johnson family and her community, she has overcome significant challenges and built a brighter and more hopeful future. Emily's story is a powerful reminder of the importance of love, support, and the human spirit's capacity for growth and healing.

Emily's journey of resilience and transformation has had a profound impact on those around her, inspiring others to find strength in their own challenges and to support vulnerable children in their communities.

Emily's classmates and friends are deeply moved by her story. Her courage in sharing her experiences and her determination to overcome adversity inspire her peers to face their own challenges with resilience. Emily's positive attitude and willingness to help others create a supportive and encouraging environment at school. Her friends admire her strength and look up to her as a role model, finding motivation in her journey to pursue their own goals and dreams.

Emily's involvement in advocacy work has inspired others to join her efforts in raising awareness about child neglect. Her story highlights the importance of providing support and stability to vulnerable children, motivating her community to take action. Emily's peers and community members participate in awareness campaigns, volunteer at local shelters, and support organizations that work to protect and care for neglected children. Her advocacy efforts have created a ripple effect, encouraging others to become advocates for change.

Emily's teachers and school staff are inspired by her resilience and dedication to her education. Her progress and achievements serve as a reminder of the importance of providing a supportive and nurturing environment for all students. Emily's story encourages educators to be more attentive to the needs of their students and to offer additional support to those facing challenges. Her journey reinforces the belief that with the right support, every child has the potential to succeed.

Emily's story has brought her community closer together. Her willingness to share her experiences and her involvement in community service have fostered a sense of unity and compassion. Community members come together to support Emily and other children in similar situations, creating a network of care and support. Emily's journey has highlighted the importance of community involvement in addressing issues of child neglect and providing a safe and nurturing environment for all children.

Emily's story serves as a beacon of hope for other children who have experienced neglect or trauma. Her resilience and determination show them that it is possible to overcome adversity and build a brighter future. Emily's willingness to mentor and support younger children provides them with a sense of connection and encouragement. Her story inspires them to believe in their own potential and to seek out the support they need to thrive.

Emily's journey has also had a profound impact on the Johnson family. Her presence in their lives has brought them immense joy and fulfilment. The Johnsons are inspired by Emily's strength and resilience, and they feel a deep sense of pride in her achievements. Emily's journey has reinforced their commitment to providing a loving and supportive home for her and has strengthened their bond as a family.

Emily's story has created a legacy of hope and inspiration. Her journey of healing and growth serves as a powerful reminder of the importance of love, support, and resilience. Emily's impact on her community and beyond continues to inspire others to take action, support vulnerable children, and create positive change. Her legacy is one of strength, compassion, and the belief that every child deserves a chance to thrive.

Emily's journey has had a lasting impact on those around her, inspiring others to find strength in their own challenges and to support vulnerable children in their communities. Her story is a testament to the power of resilience, love, and the human spirit's capacity for growth and healing.

Emily's commitment to advocacy and helping others remains a central part of her life. Her experiences have fuelled her passion for making a positive impact, and she continues to dedicate her time and energy to supporting vulnerable children and raising awareness about child neglect.

Emily remains actively involved in advocacy work, collaborating with various organizations that focus on child welfare and protection. She participates in workshops, training sessions, and conferences, where she shares her story and insights. Emily's involvement in these events helps raise awareness about the challenges faced by neglected children and the importance of providing support and stability. Her advocacy efforts continue to inspire others to take action and support vulnerable children.

Emily is frequently invited to speak at schools, community events, and conferences. Her powerful and moving speeches resonate with audiences, encouraging them to become advocates for change. Emily's ability to connect with others through her story helps raise awareness and inspire action. She uses her platform to educate the public about the signs of neglect and the resources available to support affected children.

Emily continues to mentor younger children who have experienced neglect or trauma. She volunteers as a peer mentor in her school and community programs, offering guidance and encouragement to those who need it. Emily's empathy and understanding make her a trusted and supportive figure for these children. Her mentorship provides them with a sense of connection and hope, reinforcing the importance of having a strong support system.

Emily takes an active role in creating awareness campaigns to educate the public about child neglect. She works with community organizations to develop informational materials, such as brochures, posters, and social media content. Emily's creative talents shine as she designs visually engaging materials that effectively communicate the importance of supporting neglected children. These campaigns reach a wide audience, helping to raise awareness and promote positive change.

Emily organizes fundraising events to support organizations that provide services to neglected and abused children. She plans bake sales, charity runs, and art auctions, using her creativity and organizational skills to raise funds. The money raised goes towards providing essential resources, such as clothing, school supplies, and counselling services, to children in need. Emily's efforts make a tangible difference in the lives of these children and their families.

Emily collaborates with advocacy groups to work on policy initiatives aimed at improving the lives of vulnerable children. She participates in discussions and initiatives that focus on creating systemic change. Emily's insights and experiences provide valuable perspectives that help shape advocacy efforts. Her involvement in policy work helps raise awareness and promote positive change at a broader level.

Emily's commitment to giving back to the community extends to her involvement in various volunteer activities. She volunteers at local shelters, participates in community clean-up events, and supports initiatives that promote child welfare. Emily's dedication to community service provides her with a sense of purpose and fulfilment, reinforcing her commitment to making a positive impact.

Emily's continued advocacy efforts have a lasting impact on her community and beyond. Her dedication to helping others and raising awareness about child neglect inspires those around her to get involved and make a difference. Emily's story serves as a powerful reminder of the resilience of the human spirit and the importance of providing love and stability to those in need. Her legacy of advocacy and support continues to make a positive impact, helping to create a brighter and more hopeful future for all children.

Emily's commitment to continued advocacy and helping others is a testament to her strength and determination. With the support of the Johnson family and her community, she uses her experiences to make a positive impact and inspire change. Emily's journey of healing and growth is marked by her dedication to helping others and creating a better world for all children.

Emily's journey of resilience and transformation has not only shaped her into a strong and confident individual but has also inspired her to build a lasting legacy through her work and personal achievements. Her dedication to advocacy, community service, and personal growth continues to make a positive impact on those around her.

Emily's commitment to raising awareness about child neglect and advocating for vulnerable children is a central part of her legacy. She actively participates in awareness campaigns, public speaking engagements, and policy discussions, using her voice to inspire change. Emily's efforts have helped educate the public about the importance of providing support and stability to neglected children, encouraging others to take action and support these initiatives.

Emily's role as a mentor to younger children is another significant aspect of her legacy. She volunteers as a peer mentor, offering guidance and encouragement to those who have experienced neglect or trauma. Emily's empathy and understanding make her a trusted and supportive figure, helping these children feel less alone and more hopeful about their future. Her mentorship provides a sense of connection and community, reinforcing the importance of support networks.

Emily's passion for art has led to numerous personal

achievements and contributions to her community. Her involvement in the art club and participation in exhibitions have showcased her talent and creativity. Emily's artwork often reflects her journey and experiences, providing a powerful medium for self-expression and healing. Her artistic contributions have inspired others to explore their own creativity and find solace in artistic expression.

Emily's dedication to her education and academic achievements are a testament to her resilience and determination. She has worked hard to improve her grades, receive awards, and actively participate in class discussions and group projects. Emily's commitment to her studies and her pursuit of higher education reflect her desire to build a bright and successful future. Her academic achievements serve as an inspiration to her peers, demonstrating the importance of perseverance and hard work.

Emily's involvement in community service and volunteer activities has made a tangible difference in the lives of those around her. She organizes fundraising events, volunteers at local shelters, and participates in community clean-up initiatives. Emily's dedication to giving back to her community reinforces her commitment to making a positive impact. Her efforts have helped provide essential resources and support to vulnerable children and families, creating a lasting legacy of compassion and service.

Emily's journey of personal growth and resilience is a central part of her legacy. Her ability to overcome adversity, build confidence, and embrace new opportunities serves as a powerful example to others. Emily's story of transformation and healing inspires those around her to find strength in their own challenges and to believe in their potential. Her resilience and determination continue to motivate others to pursue their dreams and create a brighter future.

Emily's story has had a profound impact on her community and beyond. Her willingness to share her experiences and advocate for change has inspired others to get involved and support vulnerable children. Emily's legacy is one of hope, resilience, and the belief that every child deserves a chance to thrive. Her journey serves as a powerful reminder of the importance of love, support, and the human spirit's capacity for growth and healing.

Emily's dedication to advocacy, community service, and

personal growth continues to build a lasting legacy. Her work and achievements inspire others to take action, support vulnerable children, and create positive change. Emily's journey is a testament to the power of resilience and the impact one person can make in the lives of others.

Emily's journey is filled with moments of joy and celebration as she reaches significant milestones and achieves personal successes. These celebrations with her loved ones reinforce her sense of accomplishment and strengthen the bonds she shares with the Johnson family and her friends.

When Emily receives her first report card with improved grades, the Johnsons throw a small family party to celebrate her hard work and dedication. They decorate the living room with balloons and streamers, and Mrs. Johnson bakes a special cake. The family gathers around to congratulate Emily, presenting her with a certificate of achievement and a heartfelt letter expressing their pride. Emily's friends from school also join the celebration, making her feel truly appreciated and valued.

Emily's artwork is selected for a school exhibition, and the Johnsons are there to support her. They attend the exhibition, taking photos and praising her creativity. Emily's art teacher, Ms. Rivera, also acknowledges her talent, further boosting her confidence. The family celebrates this achievement with a special dinner at Emily's favourite restaurant, where they toast to her success and discuss her future artistic endeavours.

Emily's participation in the school's football team leads to several moments of celebration. When she scores her first goal in a match, the Johnsons cheer for her from the sidelines, capturing the moment on camera. They celebrate her achievement with a special dinner and words of encouragement. Emily's teammates also join in the celebration, making her feel like an integral part of the team. These moments of recognition and praise help Emily build confidence in her abilities and reinforce her sense of belonging.

The Johnsons create new holiday traditions that include Emily, making her feel like an integral part of the family. Whether it's decorating the Christmas tree, carving pumpkins for Halloween, or participating in an Easter egg hunt, these shared experiences create lasting memories and strengthen their bond. Emily looks forward to these traditions, knowing that she is part of a loving and supportive family.

As Emily progresses through school, her graduation and awards ceremonies become significant milestones. The Johnsons attend these events with pride, celebrating her achievements and capturing the moments on camera. They present her with flowers and gifts, acknowledging her hard work and dedication. These celebrations reinforce Emily's sense of accomplishment and motivate her to continue pursuing her goals.

The day the adoption is finalized is one of the most significant milestones in Emily's life. The Johnsons celebrate this momentous occasion with a special family gathering. They present Emily with a personalized adoption certificate and a heartfelt letter expressing their love and commitment. The celebration is filled with joy and gratitude, marking the beginning of a new chapter in their lives. Emily feels an overwhelming sense of happiness and security, knowing that she is now a permanent member of the Johnson family.

Emily's personal milestones, such as overcoming her fears and achieving her goals, are also celebrated with her loved ones. The Johnsons acknowledge her progress and growth, offering words of encouragement and support. These celebrations help Emily feel proud of her achievements and reinforce her sense of self-worth.

Emily's journey is marked by moments of joy and celebration as she reaches significant milestones and achieves personal successes. These celebrations with her loved ones reinforce her sense of accomplishment and strengthen the bonds she shares with the Johnson family and her friends. Emily's story is a testament to the power of love, support, and the human spirit's capacity for growth and healing.

As Emily looks ahead, she feels a profound sense of confidence and hope for the future. Her journey with the Johnson family has equipped her with the resilience, strength, and support she needs to embrace the possibilities that lie ahead.

Emily is determined to pursue her dreams with unwavering dedication. She is excited about continuing her education and exploring her passions. With the support of the Johnsons, Emily plans to attend a prestigious university where she can further develop her skills and knowledge. She envisions a future where she can make a meaningful impact through her artistic talents and advocacy work. Emily's determination and hard work drive her to set ambitious goals and work tirelessly to achieve them.

Emily's future is filled with promise and potential. She is committed to building a life that reflects her values and aspirations. Emily's dedication to her education, her involvement in community service, and her passion for advocacy all contribute to her vision of a bright and fulfilling future. She is ready to face new challenges and seize new opportunities, confident in her ability to overcome obstacles and achieve her goals.

The bonds Emily has formed with the Johnson family and her friends continue to grow stronger. She cherishes the love and support she receives from her adoptive family, knowing that they will always be there for her. Emily also values the friendships she has built, which provide her with a sense of belonging and companionship. These relationships are a source of strength and comfort, reinforcing her sense of self-worth and happiness.

Emily's experiences have inspired her to give back to the community and help others who are facing similar challenges. She is passionate about raising awareness about child neglect and advocating for vulnerable children. Emily's involvement in community service and advocacy work provides her with a sense of purpose and fulfilment. She is determined to use her voice and experiences to make a positive impact and inspire change.

Emily's journey has taught her the importance of resilience and personal growth. She has developed healthy coping mechanisms to manage stress and anxiety, and she continues to work on building emotional strength. Emily's ability to navigate challenges and embrace change is a testament to her inner strength and determination. She is proud of the progress she has made and is committed to continuing her journey of self-discovery and growth.

As Emily looks to the future, she feels a sense of hope and excitement for the possibilities that lie ahead. The stability and love provided by the Johnson family have given her the foundation she needs to build a brighter and more hopeful tomorrow. Emily is ready to face whatever challenges come her way, knowing that she has the support and encouragement of those who care deeply for her.

Emily's story is one of resilience, hope, and the power of a supportive environment. With the unwavering support of the Johnson family, her teachers, and her friends, Emily is ready to embrace the future and all the possibilities it holds. Her journey is a testament to the strength of the human spirit and the importance of love and stability in fostering growth and healing.

Chapter 12
Moving Forward

Emily's decision to pursue a career in social work is driven by her personal experiences and a deep desire to make a positive impact on the lives of vulnerable children. Her journey with the Johnson family and the support she received from social services have inspired her to dedicate her life to helping others.

Emily's early years were marked by neglect and instability, which left a lasting impact on her. The intervention of social services and the unwavering support of the Johnson family played a crucial role in her healing and growth. These experiences have given Emily a unique perspective on the challenges faced by neglected and abused children. She understands the importance of providing a stable and nurturing environment, and she is determined to use her experiences to help others in similar situations.

The social workers who intervened in Emily's life made a significant impact on her. Their dedication, compassion, and commitment to her well-being inspired Emily to consider a career in social work. She saw firsthand the difference that a caring and supportive social worker can make in the lives of vulnerable children. Emily is motivated to follow in their footsteps and provide the same level of care and support to others.

Emily's journey has instilled in her a deep sense of gratitude for the support, she received. She is determined to give back to the community and help other children who are facing similar challenges. Emily believes that by becoming a social worker, she can make a meaningful difference in the lives of vulnerable children and families. Her desire to give back is a driving force behind her decision to pursue a career in social work.

Emily's involvement in advocacy work has fuelled her passion for social justice and child welfare. She has seen the impact of raising awareness and advocating for change, and she is committed to continuing this work as a social worker. Emily wants to use her voice and experiences to advocate for policies and programs that support vulnerable children and families. Her passion for advocacy is a key motivation for her career aspirations.

Emily is dedicated to pursuing the education and training necessary to become a social worker. She plans to attend a university with a strong social work program, where she can gain the knowledge and skills needed to make a positive impact. Emily is excited about the opportunities to learn from experienced professionals and to participate in internships and fieldwork that will prepare her for her future career.

Emily's long-term goals include working in child protective services, where she can directly support children and families in need. She also hopes to continue her advocacy work, raising awareness about child neglect and promoting policies that protect vulnerable children. Emily's ultimate goal is to create a positive and lasting impact on the lives of those she serves, helping them build brighter and more hopeful futures.

Emily's decision to pursue a career in social work is driven by her personal experiences, her desire to give back, and her passion for advocacy. With the support of the Johnson family and her community, she is ready to embrace this new chapter in her life and make a meaningful difference in the lives of vulnerable children and families.

Emily's journey to become a social worker is marked by dedication, hard work, and a deep commitment to making a positive impact on the lives of vulnerable children. Her educational and training experiences equip her with the knowledge and skills needed to excel in her chosen career.

Emily's interest in social work begins in high school, where she takes courses in psychology, sociology, and human development. These subjects provide her with a foundational understanding of human behaviour and social issues. Emily also participates in volunteer activities and internships that give her hands-on experience working with children and families in need. Her involvement in these activities reinforces her passion for social work and motivates her to pursue further education in the field.

With the support of the Johnson family, Emily researches universities with strong social work programs. She attends college fairs, meets with academic advisors, and visits campuses to find the best fit for her goals. Emily ultimately chooses a university known for its comprehensive social work curriculum and opportunities for practical experience. The Johnsons are by her side throughout the application process, providing guidance and encouragement.

Emily's undergraduate studies in social work are both challenging and rewarding. She takes a variety of courses that cover topics such as social welfare policy, child and family services, mental health, and community organization. Emily excels in her coursework, driven by her passion for helping others and her desire to make a difference. She actively participates in class discussions, group projects, and research assignments, gaining a deeper understanding of the complexities of social work.

As part of her social work program, Emily completes several field placements and internships. These experiences provide her with valuable hands-on training and the opportunity to apply her classroom knowledge in real-world settings. Emily works with child protective services, community organizations, and schools, gaining experience in case management, advocacy, and direct service provision. These placements help her develop practical skills and build professional relationships with experienced social workers.

After completing her undergraduate degree, Emily decides to pursue a Master of Social Work (MSW) to further specialize in her field. She applies to graduate programs that offer advanced training in child welfare and family services. Emily is accepted into a prestigious MSW program, where she continues to build on her knowledge and skills. Her graduate studies include advanced coursework in clinical practice, trauma-informed care, and policy analysis. Emily also completes a clinical internship, working with children and families affected by neglect and abuse.

Upon completing her MSW, Emily prepares for the licensure and certification process required to practice as a professional social worker. She studies diligently for the licensing exams, which test her knowledge of social work principles, ethics, and practice. Emily successfully passes the exams and obtains her social work license, allowing her to practice in her chosen field. She also pursues additional certifications in areas such as trauma-informed care and child welfare to enhance her expertise.

Emily is committed to lifelong learning and professional development. She regularly attends workshops, conferences, and training sessions to stay updated on the latest research and best practices in social work. Emily also joins professional organizations, such as the National Association of Social Workers (NASW), where she connects with other social workers and participates in advocacy efforts. Her dedication to continuing education ensures that she remains knowledgeable and effective in her practice.

With her education and training complete, Emily embarks on her career as a social worker with a deep sense of purpose and commitment. She works tirelessly to support vulnerable children and families, using her skills and knowledge to make a positive impact. Emily's journey through education and training has equipped her with the tools she needs to excel in her career and create lasting change in the lives of those she serves.

Emily's journey through education and training to become a social worker is a testament to her dedication, resilience, and passion for helping others. With the support of the Johnson family and her community, she is ready to make a meaningful difference in the world.

Emily's first job as a social worker is both rewarding and challenging. Her experiences in this role provide her with valuable insights and help her grow both professionally and personally.

Emily begins her career at Child Protective Services (CPS), where she is assigned to a team dedicated to supporting children and families in crisis. Her role involves conducting home visits, assessing the safety and well-being of children, and developing intervention plans to address the needs of families. Emily is eager to make a positive impact and is determined to use her skills and knowledge to help those in need.

One of the first challenges Emily faces is building trust with her clients. Many of the families she works with have experienced trauma and are wary of social workers. Emily approaches each case with empathy and patience, taking the time to listen to their concerns and understand their unique situations. She learns that building trust requires consistency, honesty, and a non-judgmental attitude. Over time, Emily's clients begin to open up to her, allowing her to provide the support they need.

The emotional demands of the job are significant, and Emily quickly realizes the importance of self-care and support. She encounters heartbreaking situations, such as cases of severe neglect and abuse, which take an emotional toll on her. Emily relies on her colleagues, supervisor, and therapist for guidance and support. She also practices mindfulness and engages in activities that help her relax and recharge. These strategies help Emily manage the emotional stress of her work and maintain her well-being.

Emily encounters bureaucratic challenges that can hinder her ability to provide timely support to families. She learns to navigate the complexities of the system, including paperwork, court procedures, and inter-agency collaboration. Emily's attention to detail and organizational skills become essential as she works to ensure that her clients receive the services they need. She also advocates for systemic changes that can improve the efficiency and effectiveness of CPS.

Managing a high caseload is another challenge Emily faces in her first job. She must balance the needs of multiple families, each with their own unique challenges and circumstances. Emily develops strong time management and prioritization skills to ensure that she can provide adequate support to all her clients. She learns to delegate tasks when necessary and to seek help from her colleagues when her workload becomes overwhelming.

Despite the challenges, Emily experiences many rewarding moments in her first job. She celebrates the successes of her clients, such as when a family successfully completes a reunification plan or when a child finds a safe and loving foster home. These successes reinforce Emily's commitment to her work and remind her of the positive impact she can make. She takes pride in the progress her clients achieve and finds fulfilment in knowing that she has played a role in their journey.

Emily's first job provides her with numerous opportunities for learning and growth. She attends training sessions, workshops, and conferences to stay updated on best practices and new developments in the field of social work. Emily also seeks feedback from her supervisor and colleagues to improve her skills and effectiveness. Her dedication to continuous learning helps her become a more competent and confident social worker.

Emily's experiences in her first job reaffirm her passion for social work and her commitment to helping vulnerable children and families. She is determined to continue making a positive impact and to advocate for systemic changes that can improve the lives of those she serves. Emily's journey as a social worker is just beginning, and she is excited about the opportunities and challenges that lie ahead.

Emily's first job as a social worker is filled with both challenges and rewards. Her experiences help her grow professionally and personally, reinforcing her commitment to making a positive impact on the lives of vulnerable children and families.

Emily's dedication to helping other children in similar situations is a testament to her compassion and commitment to making a positive impact. Her efforts extend beyond her professional role as a social worker, as she actively engages in various initiatives to support and uplift vulnerable children.

Emily volunteers as a mentor for children who have experienced neglect or trauma. She participates in programs at local schools and community centres, offering guidance and support to those in need. Emily's empathy and understanding make her a trusted figure for these children, who often feel isolated and misunderstood. Her mentorship provides them with a sense of connection and hope, helping them navigate their own challenges with greater confidence.

Emily continues to raise awareness about child neglect through advocacy and public speaking engagements. She collaborates with organizations that focus on child welfare, participating in awareness campaigns and educational workshops. Emily shares her story and insights, highlighting the importance of early intervention and support for neglected children. Her efforts help educate the public and encourage community involvement in addressing these critical issues.

Emily works with community organizations to create safe spaces for children to express themselves and receive support. She helps establish support groups and recreational programs that provide a nurturing environment for children to heal and grow. Emily's involvement in these initiatives ensures that children have access to the resources and care they need to thrive. Her dedication to creating safe spaces reinforces her commitment to fostering a supportive community for all children.

Emily organizes fundraising events to support organizations that provide services to neglected and abused children. She plans charity runs, art auctions, and community fairs, using her creativity and organizational skills to raise funds. The money raised goes towards providing essential resources, such as clothing, school supplies, and counselling services, to children in need. Emily's efforts make a tangible difference in the lives of these children and their families, ensuring they have the support they need to overcome their challenges.

Emily collaborates with schools to implement programs that support the well-being of students. She works with teachers and counsellors to identify children who may be at risk and to provide them with the necessary support. Emily's involvement in school-based initiatives helps create a more inclusive and supportive environment for all students. Her efforts ensure that children receive the care and attention they need to succeed academically and personally.

Emily's efforts to help other children have a profound impact on her community. Her dedication to advocacy, mentorship, and support services inspires others to get involved and make a difference. Emily's story serves as a powerful reminder of the importance of providing love and stability to vulnerable children. Her work helps create a more compassionate and supportive community, where every child has the opportunity to thrive.

Emily finds personal fulfilment in her efforts to help others. Knowing that she is making a positive impact on the lives of vulnerable children gives her a sense of purpose and satisfaction. Emily's dedication to helping others is a reflection of her own journey of healing and growth. Her experiences have shaped her into a compassionate and resilient individual, committed to making a difference in the world.

Emily's efforts to help other children in similar situations highlight her compassion, dedication, and commitment to making a positive impact. Her work as a mentor, advocate, and community leader continues to inspire and uplift those around her, creating a brighter and more hopeful future for all children.

Emily understands the importance of having a strong support network, both for herself and her clients. Her efforts to build and maintain these networks are crucial in providing the necessary support and resources for those in need.

Emily's adoptive family, the Johnsons, remain her primary source of support. Their unwavering love and encouragement provide her with a stable foundation. Emily also maintains close relationships with her friends, who offer companionship and understanding. These connections help Emily navigate the challenges of her career and personal life, providing her with a sense of belonging and security.

Emily seeks guidance from experienced social workers and mentors in her field. She regularly meets with her supervisor and colleagues to discuss cases, share insights, and seek advice. These professional relationships provide Emily with valuable support and help her develop her skills and knowledge. Her mentors offer encouragement and guidance, helping her navigate the complexities of her role as a social worker.

Recognizing the emotional demands of her job, Emily continues to work with her therapist, Dr. Collins. Regular therapy sessions provide her with a safe space to process her emotions and develop healthy coping mechanisms. Dr. Collins helps Emily manage stress and maintain her well-being, ensuring that she can provide the best support to her clients.

Emily joins professional organizations, such as the National Association of Social Workers (NASW), where she connects with other social workers and participates in advocacy efforts. These organizations offer networking opportunities, resources, and training sessions that help Emily stay updated on best practices and new developments in the field. Being part of a professional community reinforces her sense of purpose and commitment to her career.

Emily works diligently to connect her clients with community resources that can provide additional support. She collaborates with local shelters, food banks, and counselling services to ensure that her clients have access to the necessary resources. Emily's knowledge of available services helps her create comprehensive support plans that address the unique needs of each family.

Emily helps establish support groups for children and families affected by neglect and trauma. These groups provide a safe space for individuals to share their experiences, receive guidance, and build connections with others who understand their challenges. Emily facilitates group sessions, offering support and encouragement to participants. The sense of community and belonging that these groups provide is invaluable in the healing process.

Emily collaborates with schools to create supportive environments for her clients. She works with teachers, counsellors, and administrators to identify at-risk students and develop intervention plans. Emily's involvement in school-based initiatives ensures that children receive the academic and emotional support they need to succeed. Her partnerships with schools help create a network of care that extends beyond the home.

Emily advocates for her clients' rights and ensures they have access to legal support when needed. She works with legal aid organizations to provide representation and guidance for families navigating the legal system. Emily's advocacy efforts help protect her clients' rights and ensure they receive fair treatment and support.

Emily establishes peer mentorship programs that connect her clients with individuals who have successfully navigated similar challenges. These mentors offer guidance, support, and encouragement, helping clients build confidence and resilience. Emily's efforts to create these programs provide her clients with valuable role models and a sense of hope for the future.

Emily's ability to build strong relationships with her clients is a key aspect of her support network. She approaches each case with empathy and understanding, taking the time to listen to her clients' concerns and needs. Emily's genuine care and commitment help her build trust and rapport with her clients, ensuring they feel supported and valued.

Emily's efforts to build a support network for herself and her clients highlight her dedication to providing comprehensive care and support. Her personal and professional networks play a crucial role in her ability to make a positive impact on the lives of vulnerable children and families.

Emily's journey as a social worker brings her immense personal fulfilment, as she dedicates her life to helping others and making a positive impact on her community. Her work is not just a career but a calling that resonates deeply with her values and experiences.

Emily finds profound satisfaction in knowing that her efforts are making a tangible difference in the lives of vulnerable children and families. Each success story, whether it's a child finding a safe home or a family overcoming challenges, reinforces her commitment to her work. The gratitude and appreciation she receives from those she helps provide her with a sense of purpose and fulfilment. Emily's ability to create positive change in her clients' lives is a constant source of motivation and joy.

The relationships Emily builds with her clients, colleagues, and community members are a significant source of personal fulfilment. She values the trust and connections she forms with the children and families she supports. These relationships are built on empathy, understanding, and mutual respect, and they enrich Emily's life in countless ways. The bonds she creates with her clients remind her of the importance of human connection and the impact of compassionate care.

Emily takes great pride in witnessing the growth and resilience of the children and families, she works with. Seeing her clients overcome obstacles, build confidence, and achieve their goals is incredibly rewarding. Emily's role in their journey of healing and empowerment fills her with a deep sense of accomplishment. She is inspired by their strength and determination, and their progress reinforces her belief in the power of support and advocacy.

Emily's work as a social worker provides her with ongoing opportunities for learning and personal development. She is constantly expanding her knowledge and skills through training sessions, workshops, and professional development courses. This continuous learning keeps her engaged and passionate about her work. Emily's dedication to self-improvement ensures that she can provide the best possible support to her clients and stay at the forefront of her field.

Emily's involvement in advocacy work brings her a deep sense of fulfilment. She is passionate about raising awareness and promoting policies that protect and support vulnerable children. Emily's efforts to advocate for systemic change and social justice align with her values and aspirations. Knowing that she is contributing to a larger movement for positive change gives her a sense of purpose and fulfilment. Her advocacy work allows her to use her voice and experiences to inspire others and make a lasting impact.

Emily's journey as a social worker has also been a journey of personal growth and self-discovery. She has developed resilience, empathy, and a deeper understanding of herself and others. Emily's work challenges her to confront difficult situations and emotions, helping her grow both personally and professionally. The reflections and insights she gains from her experiences enrich her life and shape her perspective.

Emily feels a deep sense of gratitude for the opportunity to do meaningful work that aligns with her passions and values. She appreciates the support of the Johnson family, her colleagues, and her community, which enables her to pursue her career with dedication and enthusiasm. Emily's gratitude extends to the children and families she works with, who inspire her every day with their courage and resilience.

Emily's work as a social worker brings her immense personal fulfilment, as she dedicates her life to helping others and making a positive impact. Her journey is marked by meaningful relationships, continuous learning, and a deep sense of purpose. Emily's commitment to her work and her clients is a testament to her compassion, resilience, and dedication to creating a better world for all children.

Emily's career as a social worker is filled with both rewarding moments and significant challenges. Her ability to navigate these obstacles and find solutions is a testament to her resilience, dedication, and commitment to making a positive impact.

One of the most significant challenges Emily faces is the emotional toll of her work. Dealing with cases of severe neglect, abuse, and trauma can be overwhelming and distressing. Emily often feels the weight of her clients' pain and struggles, which can lead to emotional exhaustion. To overcome this, Emily prioritizes self-care and seeks support from her therapist, Dr. Collins. Regular therapy sessions help her process her emotions and develop healthy coping mechanisms. Emily also practices mindfulness and engages in activities that bring her joy and relaxation, such as painting and spending time in nature.

Managing a high caseload is another challenge Emily encounters in her career. The demands of her job often require her to juggle multiple cases simultaneously, each with its own unique complexities. To address this, Emily develops strong time management and organizational skills. She creates detailed schedules and prioritizes tasks to ensure that each client receives the attention and support they need. Emily also collaborates with her colleagues, seeking their assistance and sharing resources to manage the workload effectively.

Navigating the bureaucratic aspects of social work can be frustrating and time consuming. Emily often encounters challenges related to paperwork, court procedures, and inter-agency collaboration. These hurdles can delay the provision of services and support to her clients. To overcome this, Emily becomes well-versed in the policies and procedures of her organization. She maintains meticulous records and stays organized to ensure that all necessary documentation is completed accurately and on time. Emily also advocates for systemic changes that can streamline processes and improve efficiency.

Establishing trust with clients who have experienced trauma and neglect can be challenging. Many of Emily's clients are wary of social workers and may be reluctant to open up. Emily approaches each case with empathy, patience, and a non-judgmental attitude. She takes the time to listen to her clients' concerns and validate their feelings. By consistently showing compassion and understanding, Emily gradually builds trust and rapport with her clients, creating a safe space for them to share their experiences and seek support.

Maintaining a healthy work-life balance is essential for Emily's well-being, but it can be challenging given the demands of her job. The emotional and physical toll of her work can sometimes spill over into her personal life. To address this, Emily sets clear boundaries between her professional and personal time. She ensures that she takes regular breaks and schedules time for activities that bring her joy and relaxation. Emily also seeks support from her family and friends, who provide her with a sense of stability and comfort.

Advocating for her clients' rights and needs is a crucial part of Emily's role, but it can be challenging when faced with systemic barriers and resistance. Emily often encounters situations where she must navigate complex legal and policy issues to ensure her clients receive the support they deserve. To overcome this, Emily stays informed about relevant laws and policies and collaborates with legal aid organizations. She uses her knowledge and skills to advocate effectively for her clients, ensuring their voices are heard and their rights are protected.

The field of social work is constantly evolving, and staying updated on best practices and new developments is essential. Emily faces the challenge of balancing her workload with the need for continuous learning and professional development. To address this, she actively seeks out training opportunities, workshops, and conferences. Emily also engages in peer supervision and networking with other social workers to share knowledge and experiences. Her commitment to continuous learning ensures that she remains effective and knowledgeable in her practice.

Emily's ability to overcome the challenges she faces in her career is a testament to her resilience, dedication, and commitment to making a positive impact. Her strategies for managing emotional stress, high caseloads, bureaucratic hurdles, and building trust with clients enable her to provide the best possible support to those in need. Emily's journey as a social worker is marked by her unwavering determination to create positive change and support vulnerable children and families.

Emily's journey of growth and development continues to evolve, both in her career as a social worker and in her personal life.

Her commitment to learning, self-improvement, and making a positive impact drives her to reach new heights.

Emily is dedicated to staying updated on the latest developments in social work. She regularly attends workshops, seminars, and conferences to enhance her knowledge and skills. Emily also pursues advanced certifications in areas such as trauma-informed care, child welfare, and family therapy. These certifications enable her to provide specialized support to her clients and stay at the forefront of her field.

Emily's expertise and dedication are recognized by her colleagues and supervisors leading to opportunities for leadership roles. She takes on responsibilities such as supervising interns, leading team meetings, and coordinating community outreach programs. Emily's leadership skills help her mentor and guide other social workers, fostering a collaborative and supportive work environment.

Emily becomes involved in research projects that focus on improving social work practices and policies. She collaborates with academic institutions and advocacy groups to conduct studies and publish findings. Emily's research contributes to the development of evidence-based practices that enhance the effectiveness of social work interventions. Her advocacy efforts continue to raise awareness about child neglect and promote systemic changes that benefit vulnerable children and families.

Emily actively participates in professional organizations and networks with other social workers, researchers, and advocates. These connections provide her with valuable insights, resources, and opportunities for collaboration. Emily's involvement in professional communities helps her stay informed about best practices and innovative approaches in social work.

Emily prioritizes self-care and well-being to maintain her physical and emotional health. She practices mindfulness, engages in regular exercise, and enjoys hobbies such as painting and hiking. Emily's commitment to self-care ensures that she can continue to provide effective support to her clients while maintaining her own well-being.

Emily continues to nurture her relationships with the Johnson family and her friends. She values the love and support they provide, and she makes time for meaningful connections and shared experiences. Emily's strong support network reinforces her sense of belonging and happiness, contributing to her overall well-being.

Emily sets personal goals and celebrates her achievements, both big and small. Whether it's completing a challenging project at work, learning a new skill, or achieving a personal milestone, Emily takes pride in her accomplishments. These moments of recognition and celebration boost her confidence and motivate her to continue striving for success.

Emily remains actively involved in her community, volunteering her time and skills to support local initiatives. She participates in community events, mentors young people, and advocates for social justice. Emily's dedication to giving back to her community provides her with a sense of purpose and fulfilment.

Emily's journey of continued growth and development is marked by her commitment to learning, self-improvement, and making a positive impact. She is excited about the future and the opportunities it holds. Emily's dedication to her career and personal growth ensures that she will continue to make a meaningful difference in the lives of vulnerable children and families.

Emily's story is a testament to the power of resilience, dedication, and the human spirit's capacity for growth and healing. With the support of the Johnson family and her community, she is ready to embrace the future with confidence and hope.

Emily's dedication to her work as a social worker has a profound impact on the lives of the children and families, she supports. Her compassion, resilience, and commitment to making a positive difference are evident in the transformative changes she helps bring about.

One of Emily's most rewarding experiences is reuniting children with their families after a period of separation. She works tirelessly to support parents in addressing the issues that led to their children being placed in care. Emily provides counselling, resources, and guidance to help parents create a safe and nurturing environment for their children. When a family successfully completes their reunification plan, Emily feels immense joy and satisfaction. The smiles and tears of happiness from both the parents and children are a testament to the positive impact of her work.

Emily's efforts to find safe and loving foster homes for children in crisis make a significant difference in their lives. She carefully matches children with foster families who can provide the stability and care they need. Emily's support doesn't end with placement; she continues to check in with both the children and foster families, ensuring that everyone is adjusting well. The sense of security and belonging that these children experience in their new homes is a direct result of Emily's dedication and compassion.

Emily's work with teenagers who have experienced neglect and trauma is particularly impactful. She mentors these young individuals, helping them build confidence and develop life skills. Emily organizes workshops on topics such as self-esteem, goal-setting, and healthy relationships. Her guidance and encouragement empower these teenagers to believe in themselves and pursue their dreams. Seeing them graduate from high school, secure jobs, or enrol in college fills Emily with pride and reinforces her commitment to supporting vulnerable youth.

Emily's advocacy efforts extend beyond individual cases. She works with community organizations and policymakers to address systemic issues that affect vulnerable children and families. Emily's involvement in advocacy campaigns helps raise awareness about child neglect and the importance of early intervention. Her contributions to policy discussions and research initiatives promote positive changes that benefit the broader community. Emily's ability to influence systemic change is a testament to her dedication to creating a better future for all children.

Emily understands the importance of a strong support network for both her clients and herself. She helps establish support groups for parents, children, and foster families, providing a safe space for them to share their experiences and receive guidance. Emily's efforts to build these networks foster a sense of community and belonging, helping individuals feel less isolated and more supported. The positive feedback and gratitude she receives from participants highlight the difference these support networks make in their lives.

Emily's work brings her immense personal fulfilment.

Knowing that she is making a positive impact on the lives of vulnerable children and families gives her a sense of purpose and satisfaction. Emily's dedication to her clients and her commitment to continuous learning and growth ensure that she remains an effective and compassionate social worker. Her journey is marked by meaningful relationships, transformative changes, and a deep sense of fulfilment.

Emily's dedication to her work as a social worker has a profound impact on the lives of the children and families, she supports. Her compassion, resilience, and commitment to making a positive difference are evident in the transformative changes she helps bring about.

Emily's story is a testament to the power of love, support, and the human spirit's capacity for growth and healing.

As Emily reflects on her journey and the incredible support she has received, she feels a profound sense of optimism and determination for the future. Her experiences have shaped her into a resilient, compassionate, and empowered individual, ready to embrace the possibilities that lie ahead.

Emily is excited about the endless opportunities that await her. She looks forward to continuing her education, exploring her passions, and pursuing her dreams. With the support of the Johnson family and her community, Emily is confident in her ability to achieve her goals and make a meaningful impact. She is determined to use her skills and knowledge to create positive change and support vulnerable children and families.

Emily's vision for the future is filled with promise and potential. She is committed to building a life that reflects her values and aspirations. Emily's dedication to her career as a social worker, her involvement in advocacy, and her passion for helping others all contribute to her vision of a bright and fulfilling future. She is ready to face new challenges and seize new opportunities, confident in her ability to overcome obstacles and achieve her goals.

The bonds Emily has formed with the Johnson family and her friends continue to grow stronger. She cherishes the love and support she receives from her adoptive family, knowing that they will always be there for her. Emily also values the friendships she has built, which provide her with a sense of belonging and companionship. These relationships are a source of strength and comfort, reinforcing her sense of self-worth and happiness.

Emily's experiences have inspired her to give back to the community and help others who are facing similar challenges. She is passionate about raising awareness about child neglect and advocating for vulnerable children. Emily's involvement in community service and advocacy work provides her with a sense of purpose and fulfilment. She is determined to use her voice and experiences to make a positive impact and inspire change.

Emily's journey has taught her the importance of resilience and personal growth. She has developed healthy coping mechanisms to manage stress and anxiety, and she continues to work on building emotional strength. Emily's ability to navigate challenges and embrace change is a testament to her inner strength and determination. She is proud of the progress she has made and is committed to continuing her journey of self-discovery and growth.

As Emily looks to the future, she feels a sense of hope and excitement for the possibilities that lie ahead. The stability and love provided by the Johnson family have given her the foundation she needs to build a brighter and more hopeful tomorrow. Emily is ready to face whatever challenges come her way, knowing that she has the support and encouragement of those who care deeply for her.

Emily's story is one of resilience, hope, and the power of a supportive environment. With the unwavering support of the Johnson family, her teachers, and her friends, Emily is ready to embrace the future and all the possibilities it holds. Her journey is a testament to the strength of the human spirit and the importance of love and stability in fostering growth and healing.

Chapter 13
Mentorship and Leadership

Emily's journey of growth and resilience naturally leads her to take on a mentorship role, where she can share her experiences and knowledge with new social workers and young people in care. Her dedication to helping others and her compassionate nature make her an inspiring and effective mentor.

Emily understands the challenges that new social workers face as they navigate their roles. She offers guidance and support to help them build confidence and develop their skills. Emily shares her own experiences, providing practical advice on managing caseloads, building trust with clients, and navigating bureaucratic hurdles. Her empathetic approach helps new social workers feel understood and supported.

Emily takes on the responsibility of leading training sessions for new social workers. She organizes workshops and seminars that cover essential topics such as trauma-informed care, child welfare policies, and effective communication strategies. Emily's engaging and informative sessions equip new social workers with the knowledge and tools they need to succeed in their roles.

Emily fosters a supportive and collaborative environment for new social workers. She encourages open communication and peer support, creating a space where they can share their challenges and successes. Emily's mentorship helps build a sense of community and camaraderie among new social workers, reinforcing the importance of teamwork and mutual support.

Emily's personal experiences make her a relatable and trusted mentor for young people in care. She takes the time to build genuine connections with them, listening to their stories and validating their feelings. Emily's ability to empathize with their struggles helps young people feel understood and supported.

Emily provides guidance and encouragement to young people in care, helping them navigate their challenges and pursue their goals. She offers practical advice on academic success, career planning, and personal development. Emily's mentorship empowers young people to believe in themselves and strive for a brighter future.

Emily organizes workshops and activities that promote personal growth and skill development for young people in care. These activities include life skills training, creative arts sessions, and leadership development programs. Emily's efforts provide young people with valuable opportunities to learn, grow, and build confidence.

Emily ensures that the young people she mentors have access to a safe and nurturing environment. She collaborates with community organizations to provide resources and support services that address their needs. Emily's commitment to creating a supportive environment helps young people feel secure and valued.

Emily's mentorship has a profound impact on both new social workers and young people in care. Her guidance and support help new social workers build confidence and develop their skills, ensuring they can provide effective support to their clients. For young people in care, Emily's mentorship provides a sense of connection, encouragement, and hope. Her efforts inspire them to believe in their potential and pursue their dreams.

Emily's role as a mentor is a testament to her dedication to helping others and her commitment to making a positive impact. Her journey of growth and resilience continues to inspire those around her, creating a legacy of compassion, support, and empowerment.

Emily's dedication, expertise, and passion for social work naturally lead her to take on leadership roles within her organization. Her journey into leadership is marked by her commitment to making a positive impact and her ability to inspire and guide others.

Emily's first leadership role comes when she is appointed as a team lead within her department. In this position, she is responsible for overseeing a group of social workers, providing guidance, and ensuring that cases are managed effectively. Emily's empathetic and supportive approach helps her team members feel valued and motivated. She fosters a collaborative environment where everyone's input is respected, and challenges are addressed collectively.

Recognizing Emily's expertise and dedication to continuous learning, her organization appoints her as a training coordinator. In this role, Emily is responsible for organizing and leading training sessions for new social workers. She develops comprehensive training programs that cover essential topics such as trauma-informed care, child welfare policies, and effective communication strategies. Emily's engaging and informative sessions equip new social workers with the knowledge and tools they need to succeed in their roles.

Emily's success as a team lead and training coordinator leads to her promotion to program manager. In this role, she oversees multiple programs within her organization, ensuring that they run smoothly and effectively. Emily is responsible for developing program strategies, managing budgets, and evaluating program outcomes. Her ability to think strategically and her commitment to excellence help her drive positive changes and improvements within the organization.

Emily's dedication and leadership skills are further recognized when she is promoted to the position of Director of Child Welfare Services. In this role, Emily oversees all child welfare programs and services within the organization. She is responsible for setting the vision and direction for the department, developing policies and procedures, and ensuring that the organization's goals are met. Emily's leadership helps create a culture of excellence and compassion, where the well-being of children and families is always the top priority.

Emily's leadership style is characterized by her ability to inspire and motivate others. She leads by example, demonstrating dedication, empathy, and a commitment to making a positive impact. Emily's team members look up to her as a role model and are motivated by her passion and drive. Her ability to connect with others on a personal level helps create a supportive and collaborative work environment.

As a leader, Emily is committed to driving positive change

within her organization and the broader community. She advocates for policies and practices that support vulnerable children and families, and she works tirelessly to improve the effectiveness of social work interventions. Emily's leadership helps create a culture of continuous improvement, where innovative ideas and best practices are embraced.

Emily's leadership extends beyond her organization as she builds strong partnerships with other agencies, community organizations, and policymakers. She collaborates with these partners to address systemic issues and create comprehensive support networks for children and families. Emily's ability to build and maintain these partnerships enhances the organization's capacity to provide effective and holistic support.

Emily is dedicated to mentoring and developing future leaders within her organization. She identifies and nurtures talent, providing guidance and opportunities for growth. Emily's mentorship helps prepare the next generation of social workers and leaders, ensuring that the organization continues to thrive and make a positive impact.

Emily's progression into leadership roles within her organization is a testament to her dedication, expertise, and passion for making a positive impact. Her ability to inspire and guide others, drive positive change, and build strong partnerships ensures that she continues to make a meaningful difference in the lives of vulnerable children and families.

Emily's commitment to supporting children and families extends to her involvement in developing innovative programs that address their unique needs. Her creativity, dedication, and deep understanding of the challenges faced by vulnerable populations drive her to create impactful initiatives.

Emily recognizes the importance of early intervention in preventing long-term negative outcomes for children at risk. She collaborates with her colleagues to develop programs that identify and support children and families in the early stages of crisis. These programs include:

Emily helps design comprehensive family support services that provide resources and guidance to parents struggling with various challenges. These services include parenting classes, counselling, and access to community resources. Emily's goal is to empower parents with the skills and knowledge they need to create a safe and nurturing environment for their children.

Understanding the critical role schools play in a child's life, Emily works with educators to implement school-based intervention programs. These programs provide support to students facing academic, behavioural, or emotional difficulties. Emily's initiatives include after-school tutoring, mentoring programs, and mental health services. By addressing issues early on, these programs help students succeed academically and personally.

Emily's experience with trauma-informed care informs her approach to developing programs that support children who have experienced trauma. She advocates for and helps implement trauma-informed practices across various settings, including schools, foster care, and community organizations. Key components of these programs include:

Emily organizes training sessions for educators, social workers, and healthcare providers on trauma-informed care principles. These sessions equip professionals with the knowledge and skills to recognize and respond to the effects of trauma. Emily's training programs emphasize the importance of creating safe and supportive environments for children.

Emily helps establish therapeutic services that provide specialized support to children affected by trauma. These services include individual and group therapy, art therapy, and play therapy. Emily's initiatives ensure that children have access to the care they need to heal and thrive.

Emily is passionate about empowering young people to reach their full potential. She develops programs that provide opportunities for personal growth, skill development, and leadership.

Emily creates youth leadership development programs that encourage young people to take on leadership roles in their communities. These programs include workshops on public speaking, project management, and community organizing. Emily's goal is to inspire young people to become advocates for positive change.

Emily designs programs that prepare young people for successful transitions to college and careers. These programs offer career counselling, college application assistance, and job readiness training. Emily's initiatives help young people set and achieve their goals, providing them with the tools they need to succeed.

Emily's commitment to supporting children and families extends to her work in the community. She develops outreach programs that connect families with essential resources and support services.

Emily organizes community resource fairs that bring together various service providers in one location. These fairs offer families access to healthcare, housing assistance, legal aid, and other essential services. Emily's efforts ensure that families have the support they need to overcome challenges and thrive.

Emily helps establish parent support groups that provide a safe space for parents to share their experiences and receive guidance. These groups offer peer support, parenting workshops, and access to resources. Emily's initiatives help parents build strong support networks and develop effective parenting strategies.

Emily's involvement in developing new programs to support children and families highlights her dedication, creativity, and commitment to making a positive impact. Her innovative initiatives address the unique needs of vulnerable populations, providing them with the resources and support they need to thrive.

Emily's dedication to child welfare extends beyond her professional role as a social worker. She actively engages with her community to raise awareness about child welfare issues and to foster a supportive environment for vulnerable children and families.

Emily takes the initiative to organize community events that focus on raising awareness about child welfare. She plans and hosts events such as family fun days, educational workshops, and awareness walks. These events bring together community members, local organizations, and service providers to share information and resources. Emily's efforts help create a sense of community and encourage collective action to support vulnerable children.

Emily conducts educational workshops for parents, teachers, and community members. These workshops cover topics such as recognizing signs of neglect and abuse, understanding the impact of trauma, and learning effective parenting strategies. Emily's workshops provide valuable information and practical tools that empower participants to support children in their care. Her engaging and informative presentations help raise awareness and promote positive change.

Emily collaborates with local organizations, such as schools, healthcare providers, and non-profits, to address child welfare issues. She works with these partners to develop and implement programs that provide comprehensive support to children and families. Emily's collaborative approach ensures that resources are effectively utilized and that services are accessible to those in need. Her partnerships strengthen the community's capacity to support vulnerable children.

Emily is actively involved in advocacy campaigns that aim to influence policy and raise public awareness about child welfare issues. She participates in campaigns that highlight the importance of early intervention, adequate funding for child welfare services, and the need for trauma-informed care. Emily's advocacy efforts include writing articles, speaking at public forums, and engaging with policymakers. Her passion and dedication help drive positive changes at both the local and broader levels.

Emily develops and implements community outreach programs that connect families with essential resources and support services. She organizes resource fairs, where families can access information about healthcare, housing, legal aid, and other services. Emily's outreach programs ensure that families are aware of the support available to them and can easily access the help they need. Her efforts help create a more informed and connected community.

Emily is passionate about engaging young people in her community and empowering them to become advocates for change. She organizes youth engagement initiatives, such as leadership development programs, volunteer opportunities, and peer support groups. These initiatives provide young people with the skills and confidence to take on leadership roles and make a positive impact in their community. Emily's efforts inspire the next generation to become active participants in promoting child welfare.

Emily uses her voice to raise awareness about child welfare issues through public speaking and media engagement. She speaks at community events, conferences, and schools, sharing her experiences and insights. Emily also engages with local media, participating in interviews and writing opinion pieces. Her ability to communicate effectively and passionately helps raise awareness and mobilize community support for child welfare initiatives.

Emily's community engagement efforts contribute to building a supportive and compassionate community. Her initiatives foster a sense of collective responsibility and encourage community members to take action to support vulnerable children and families. Emily's dedication to raising awareness and promoting positive change helps create a community where every child has the opportunity to thrive.

Emily's efforts to engage with the community and raise awareness about child welfare issues highlight her commitment to making a positive impact. Her initiatives foster a supportive environment and encourage collective action to support vulnerable children and families.

Emily's advocacy work is a crucial aspect of her commitment to improving the lives of vulnerable children and families. Her efforts at both local and national levels aim to influence policy changes and raise awareness about child welfare issues.

Emily actively engages with her local community to raise awareness about child welfare issues. She organizes town hall meetings, community forums, and workshops to educate residents about the signs of neglect and abuse, the importance of early intervention, and available resources. Emily's outreach efforts help create a more informed and supportive community, encouraging collective action to protect vulnerable children.

Emily works closely with local government officials, including city council members and school board representatives, to advocate for policies that support child welfare. She presents data, shares case studies, and provides recommendations for improving services and resources for children and families. Emily's collaboration with local officials helps ensure that child welfare issues are prioritized in community planning and decision-making.

Emily partners with local schools to implement programs that support students' well-being. She advocates for the inclusion of mental health services, anti-bullying initiatives, and trauma-informed practices in school policies. Emily's efforts help create a safer and more supportive environment for students, promoting their academic and personal success.

Emily's dedication to child welfare extends to the national level, where she advocates for policy changes that benefit vulnerable children and families. She collaborates with national organizations, such as the National Association of Social Workers (NASW), to develop and promote policy recommendations. Emily's advocacy focuses on issues such as funding for child welfare services, access to mental health care, and the implementation of trauma-informed practices.

Emily's expertise and passion for child welfare lead to opportunities to testify before parliamentary committees. She shares her experiences and insights, providing valuable perspectives on the challenges faced by social workers and the children they serve. Emily's testimony helps inform lawmakers about the critical need for policy changes and increased support for child welfare programs.

Emily participates in national advocacy campaigns that aim to raise awareness and drive policy changes. She collaborates with advocacy groups to organize events, create educational materials, and engage with the media. Emily's involvement in these campaigns helps amplify the voices of vulnerable children and families, bringing attention to their needs and advocating for systemic change.

Emily's advocacy efforts contribute to meaningful policy changes at both local and national levels. Her work helps secure increased funding for child welfare services, the implementation of trauma-informed practices, and improved access to mental health care. Emily's ability to influence policy changes ensures that vulnerable children and families receive the support they need to thrive.

Emily's advocacy work raises awareness about child welfare issues, helping to educate the public and policymakers about the importance of early intervention and support. Her efforts help create a more informed and compassionate society, where the well-being of children is a priority.

Emily's advocacy work inspires and empowers others to get involved and make a difference. Her dedication and passion serve as a powerful example, motivating community members, social workers, and policymakers to take action. Emily's efforts help build a network of advocates who are committed to improving the lives of vulnerable children and families.

Emily's advocacy work at local and national levels highlights her commitment to making a positive impact and influencing policy changes. Her efforts help create a more supportive and informed society, ensuring that vulnerable children and families receive the care and resources they need.

Emily's ability to build strong partnerships with other organizations is a key factor in enhancing support services for vulnerable children and families. Her collaborative approach ensures that resources are effectively utilized, and that comprehensive care is provided.

Emily begins by identifying organizations that share a common goal of supporting children and families. These may include local non-profits, healthcare providers, educational institutions, and government agencies. Emily conducts thorough research to understand the services each organization offers and how they align with the needs of her clients.

Emily reaches out to potential partners to establish relationships and explore opportunities for collaboration. She attends networking events, community meetings, and conferences to connect with representatives from these organizations. Emily's approachable and empathetic nature helps her build trust and rapport with potential partners, laying the foundation for successful collaborations.

Once relationships are established, Emily works with her partners to develop collaborative plans that address the needs of children and families. She organizes joint meetings and workshops to discuss goals, share resources, and develop strategies. Emily's ability to facilitate open and productive discussions ensures that all partners are aligned and committed to the shared objectives.

Emily's partnerships lead to the creation of integrated support services that provide comprehensive care to children and families. For example, she collaborates with healthcare providers to offer medical and mental health services, with schools to provide educational support, and with non-profits to offer housing and financial assistance. Emily's efforts ensure that her clients have access to a wide range of services that address their holistic needs.

Emily emphasizes the importance of resource sharing and coordination among partner organizations. She develops systems for sharing information, tracking progress, and coordinating services. Emily's approach ensures that there is no duplication of efforts and that resources are used efficiently. Her coordination efforts help create a seamless support network for children and families.

Emily collaborates with her partners on joint advocacy efforts to raise awareness and influence policy changes. Together, they organize campaigns, write policy briefs, and engage with policymakers to advocate for the needs of vulnerable children and families. Emily's ability to unite multiple organizations amplifies their collective voice and increases the impact of their advocacy efforts.

Emily and her partners regularly evaluate the effectiveness of their collaborative efforts. They collect data, gather feedback from clients, and assess outcomes to identify areas for improvement. Emily's commitment to continuous improvement ensures that the support services provided are effective and responsive to the needs of children and families.

Emily's partnerships create a strong network of support that benefits the entire community. Her collaborative approach fosters a sense of unity and shared responsibility among organizations. Emily's efforts help build a community where children and families have access to the resources and support, they need to thrive.

Emily's ability to build partnerships with other organizations enhances support services for vulnerable children and families. Her collaborative approach ensures that resources are effectively utilized, and that comprehensive care is provided. Emily's dedication to creating a strong network of support highlights her commitment to making a positive impact.

Emily's dedication to her career as a social worker is unwavering, but balancing her professional responsibilities with her personal life presents significant challenges. Her journey is marked by moments of struggle and resilience as she navigates the complexities of maintaining a healthy work-life balance.

The emotional demands of Emily's job can be overwhelming. Dealing with cases of severe neglect, abuse, and trauma takes a toll on her mental and emotional well-being. Emily often finds herself carrying the weight of her clients' pain, which can lead to emotional exhaustion. To manage this, she prioritizes self-care and seeks support from her therapist, Dr. Collins. Regular therapy sessions provide Emily with a safe space to process her emotions and develop healthy coping mechanisms.

Balancing a high caseload with personal commitments is a constant challenge for Emily. Her job requires her to be available for her clients, often outside of regular working hours. This can make it difficult for her to find time for herself and her loved ones. Emily develops strong time management skills, creating detailed schedules and setting boundaries to ensure she can meet her professional responsibilities while also making time for personal activities and relationships.

Emily's demanding career can strain her personal relationships. The long hours and emotional intensity of her work sometimes leave her feeling drained and unable to fully engage with her family and friends. Emily makes a conscious effort to nurture her relationships, setting aside quality time to spend with the Johnson family and her close friends. She communicates openly with her loved ones about her challenges, seeking their understanding and support.

Emily understands the importance of self-care in maintaining her overall well-being. She incorporates self-care practices into her daily routine, such as mindfulness meditation, regular exercise, and creative activities like painting. These practices help Emily recharge and maintain her mental and physical health. She also makes time for hobbies and activities that bring her joy and relaxation, ensuring she has a healthy balance between work and personal life.

Setting and maintaining professional boundaries is crucial for Emily to prevent burnout. She learns to say no when her workload becomes overwhelming and to delegate tasks when necessary. Emily also sets clear boundaries with her clients, ensuring that she is available to support them while also protecting her own well-being. These boundaries help Emily manage her workload effectively and maintain a healthy work-life balance.

Emily recognizes the importance of seeking support from her colleagues and mentors. She regularly participates in peer supervision and support groups, where she can share her experiences and receive guidance. Emily's professional network provides her with valuable insights and encouragement, helping her navigate the challenges of her career. She also seeks support from the Johnson family, who offer her love and understanding during difficult times.

Despite the challenges, Emily finds fulfilment in her work and takes pride in her achievements. She reflects on the positive impact she has made in the lives of her clients, which reinforces her commitment to her career. Emily's ability to celebrate her successes and acknowledge her progress helps her stay motivated and resilient.

Emily's journey of balancing her career and personal life is marked by moments of struggle and resilience. Her dedication to self-care, time management, and seeking support helps her navigate the challenges and maintain a healthy work-life balance. Emily's story is a testament to her strength and determination to make a positive impact while also caring for her own well-being.

Emily's dedication to developing and implementing programs and initiatives has led to numerous successes that have positively impacted the lives of vulnerable children and families. Her efforts have been recognized and celebrated within her community and beyond.

Emily's family support services program has been a resounding success. The program provides parents with the resources and guidance they need to create a safe and nurturing environment for their children. Through parenting classes, counselling, and access to community resources, many families have been able to overcome challenges and build stronger, healthier relationships. The program's success is evident in the positive feedback from parents, who report improved parenting skills and stronger family bonds.

The school-based intervention programs that Emily helped implement have made a significant difference in the lives of students. These programs provide support to students facing academic, behavioural, or emotional difficulties. As a result, many students have shown improved academic performance, better behaviour, and enhanced emotional well-being. Teachers and school administrators have praised the programs for creating a more supportive and inclusive school environment.

Emily's trauma-informed care programs have been instrumental in supporting children who have experienced trauma. The training sessions for professionals have equipped educators, social workers, and healthcare providers with the knowledge and skills to recognize and respond to the effects of trauma. The therapeutic services established through these programs have provided children with the care they need to heal and thrive. The success of these programs is reflected in the positive outcomes for children, including improved mental health and emotional resilience.

Emily's youth empowerment programs have inspired and motivated young people to reach their full potential. The youth leadership development programs have encouraged young people to take on leadership roles in their communities, while the career and college readiness programs have prepared them for successful transitions to higher education and careers. Many participants have gone on to achieve their goals, thanks to the guidance and support provided by these programs. The success stories of these young individuals serve as a testament to the impact of Emily's initiatives.

Emily's community outreach programs have connected families with essential resources and support services. The resource fairs she organized have provided families with access to healthcare, housing assistance, legal aid, and other services. The parent support groups have offered a safe space for parents to share their experiences and receive guidance. The success of these programs is evident in the positive feedback from participants, who report feeling more supported and empowered to overcome challenges.

Emily's advocacy efforts have led to meaningful policy changes at both local and national levels. Her work has helped secure increased funding for child welfare services, the implementation of trauma-informed practices, and improved access to mental health care. Emily's ability to influence policy changes has ensured that vulnerable children and families receive the support they need to thrive. The recognition of her advocacy work by policymakers and community leaders highlights the impact of her efforts.

Emily's dedication and success have not gone unnoticed. She has received numerous awards and accolades for her contributions to child welfare and her community. These recognitions serve as a testament to the positive impact of her work and the difference she has made in the lives of vulnerable children and families.

Emily's programs and initiatives have achieved remarkable success, positively impacting the lives of vulnerable children and families. Her dedication, creativity, and commitment to making a positive difference have been recognized and celebrated within her community and beyond.

Emily's journey and dedication to social work have a profound impact on those around her, inspiring many to get involved in social work and advocacy. Her story of resilience, compassion, and commitment serves as a powerful example of the difference one person can make.

Emily frequently shares her personal story and professional experiences at schools, universities, and community events. Her journey from a vulnerable child to a dedicated social worker resonates with many, particularly students considering a career in social work. Emily's honesty about the challenges and rewards of her work provides a realistic and inspiring perspective. Her story encourages others to pursue social work, knowing that their efforts can have a meaningful impact.

Emily takes on the role of a mentor for students interested in social work. She offers guidance, support, and practical advice to help them navigate their educational and career paths. Emily's mentorship helps students build confidence and develop the skills needed to succeed in the field. Her dedication to nurturing future social workers ensures that her legacy of compassion and commitment continues.

Emily is often invited to give guest lectures and lead workshops at universities and training programs. She shares her knowledge and expertise on topics such as trauma-informed care, child welfare policies, and effective advocacy strategies. Emily's engaging and informative sessions inspire students to explore the field of social work and consider how they can contribute to positive change.

Emily's active involvement in community events and initiatives inspires others to get involved and make a difference. Her efforts to organize resource fairs, support groups, and awareness campaigns demonstrate the impact of collective action. Community members are motivated by Emily's dedication and passion, leading them to volunteer their time and resources to support vulnerable children and families.

Emily's advocacy work at both local and national levels highlights the importance of raising awareness and influencing policy changes. Her participation in campaigns and public speaking engagements encourages others to join the cause. Emily's ability to articulate the needs of vulnerable populations and advocate for systemic change inspires community members to become advocates themselves.

Emily's collaborative approach to developing and implementing programs fosters a sense of unity and shared responsibility among organizations and community members. Her partnerships with local non-profits, schools, and healthcare providers create opportunities for others to get involved and contribute to meaningful initiatives. Emily's leadership and vision inspire others to work together towards common goals.

Emily's colleagues and peers are inspired by her dedication, resilience, and compassionate approach to social work. Her ability to navigate challenges and achieve positive outcomes serves as a model for others in the field. Emily's leadership and commitment to continuous learning motivate her peers to strive for excellence in their own work.

Emily's involvement in professional organizations and her efforts to provide training and mentorship opportunities contribute to the growth and development of her colleagues. Her dedication to sharing knowledge and best practices helps create a culture of continuous improvement within her organization. Emily's impact on her peers ensures that the field of social work continues to evolve and improve.

Emily's advocacy work and contributions to child welfare have gained national recognition. Her story is shared through media outlets, conferences, and publications, reaching a wider audience. Emily's ability to inspire others extends beyond her immediate community, encouraging individuals across the country to get involved in social work and advocacy.

The impact of Emily's work creates a ripple effect, inspiring others to take action and make a difference. Her story of resilience and dedication serves as a powerful reminder of the importance of compassion, support, and advocacy. Emily's influence encourages individuals and organizations to work towards creating a better future for vulnerable children and families.

Emily's story and work inspire others to get involved in social work and advocacy, creating a lasting impact on her community and beyond. Her dedication, compassion, and commitment to making a positive difference serve as a powerful example for all.

As Emily reflects on her journey and the impact she has made, she feels a profound sense of optimism and determination for the future. Her experiences have shaped her into a resilient, compassionate, and empowered individual, ready to embrace new opportunities and continue making a positive difference.

Emily is committed to expanding her advocacy efforts to reach a broader audience and influence more significant policy changes. She plans to collaborate with national organizations and policymakers to advocate for comprehensive child welfare reforms. Emily's goal is to ensure that all children have access to the support and resources they need to thrive.

Emily is excited about developing new and innovative programs that address emerging challenges faced by vulnerable children and families. She aims to create initiatives that focus on mental health, educational support, and community engagement. Emily's vision includes leveraging technology and research to design programs that are both effective and accessible.

Building on her success in creating strong community partnerships, Emily plans to further strengthen these relationships and explore new collaborations. She envisions a network of organizations working together to provide holistic support to children and families. Emily's efforts will focus on enhancing coordination and resource sharing to maximize the impact of community services.

Emily is passionate about mentoring the next generation of social workers and advocates. She plans to establish mentorship programs that provide guidance, support, and professional development opportunities for students and new professionals. Emily's goal is to inspire and equip future leaders with the skills and knowledge they need to make a meaningful impact.

Emily is dedicated to continuous learning and professional growth. She plans to pursue advanced education, such as a doctoral degree in social work or public policy, to deepen her expertise and expand her influence. Emily's commitment to education reflects her desire to stay at the forefront of her field and contribute to the development of best practices.

Emily's journey has instilled in her a deep sense of confidence and determination. She is proud of the progress she has made and the positive impact she has had on the lives of vulnerable children and families. Emily's experiences have taught her the importance of resilience, empathy, and the power of collective action.

As she looks to the future, Emily is filled with hope and excitement for the possibilities that lie ahead. She is ready to embrace new challenges and opportunities, confident in her ability to make a difference. Emily's dedication to her work and her unwavering commitment to supporting children and families ensure that her impact will continue to grow.

Emily's story is a testament to the strength of the human spirit and the importance of love, support, and advocacy. With the support of the Johnson family, her colleagues, and her community, Emily is ready to continue her journey and create a brighter future for all children.

Chapter 14
Personal Life and Relationships

Emily understands the importance of having a strong support network outside of her professional life. She makes a conscious effort to build and maintain friendships that provide her with joy, companionship, and a sense of balance.

Emily actively seeks out social groups and clubs that align with her interests and hobbies. She joins a local art club where she can share her passion for painting and connect with others who appreciate creativity. Emily also participates in a book club, where she enjoys discussing literature and exploring new genres with fellow book enthusiasts. These groups provide her with opportunities to meet new people and build meaningful connections.

Emily regularly attends community events, such as festivals, fairs, and charity runs. She enjoys the vibrant atmosphere and the chance to engage with her neighbours and community members. Emily's friendly and approachable nature helps her strike up conversations and make new friends. These events also allow her to stay connected with her community and contribute to local causes.

Emily takes the initiative to organize social gatherings with her friends and colleagues. She hosts dinner parties, game nights, and movie marathons at her home, creating a warm and welcoming environment for her guests. Emily's efforts to bring people together help strengthen her friendships and create lasting memories. Her gatherings are filled with laughter, good food, and meaningful conversations.

Emily's commitment to giving back extends to her personal life, where she volunteers for various causes and organizations. She participates in community clean-up events, mentors young people and supports local shelters. Volunteering not only allows Emily to make a positive impact but also provides her with opportunities to meet like-minded individuals who share her passion for helping others. The friendships she forms through volunteering are built on shared values and a sense of purpose.

Emily makes a conscious effort to stay connected with her friends, even when her work schedule is demanding. She regularly checks in with her friends through phone calls, text messages, and social media. Emily values the importance of maintaining these connections and makes time for regular catch-ups and outings. Whether it's grabbing coffee, going for a hike, or simply chatting over the phone, Emily's efforts to stay connected help her nurture her friendships.

Emily understands the importance of balancing her work and personal life to maintain her well-being. She sets boundaries to ensure that she has time for herself and her friends. Emily schedules regular breaks and vacations, allowing her to recharge and spend quality time with her loved ones. Her ability to balance her professional responsibilities with her personal life helps her maintain strong and fulfilling friendships.

Emily's efforts to build and maintain friendships outside of work highlight her commitment to creating a balanced and fulfilling life. Her social connections provide her with joy, support, and a sense of belonging, enriching her personal life and contributing to her overall well-being.

Emily's experiences with romantic relationships are deeply influenced by her past, particularly her early years marked by neglect and instability. Her journey towards building healthy and fulfilling romantic relationships is one of self-discovery, healing, and growth.

Emily's early experiences with neglect have left her with trust issues that she must navigate in her romantic relationships. She often finds it challenging to fully trust her partners, fearing that they might abandon or hurt her. Emily works through these trust issues with the help of her therapist, Dr. Collins. Therapy sessions provide her with a safe space to explore her fears and develop strategies to build trust. Emily's willingness to be vulnerable and open with her partners helps her gradually overcome these challenges.

Emily's past experiences have made her value stability and

security in her romantic relationships. She seeks partners who are reliable, supportive, and understanding. Emily is drawn to individuals who can provide a sense of safety and consistency, qualities that were lacking in her early life. Her relationships are built on mutual respect and a shared commitment to creating a stable and nurturing environment.

Effective communication and setting healthy boundaries are essential aspects of Emily's romantic relationships. She understands the importance of expressing her needs and feelings openly and honestly. Emily's past experiences have taught her the value of clear communication in building strong and healthy relationships. She also sets boundaries to protect her emotional well-being, ensuring that her relationships are balanced and respectful.

Emily's journey towards building fulfilling romantic relationships involves embracing vulnerability. She recognizes that being open and honest about her past and her emotions is crucial for deepening her connections with her partners. Emily's willingness to share her story and her struggles helps her build intimacy and trust. Her partners appreciate her authenticity and the strength it takes to be vulnerable.

Emily's past relationships have provided her with valuable lessons about herself and what she needs in a partner. She reflects on her experiences to identify patterns and areas for growth. Emily's ability to learn from her past relationships helps her make more informed choices in her current and future relationships. She is committed to personal growth and continuously works on becoming a better partner.

The support and love of the Johnson family play a significant role in Emily's romantic relationships. Their unwavering support provides her with a strong foundation and a sense of security. Emily often seeks advice and guidance from the Johnsons, who offer her valuable insights and encouragement. Their presence in her life reinforces her belief in the importance of healthy and supportive relationships.

Balancing her demanding career with her romantic relationships is a challenge that Emily navigates with care. She makes a conscious effort to prioritize her personal life and ensure that she has time for her partner. Emily's ability to set boundaries and manage her time effectively helps her maintain a healthy balance between her professional and personal life. Her partners appreciate her dedication to her career and her commitment to making time for their relationship.

Emily's journey towards building healthy and fulfilling romantic relationships is ongoing. She is optimistic about the future and excited about the possibilities that lie ahead. Emily's experiences have taught her the importance of resilience, communication, and mutual support in relationships. She is confident in her ability to build strong and loving connections with her partners, creating a future filled with love and happiness.

Emily's experiences with romantic relationships are deeply influenced by her past, but her journey of healing and growth has equipped her with the tools to build healthy and fulfilling connections. Her story is a testament to the power of resilience, vulnerability, and the human spirit's capacity for love and connection.

Emily's relationship with the Johnson family remains a cornerstone of her life, providing her with unwavering support, love, and a sense of belonging. Her bond with the Johnsons continues to grow stronger, even as she navigates her career and personal challenges.

The Johnsons have always been a source of emotional support for Emily. They celebrate her successes, offer guidance during difficult times, and provide a safe space for her to express her feelings. Emily often turns to them for advice and reassurance, knowing that their love and support are unconditional. The Johnsons' presence in her life reinforces her sense of stability and security.

Emily cherishes the family traditions she shares with the Johnsons. Whether it's holiday celebrations, weekend outings, or family dinners, these moments create lasting memories and strengthen their bond. Emily looks forward to these traditions, knowing that they are a testament to the love and unity of the Johnson family.

Emily enjoys participating in various activities with the Johnsons, such as hiking, cooking, and attending community events. These shared experiences provide opportunities for quality time and deepen their connection. The Johnsons' involvement in Emily's life helps her feel valued and appreciated.

The Johnsons are incredibly proud of Emily's achievements and are always there to support her career aspirations. They attend her public speaking engagements, celebrate her professional milestones, and offer encouragement during challenging times. Their belief in her abilities motivates Emily to continue pursuing her goals with confidence.

Emily has made efforts to reconnect with her biological siblings. She reaches out to them through social media and occasional visits, hoping to rebuild their relationship. While the process is gradual and sometimes challenging, Emily values the opportunity to reconnect with her siblings and understand their experiences. These connections provide her with a sense of continuity and a deeper understanding of her past.

Emily's contact with her biological parents remains limited. The neglect and instability she experienced in her early years have left deep emotional scars, making it difficult for her to fully reconcile with them. However, Emily occasionally communicates with her biological parents, seeking closure and understanding. She approaches these interactions with caution, prioritizing her emotional well-being.

Emily continues to work with her therapist, Dr. Collins, to navigate her feelings about her biological family. Therapy sessions provide her with a safe space to process her emotions and develop healthy coping mechanisms. Dr. Collins helps Emily explore her past and find ways to integrate her experiences into her present life. This therapeutic support is crucial in helping Emily maintain her emotional balance.

Emily strives to balance her relationships with the Johnsons and her biological family. She acknowledges the importance of both connections and works to maintain a healthy equilibrium. Emily's ability to navigate these relationships with empathy and resilience reflects her growth and maturity.

Emily's ongoing relationship with the Johnsons and her efforts to reconnect with her biological family, highlight her commitment to building meaningful connections. Her journey is marked by love, support, and a deep sense of belonging, which continue to shape her life in positive ways.

Emily's dedication to her career as a social worker is unwavering, but she understands the importance of maintaining a healthy work-life balance to ensure her well-being and effectiveness. Her efforts to achieve this balance are marked by intentional strategies and a commitment to self-care.

Emily recognizes the importance of setting clear boundaries between her work and personal life. She establishes specific working hours and makes a conscious effort to stick to them. Emily avoids checking work emails or taking work-related calls outside of these hours, ensuring that she has time to unwind and focus on her personal life. By setting these boundaries, she creates a clear separation between her professional responsibilities and personal time.

Self-care is a crucial aspect of Emily's routine. She incorporates activities that promote her physical, mental, and emotional well-being into her daily schedule. Emily practices mindfulness meditation, which helps her manage stress and stay grounded. She also engages in regular exercise, such as yoga and hiking, to maintain her physical health. Creative activities like painting provide her with a sense of relaxation and fulfilment. Emily's commitment to self-care ensures that she remains resilient and capable of handling the demands of her job.

Effective time management is essential for Emily to balance her work and personal life. She uses tools like planners and digital calendars to organize her tasks and appointments. Emily prioritizes her workload, focusing on the most critical tasks first and delegating when necessary. By managing her time efficiently, she ensures that she can meet her professional responsibilities while also making time for herself and her loved ones.

Emily understands the importance of taking regular breaks and vacations to recharge. She schedules short breaks throughout her workday to rest and rejuvenate. Emily also plans vacations and weekend getaways to disconnect from work and spend quality time with her family and friends. These breaks help her return to work with renewed energy and focus.

Emily values the support of her colleagues, friends, and family in maintaining a healthy work-life balance. She regularly participates in peer supervision and support groups, where she can share her experiences and receive guidance. Emily's professional network provides her with valuable insights and encouragement. She also leans on the Johnson family for emotional support and advice, knowing that their love and understanding are always available.

Emily makes time for hobbies and interests that bring her joy and relaxation. She enjoys painting, reading, and exploring nature. These activities provide her with a sense of fulfilment and help her unwind after a busy day. Emily's commitment to pursuing her passions outside of work contributes to her overall well-being and happiness.

Building and maintaining social connections is an important part of Emily's work-life balance. She regularly spends time with her friends, attending social gatherings, and participating in community events. Emily's social connections provide her with companionship, support, and a sense of belonging. These relationships enrich her personal life and help her stay grounded.

Emily takes time to reflect on her achievements and celebrate her successes, both big and small. Acknowledging her accomplishments helps her stay motivated and reinforces her sense of purpose. Emily's ability to recognize and celebrate her progress contributes to her overall well-being and satisfaction.

Emily's efforts to achieve a healthy work-life balance are marked by intentional strategies and a commitment to self-care. Her dedication to setting boundaries, prioritizing self-care, managing her time effectively, and seeking support ensures that she can maintain her well-being while excelling in her career. Emily's journey is a testament to the importance of balance and self-care in achieving personal and professional fulfilment.

Emily's personal hobbies and interests play a crucial role in her overall well-being, providing her with joy, relaxation, and a sense of fulfilment. These activities allow her to unwind and recharge, balancing the demands of her professional life.

Emily has a deep passion for painting, which serves as a creative outlet and a source of relaxation. She enjoys experimenting with different mediums, such as watercolours, acrylics, and oils. Emily often spends her weekends in her home studio, surrounded by canvases and art supplies. The process of creating art allows her to express her emotions and find peace. Her paintings often reflect her inner thoughts and experiences, making each piece unique and personal.

Emily is an avid reader who finds solace and inspiration in books. She enjoys exploring various genres, from classic literature to contemporary fiction and non-fiction. Emily is a member of a local book club, where she meets with fellow book enthusiasts to discuss their latest reads. These gatherings provide her with intellectual stimulation and the opportunity to connect with others who share her love for literature. Emily's favourite authors include Jane Austen, Toni Morrison, and Haruki Murakami.

Spending time in nature is one of Emily's favourite ways to relax and recharge. She enjoys hiking and taking long walks in nearby parks and nature reserves. The fresh air, scenic views, and physical activity help her clear her mind and reduce stress. Emily often brings her sketchbook along on these outings, capturing the beauty of the natural world through her drawings. Her love for nature also inspires her to advocate for environmental conservation and sustainability.

Emily practices yoga and mindfulness meditation to maintain her physical and mental well-being. She attends yoga classes at a local studio and incorporates mindfulness exercises into her daily routine. These practices help her stay grounded, manage stress, and improve her overall health. Emily finds that yoga and meditation provide her with a sense of inner peace and balance, allowing her to approach her work and personal life with greater clarity and focus.

Emily enjoys experimenting in the kitchen, trying out new recipes and creating delicious meals. Cooking and baking are therapeutic activities for her, allowing her to unwind and express her creativity. She often invites friends and family over for dinner parties, where she can share her culinary creations and enjoy good company. Emily's specialties include homemade pasta, gourmet desserts, and international cuisine. Her love for cooking also extends to exploring local farmers' markets and sourcing fresh, seasonal ingredients.

Giving back to the community is an important aspect of Emily's life. She volunteers her time and skills to support various causes and organizations. Emily participates in community clean-up events, mentors young people, and helps organize charity fundraisers.

Volunteering provides her with a sense of purpose and fulfilment, reinforcing her commitment to making a positive impact. The connections she forms through her volunteer work enrich her life and inspire her to continue giving back.

Emily's personal hobbies and interests bring her joy and fulfilment, providing a healthy balance to her professional responsibilities. These activities allow her to express her creativity, connect with others, and maintain her well-being. Emily's dedication to her hobbies reflects her commitment to living a balanced and fulfilling life.

Emily's commitment to self-care is essential for maintaining her mental and emotional well-being. She adopts a variety of practices that help her manage stress, stay grounded, and maintain a healthy balance between her professional and personal life.

Emily practices mindfulness meditation daily to help her stay present and manage stress. She sets aside time each morning to meditate, focusing on her breath and clearing her mind. This practice helps Emily start her day with a sense of calm and clarity. She also incorporates mindfulness techniques throughout her day, such as deep breathing exercises and mindful walking, to stay centred and grounded.

Physical activity is a crucial part of Emily's self-care routine. She enjoys activities like yoga, hiking, and jogging, which help her stay fit and release stress. Emily finds that regular exercise boosts her mood, increases her energy levels, and improves her overall well-being. She makes it a priority to incorporate physical activity into her daily schedule, whether it's a morning yoga session or an evening walk in the park.

Emily's passion for painting provides her with a creative outlet that helps her relax and express her emotions. She spends time in her home studio, experimenting with different mediums and techniques. Painting allows Emily to unwind and find joy in the creative process. Her artwork often reflects her inner thoughts and experiences, making it a deeply personal and fulfilling activity.

Emily finds solace in reading and journaling. She enjoys exploring various genres of literature, which provide her with intellectual stimulation and a temporary escape from the demands of her job. Emily also keeps a journal where she writes about her thoughts, feelings, and experiences. Journaling helps her process her emotions, reflect on her day, and gain insights into her personal growth.

Maintaining a balanced diet is an important aspect of Emily's self-care. She makes conscious choices to eat nutritious meals that fuel her body and mind. Emily enjoys cooking and experimenting with healthy recipes, incorporating fresh fruits, vegetables, and whole grains into her diet. She also stays hydrated by drinking plenty of water throughout the day. Emily's focus on healthy eating helps her feel energized and supports her overall well-being.

Building and maintaining social connections is vital for Emily's emotional well-being. She regularly spends time with her friends and family, attending social gatherings, and participating in community events. Emily values the companionship and support of her loved ones, which provide her with a sense of belonging and happiness. These social interactions help her stay connected and balanced.

Emily continues to work with her therapist, Dr. Collins, to navigate the emotional demands of her job and her personal life. Regular therapy sessions provide her with a safe space to explore her feelings, develop coping strategies, and gain insights into her experiences. Dr. Collins helps Emily maintain her mental health and well-being, ensuring that she can provide effective support to her clients while also caring for herself.

Emily understands the importance of setting boundaries to protect her well-being. She establishes clear boundaries between her work and personal life, ensuring that she has time to rest and recharge. Emily avoids checking work emails or taking work-related calls outside of her designated working hours. By setting these boundaries, she creates a healthy balance and prevents burnout.

Emily makes time for hobbies and interests that bring her joy and relaxation. Whether it's painting, reading, hiking, or cooking, these activities provide her with a sense of fulfilment and help her unwind. Emily's dedication to pursuing her passions outside of work contributes to her overall well-being and happiness.

Emily's self-care practices are essential for maintaining her mental and emotional well-being. Her commitment to mindfulness, regular exercise, creative outlets, healthy eating, social connections, therapeutic support, setting boundaries, and engaging in hobbies ensures that she can navigate the demands of her career while also caring for herself. Emily's story is a testament to the importance of self-care in achieving personal and professional fulfilment.

Emily's journey is marked by resilience and determination as she navigates various personal struggles. Her ability to overcome these challenges is a testament to her strength and commitment to personal growth.

Emily often experiences anxiety, particularly when faced with high-stress situations at work. The emotional demands of her job can trigger feelings of overwhelm and worry. To manage her anxiety, Emily practices mindfulness meditation and deep breathing exercises. These techniques help her stay grounded and calm during stressful moments. She also seeks support from her therapist, Dr. Collins, who provides her with strategies to cope with anxiety and build resilience.

Despite her accomplishments, Emily sometimes struggles with imposter syndrome, feeling that she is not truly deserving of her success. She worries that others may perceive her as inadequate or unqualified. To combat these feelings, Emily reflects on her achievements and the positive impact she has made in her career. She keeps a journal where she documents her successes and the feedback she receives from colleagues and clients. This practice helps her recognize her worth and build self-confidence.

Maintaining a healthy work-life balance is an ongoing challenge for Emily. The demands of her job often require her to work long hours, leaving little time for herself and her loved ones. Emily makes a conscious effort to set boundaries and prioritize self-care. She schedules regular breaks, takes vacations, and engages in activities that bring her joy. By managing her time effectively and setting clear boundaries, Emily ensures that she can fulfil her professional responsibilities while also taking care of her personal well-being.

The emotional toll of working with vulnerable children and families can lead to emotional exhaustion. Emily sometimes feels drained and overwhelmed by the weight of her clients' struggles. To cope with this, she practices self-care and seeks support from her colleagues and therapist. Emily also engages in activities that help her recharge, such as painting, hiking, and spending time with friends. These practices help her maintain her emotional well-being and prevent burnout.

Emily's past experiences with neglect have left her with trust issues that affect her relationships. She sometimes finds it challenging to fully trust her partners and fears abandonment. Emily works through these issues with the help of her therapist, who provides her with strategies to build trust and communicate effectively. She also makes a conscious effort to be open and honest with her partners, fostering healthy and supportive relationships.

Emily occasionally struggles with self-doubt, questioning her abilities and decisions. She worries that she may not be making the right choices for her clients or herself. To overcome self-doubt, Emily seeks feedback from her colleagues and mentors, who provide her with valuable insights and reassurance. She also reflects on her past successes and the positive impact she has made, reminding herself of her capabilities and strengths.

Emily's early experiences with neglect and instability have left emotional scars that she continues to navigate. She seeks closure by reconnecting with her biological family and exploring her past with the support of her therapist. Emily's journey of healing involves acknowledging her experiences, processing her emotions, and integrating her past into her present life. This process helps her find peace and move forward with a sense of acceptance and resilience.

Emily's ability to overcome personal struggles is a testament to her strength, resilience, and commitment to personal growth. Her journey is marked by self-awareness, determination, and a dedication to maintaining her well-being. Emily's story serves as an inspiration to others, highlighting the importance of self-care, support, and perseverance in overcoming challenges.

Emily's journey is filled with significant personal milestones that mark her growth, achievements, and the meaningful moments she cherishes. These milestones are celebrated with joy and gratitude, reflecting the love and support she receives from those around her.

Emily's birthdays are special occasions that she celebrates with her loved ones. Each year, the Johnson family, and her friends come together to make her birthday memorable. They organize surprise parties, prepare her favourite meals, and shower her with thoughtful gifts. Emily's birthdays are filled with laughter, love, and heartfelt moments, reminding her of the strong bonds she shares with her family and friends.

Emily celebrates important anniversaries that mark significant events in her life. One such anniversary is the day she was adopted by the Johnson family. Each year, they commemorate this special day with a family gathering, reflecting on the journey they have shared and the love that has grown between them. This anniversary is a reminder of the stability and support the Johnsons have provided, and it holds a special place in Emily's heart.

Emily's dedication to her career as a social worker has led to numerous professional achievements. She celebrates milestones such as receiving advanced certifications, being promoted to leadership roles, and successfully implementing new programs. These achievements are recognized and celebrated by her colleagues and mentors, who appreciate her hard work and commitment. Emily takes pride in her accomplishments and uses these moments to reflect on her growth and the positive impact she has made.

Emily's pursuit of continuous learning is marked by significant educational milestones. She celebrates completing advanced training programs, earning certifications, and pursuing higher education. Each educational achievement is a testament to her dedication to personal and professional growth. Emily's family and friends celebrate these milestones with her, acknowledging the effort and determination she has invested in her education.

Emily's journey of personal growth is filled with milestones that reflect her resilience and self-discovery. She celebrates moments of overcoming challenges, building healthy relationships and achieving a balanced work-life dynamic. These milestones are celebrated with gratitude and self-reflection, as Emily acknowledges the progress she has made and the strength she has developed. Her personal growth milestones are a source of inspiration and motivation for her continued journey.

Emily's contributions to her community are celebrated through various recognitions and awards. She receives accolades for her advocacy work, volunteer efforts, and the positive impact of her programs. These recognitions are celebrated with her colleagues, community members, and the Johnson family, who take pride in her achievements. Emily's community impact milestones highlight her commitment to making a difference and the appreciation of those she serves.

In addition to formal milestones, Emily cherishes special moments that hold personal significance. These include reconnecting with her biological siblings, achieving personal goals, and creating lasting memories with her loved ones. Each special moment is celebrated with joy and gratitude, adding to the tapestry of her life's journey.

Emily's personal milestones are celebrated with love, gratitude, and a sense of accomplishment. These moments reflect her growth, achievements, and the meaningful connections she has built. Emily's journey is marked by resilience, dedication, and the unwavering support of her family and friends.

Emily's journey is enriched by the supportive relationships she has cultivated with friends, family, and colleagues. These connections provide her with love, encouragement, and a sense of belonging, helping her navigate the challenges of her career and personal life.

The Johnson family remains Emily's primary source of support and stability. Their unwavering love and encouragement have been a constant in her life since her adoption. The Johnsons celebrate her successes, offer guidance during difficult times, and provide a safe space for her to express her feelings. Their presence in her life reinforces her sense of security and belonging.

Emily also maintains close relationships with he extended family members, including aunts, uncles, and cousins. Family gatherings and celebrations are filled with warmth and joy, creating lasting memories. Emily values the strong family bonds and the sense of community they provide.

Emily has a close-knit group of friends who offer companionship, understanding, and support. They share common interests and enjoy spending time together, whether it's attending social events, exploring new hobbies, or simply catching up over coffee. Emily's friends provide her with a sense of belonging and help her unwind from the demands of her job.

Emily actively participates in social groups and clubs that align with her interests, such as an art club and a book club. These groups provide her with opportunities to meet new people and build meaningful connections. The friendships she forms through these activities enrich her life and offer a sense of community.

Emily seeks guidance from experienced social workers and mentors in her field. She regularly meets with her supervisor and colleagues to discuss cases, share insights, and seek advice. These professional relationships provide Emily with valuable support and help her develop her skills and knowledge. Her mentors offer encouragement and guidance, helping her navigate the complexities of her role as a social worker.

Emily's colleagues are an essential part of her support network. They collaborate on cases, share resources, and provide emotional support during challenging times. Emily values the camaraderie and mutual respect she shares with her peers, which create a positive and supportive work environment.

Emily is an active member of professional organizations, such as the National Association of Social Workers (NASW). These organizations offer networking opportunities, resources, and training sessions that help Emily stay updated on best practices and new developments in the field. Being part of a professional community reinforces her sense of purpose and commitment to her career.

Emily's involvement in volunteering and community service provides her with additional support and a sense of fulfilment. She participates in community events, mentors young people, and supports local shelters. The connections she forms through her volunteer work enrich her life and inspire her to continue giving back.

Emily collaborates with community organizations to raise awareness about child welfare issues. Her advocacy efforts help educate the public and encourage community involvement in addressing these critical issues. The support she receives from her community partners reinforces her commitment to making a positive impact.

Emily's supportive relationships with friends, family, and colleagues play a crucial role in her journey. These connections provide her with love, encouragement, and a sense of belonging, helping her navigate the challenges of her career and personal life. Emily's story is a testament to the importance of strong and supportive relationships in achieving personal and professional fulfilment.

As Emily looks to the future, she is filled with optimism and determination. Her journey has been marked by resilience, growth, and the unwavering support of her loved ones. Emily's aspirations for her personal life and relationships reflect her commitment to living a fulfilling and balanced life.

Emily dreams of building a family of her own. She envisions a future where she can provide a loving and stable home for her children, much like the one the Johnson family provided for her. Emily's experiences have taught her the importance of love, support, and stability, and she is determined to create a nurturing environment for her future family. She looks forward to the joys and challenges of parenthood, knowing that she has the strength and resilience to be a loving and supportive parent.

Emily is committed to strengthening her relationships with her friends, family, and colleagues. She values the connections she has built and is determined to nurture these relationships. Emily plans to continue spending quality time with her loved ones, participating in shared activities, and creating lasting memories. Her dedication to maintaining strong and supportive relationships ensures that she will always have a network of love and encouragement.

Emily's love for painting, reading, and nature will continue to be an important part of her life. She aspires to further develop her artistic skills, perhaps even showcasing her work in local galleries. Emily also plans to explore new hobbies and interests, embracing opportunities for personal growth and fulfilment. Her commitment to pursuing her passions ensures that she will always have outlets for creativity and relaxation.

Emily is dedicated to advancing her career as a social worker and making a positive impact on the lives of vulnerable children and families. She plans to pursue advanced education, such as a doctoral degree in social work or public policy, to deepen her expertise and expand her influence. Emily's goal is to take on leadership roles within her organization and contribute to the development of best practices in the field. Her commitment to continuous learning and professional growth ensures that she will continue to make a meaningful difference.

Emily's passion for advocacy will remain a central focus of her future aspirations. She plans to expand her advocacy efforts to reach a broader audience and influence more significant policy changes. Emily envisions collaborating with national organizations and policymakers to advocate for comprehensive child welfare reforms. Her dedication to raising awareness and driving positive change will continue to inspire others and create a lasting impact.

Emily is determined to maintain a healthy work life balance, ensuring that she can fulfil her professional responsibilities while also taking care of her personal well-being. She plans to continue practicing self-care, setting boundaries, and prioritizing her mental and emotional health. Emily's commitment to creating a balanced life ensures that she can navigate the demands of her career while also enjoying a fulfilling personal life.

As Emily looks to the future, she is filled with hope and excitement for the possibilities that lie ahead. Her journey has taught her the importance of resilience, love, and the power of supportive relationships. Emily is ready to embrace new challenges and opportunities, confident in her ability to make a positive difference. Her aspirations reflect her dedication to living a life of purpose, fulfilment, and joy.

Emily's story is a testament to the strength of the human spirit and the importance of love, support, and advocacy. With the unwavering support of the Johnson family, her friends, and her community, Emily is ready to continue her journey and create a brighter future for herself and those she serves.

Chapter 15
Legacy and Impact

As Emily sits in her cozy home, surrounded by the warmth of her loved ones and the memories of her journey, she takes a moment to reflect on her career achievements and the profound impact she has made on the lives of vulnerable children and families.

Emily's career as a social worker is marked by numerous milestones that highlight her dedication and expertise. She recalls the day she received her advanced certification in trauma-informed care, a testament to her commitment to providing specialized support to children who have experienced trauma. Emily's promotion to Director of Child Welfare Services stands out as a significant achievement, reflecting her leadership skills and the trust her organization places in her.

Emily takes pride in the programs she has developed and implemented, each designed to address the unique needs of vulnerable populations. The family support services program, which provides parents with resources and guidance, has helped countless families create safe and nurturing environments for their children. The school-based intervention programs have made a significant difference in the lives of students, improving their academic performance and emotional well-being. Emily's trauma-informed care programs have provided essential support to children affected by trauma, helping them heal and thrive.

Emily's advocacy efforts have led to meaningful policy changes at both local and national levels. She reflects on her testimony before congressional committees, where she shared her experiences and insights to inform lawmakers about the critical need for child welfare reforms. Emily's ability to influence policy changes has ensured that vulnerable children and families receive the support they need to thrive. Her advocacy work has raised awareness about child welfare issues and inspired others to join the cause.

Emily's contributions to her community are a source of immense pride. She recalls organizing resource fairs that connected families with essential services, from healthcare to housing assistance. The positive feedback from participants highlights the impact of these initiatives. Emily's involvement in community events and volunteer work has strengthened her connections with her neighbours and created a sense of unity and collective responsibility.

Reflecting on her journey, Emily acknowledges the personal growth and resilience she has developed along the way. Her experiences have taught her the importance of self-care, setting boundaries, and seeking support. Emily's ability to navigate challenges and maintain a healthy work-life balance is a testament to her strength and determination. She takes pride in her achievements and the progress she has made, both personally and professionally.

Emily's story and work have inspired many to get involved in social work and advocacy. She recalls the students she has mentored, the colleagues she has guided, and the community members she has motivated to take action. Emily's ability to inspire others is one of her most cherished achievements, as it ensures that her legacy of compassion and commitment will continue to make a positive impact.

As Emily reflects on her career achievements and the impact she has made, she feels a profound sense of fulfilment and gratitude. Her journey is a testament to the power of resilience, dedication, and the human spirit's capacity for growth and healing. Emily's legacy is one of love, support, and advocacy, and she looks forward to continuing her work and making a difference in the lives of vulnerable children and families.

Emily's legacy is built on her unwavering dedication to making a positive impact through her work and personal contributions. Her efforts extend beyond her immediate responsibilities, creating a lasting influence on the lives of vulnerable children, families, and the broader community.

Emily's development of innovative programs has left a lasting mark on the field of social work. Her family support services, school-based interventions, and trauma-informed care programs have provided essential support to countless children and families. These programs have become models for best practices, inspiring other organizations to adopt similar approaches. Emily's commitment to continuous improvement ensures that her programs evolve to meet the changing needs of the community.

Emily's leadership roles within her organization have allowed her to mentor and guide new social workers. She shares her knowledge and experiences, helping them develop the skills and confidence needed to succeed in their roles. Emily's mentorship fosters a culture of collaboration and support, ensuring that future generations of social workers are well-equipped to make a positive impact. Her influence extends beyond her immediate team, shaping the practices and values of the entire organization.

Emily's advocacy efforts have led to significant policy changes that benefit vulnerable children and families. Her work with policymakers and community organizations has raised awareness about critical child welfare issues and driven systemic change. Emily's ability to influence policy ensures that her impact is felt on a broader scale, creating a more supportive and equitable environment for all children. Her advocacy work continues to inspire others to join the cause and advocate for positive change.

Emily's active involvement in her community has created a lasting legacy of support and unity. She organizes events, volunteers her time, and collaborates with local organizations to address the needs of vulnerable populations. Emily's efforts have strengthened community bonds and encouraged collective action. Her dedication to giving back inspires others to get involved and make a difference in their own communities.

Emily's ability to build and maintain strong relationships with her friends, family, and colleagues is a testament to her compassionate and empathetic nature. These relationships provide her with a support network that enriches her life and enhances her ability to make a positive impact. Emily's commitment to nurturing these connections ensures that her legacy is one of love, support, and mutual respect.

Emily's story and work have inspired many to pursue careers

in social work and advocacy. Her journey of resilience, dedication, and personal growth serves as a powerful example of the difference one person can make. Emily's ability to inspire others ensures that her legacy continues to grow, as more individuals are motivated to follow in her footsteps and contribute to positive change.

Emily's legacy is not just about the impact she has made so far, but also about the future she envisions. She is committed to continuing her work, expanding her advocacy efforts, and developing new programs that address emerging challenges. Emily's dedication to personal and professional growth ensures that she will continue to make a meaningful difference in the lives of vulnerable children and families.

Emily's legacy is built on a foundation of compassion, resilience, and a commitment to making a positive impact. Her professional and personal contributions have created lasting change, inspiring others to join her in the pursuit of a better future for all children.

Emily's dedication to social work extends beyond her immediate responsibilities. She is passionate about inspiring and mentoring the next generation of social workers and advocates, ensuring that her legacy of compassion and commitment continues to make a positive impact.

Emily takes an active role in mentoring students and interns who are pursuing careers in social work. She offers guidance, support, and practical advice to help them navigate their educational and professional journeys. Emily shares her experiences, providing insights into the challenges and rewards of the field. Her mentorship helps students build confidence, develop essential skills, and gain a deeper understanding of the impact they can make.

Emily is frequently invited to give guest lectures and lead workshops at universities and training programs. She shares her knowledge on topics such as trauma-informed care, child welfare policies, and effective advocacy strategies. Emily's engaging and informative sessions inspire students to explore the field of social work and consider how they can contribute to positive change. Her ability to connect with students and convey the importance of their work leaves a lasting impression.

Recognizing the importance of hands-on experience, Emily collaborates with her organization to create internship opportunities for aspiring social workers. She designs comprehensive internship programs that provide students with practical experience in various aspects of social work. Emily ensures that interns receive mentorship, supervision, and opportunities to apply their knowledge in real-world settings. These internships help students develop their skills and prepare for successful careers in social work.

Emily is committed to the continuous professional development of her colleagues and peers. She organizes training sessions, workshops, and seminars that cover essential topics and emerging trends in social work. Emily's efforts to provide ongoing education and support help ensure that social workers are equipped with the latest knowledge and best practices. Her dedication to professional development fosters a culture of learning and growth within her organization.

Emily's advocacy work includes efforts to raise awareness about the importance of social work and the critical role social workers play in supporting vulnerable populations. She participates in campaigns that highlight the impact of social work and encourage others to join the field. Emily's ability to articulate the value of social work and advocate for systemic change inspires others to consider careers in social work and advocacy.

Emily understands the importance of a strong support network for social workers. She actively participates in professional organizations and networks with other social workers, researchers, and advocates. Emily's involvement in these communities provides her with valuable insights, resources, and opportunities for collaboration. She encourages her mentees and colleagues to build their own support networks, emphasizing the importance of mutual support and collaboration in the field.

Emily believes in recognizing and celebrating the achievements of her mentees and colleagues. She acknowledges their successes, provides positive feedback, and encourages them to take pride in their accomplishments. Emily's efforts to celebrate achievements help build confidence and motivation, reinforcing the importance of their work and the positive impact they are making.

Emily's efforts to inspire and mentor the next generation of social workers and advocates highlight her commitment to making a lasting impact. Her dedication to mentorship, professional development, and advocacy ensures that her legacy of compassion and commitment continues to inspire others and create positive change.

Emily's dedication and impact have not gone unnoticed. She has received numerous accolades and recognition from her community and peers, highlighting the profound difference she has made in the lives of vulnerable children and families.

Emily was honoured with the Community Service Award by her local government for her outstanding contributions to child welfare and community support. This award recognizes her tireless efforts to improve the lives of children and families through innovative programs and advocacy work. The ceremony was attended by community leaders, colleagues, and the Johnson family, who celebrated Emily's achievements with pride.

Emily received the prestigious Social Worker of the Year award from the National Association of Social Workers (NASW). This award acknowledges her exceptional dedication, leadership, and impact in the field of social work. Emily's colleagues and mentors nominated her for this honour, highlighting her commitment to excellence and her ability to inspire others. The award ceremony was a moment of great pride for Emily, as she stood among her peers and received recognition for her hard work and dedication.

Emily's advocacy efforts were recognized with the Advocacy Excellence Award from a national child welfare organization. This award celebrates her success in raising awareness about child welfare issues and influencing policy changes. Emily's ability to articulate the needs of vulnerable children and families and drive systemic change earned her this well-deserved recognition. The award ceremony was attended by policymakers, advocates, and community members who applauded Emily's contributions.

Emily's work has been featured in local newspapers, magazines, and television programs. These media features highlight her innovative programs, advocacy efforts, and the positive impact she has made in the community. Emily's story serves as an inspiration to others, encouraging them to get involved and make a difference. The media coverage also helps raise awareness about the importance of child welfare and the critical role social workers play in supporting vulnerable populations.

Emily is often invited to speak at community events, conferences, and schools. Her engaging and informative presentations provide valuable insights into child welfare issues and the importance of advocacy. Emily's ability to connect with her audience and share her experiences has made her a sought-after speaker. These engagements provide her with opportunities to inspire others and promote positive change.

The families and individuals Emily has supported often express their gratitude through heartfelt testimonials. These testimonials highlight the difference Emily has made in their lives, from reuniting families to providing essential resources and support. The positive feedback from her clients and community members reinforces the impact of her work and the importance of her dedication.

Emily's colleagues and peers hold her in high regard, recognizing her as a leader and mentor in the field of social work. They appreciate her willingness to share her knowledge, provide guidance, and support their professional growth. Emily's collaborative approach and commitment to excellence have earned her the respect and admiration of her peers.

Emily's involvement in professional organizations and networks has led to recognition from her peers across the country. She is often invited to participate in panels, workshops, and collaborative projects, where her expertise and insights are highly valued. Emily's contributions to the professional community help shape best practices and drive positive change in the field of social work.

Emily's recognition from the community and her peers is a testament to her dedication, impact, and commitment to making a positive difference. Her awards, media features, public speaking engagements, and peer appreciation highlight the profound influence she has had on the lives of vulnerable children and families.

Emily's commitment to continuing education and professional development is a cornerstone of her career. She understands the importance of staying updated with the latest knowledge, skills, and best practices in the field of social work. Her dedication to lifelong learning ensures that she can provide the highest quality support to vulnerable children and families.

Emily is dedicated to furthering her education by pursuing advanced degrees. She has completed a master's degree in social work (MSW) and is currently considering enrolling in a doctoral program. Emily's goal is to deepen her expertise in child welfare and trauma-informed care, allowing her to contribute to the development of best practices and policies in the field. Her pursuit of advanced education reflects her commitment to continuous learning and professional growth.

Emily regularly attends workshops, seminars, and conferences to stay informed about the latest developments in social work. These events provide her with opportunities to learn from experts, network with peers, and gain new insights into emerging trends and challenges. Emily actively participates in sessions on topics such as trauma-informed care, child welfare policies, and advocacy strategies. Her engagement in these events helps her stay at the forefront of her field and apply new knowledge to her practice.

Emily is committed to obtaining professional certifications that enhance her skills and knowledge. She has earned certifications in areas such as trauma-informed care, child welfare, and mental health counselling. These certifications demonstrate her expertise and dedication to providing specialized support to her clients. Emily's pursuit of professional certifications ensures that she can offer the highest quality services and stay updated with best practices.

Emily values the importance of peer supervision and regularly participates in supervision groups with her colleagues. These groups provide a supportive environment where social workers can share their experiences, discuss challenging cases, and seek guidance. Emily's involvement in peer supervision helps her gain new perspectives, develop problem-solving skills, and receive constructive feedback. This collaborative approach to professional development enhances her ability to provide effective support to her clients.

Emily is dedicated to staying informed about the latest research and evidence-based practices in social work. She regularly reads academic journals, research articles, and publications related to child welfare and trauma-informed care. Emily's commitment to staying updated with current research ensures that her practice is informed by the latest findings and best practices. She applies this knowledge to develop innovative programs and interventions that address the needs of vulnerable children and families.

Emily is an active member of professional organizations such as the National Association of Social Workers (NASW). These organizations provide her with access to resources, training opportunities, and a network of professionals in the field. Emily's involvement in professional organizations allows her to stay connected with her peers, participate in advocacy efforts, and contribute to the advancement of the social work profession. Her engagement in these organizations reflects her commitment to continuous professional development.

Emily's dedication to continuing education extends to her role as a mentor and educator. She regularly mentors students and new social workers, sharing her knowledge and experiences to help them develop their skills. Emily also leads training sessions and workshops, providing valuable insights into best practices and emerging trends. Her commitment to mentoring and teaching ensures that the next generation of social workers is well-equipped to make a positive impact.

Emily's commitment to continuing education and professional development is a testament to her dedication to providing the highest quality support to vulnerable children and families. Her pursuit of advanced degrees, professional certifications, and engagement in research and professional organizations ensures that she remains at the forefront of her field. Emily's dedication to lifelong learning reflects her passion for social work and her commitment to making a meaningful difference.

Emily's dedication to sharing her experiences and knowledge extends to her involvement in writing and public speaking. Through these platforms, she reaches a wider audience, raising awareness about child welfare issues and inspiring others to take action. Emily regularly writes articles for professional journals, magazines, and online platforms.

Her articles cover a range of topics, including trauma informed care, child welfare policies, and effective advocacy strategies. Emily's writing is informed by her extensive experience and research, providing valuable insights and practical advice for social workers and advocates. Her articles are well-received by her peers and contribute to the ongoing dialogue about best practices in the field. Emily's ability to articulate complex issues in a clear and engaging manner makes her writing accessible and impactful.

Emily has authored several books that delve into her experiences and the lessons she has learned throughout her career. Her books provide a comprehensive look at the challenges and rewards of social work, offering guidance and inspiration to both new and experienced professionals. Emily's writing is deeply personal, reflecting her journey of resilience and growth. Her books have been praised for their authenticity and practical insights, making them valuable resources for anyone interested in child welfare and advocacy.

Emily is a sought-after speaker at conferences, workshops, and community events. Her engaging and informative presentations cover a wide range of topics, from trauma-informed care to effective advocacy. Emily's ability to connect with her audience and share her experiences in a relatable manner makes her a compelling speaker. She often uses storytelling to illustrate key points, drawing on her own experiences and those of the children and families she has supported. Emily's speeches inspire and motivate others to get involved and make a difference.

In addition to speaking at conferences and events, Emily is frequently invited to give guest lectures at universities and training programs. She shares her knowledge and experiences with students, providing them with valuable insights into the field of social work. Emily's lectures cover essential topics such as child welfare policies, trauma-informed care, and advocacy strategies. Her ability to engage with students and convey the importance of their work leaves a lasting impression, inspiring many to pursue careers in social work and advocacy.

Emily's expertise and dedication have led to numerous media appearances, including interviews on television, radio, and podcasts.

She uses these opportunities to raise awareness about child welfare issues and advocate for policy changes. Emily's media engagements help amplify her message and reach a broader audience, encouraging public support for vulnerable children and families. Her ability to communicate effectively and passionately makes her a powerful advocate and spokesperson.

Emily often collaborates with other professionals on writing projects, contributing chapters to books, co-authoring articles, and participating in research studies. These collaborations allow her to share her knowledge and insights with a wider audience and contribute to the development of best practices in the field. Emily's collaborative approach reflects her commitment to continuous learning and professional growth.

Emily's involvement in writing and speaking highlights her dedication to sharing her experiences and knowledge with others. Through her articles, books, speeches, and media engagements, she raises awareness about child welfare issues and inspires others to take action. Emily's ability to communicate effectively and passionately ensures that her message reaches a wide audience, making a lasting impact on the field of social work and advocacy.

Emily's dedication to supporting vulnerable children and families drives her continuous efforts to expand and improve the programs she has developed. Her commitment to innovation and excellence ensures that these programs remain effective and responsive to the evolving needs of the community.

Emily begins by conducting thorough assessments to identify emerging needs within the community. She collaborates with her colleagues, community partners, and clients to gather insights and feedback. Emily's ability to listen and understand the unique challenges faced by children and families allows her to develop targeted solutions. This proactive approach ensures that her programs address the most pressing issues and provide relevant support.

To expand and improve her programs, Emily actively seeks funding and resources from various sources. She writes grant proposals, engages with donors, and partners with local businesses and organizations. Emily's ability to articulate the impact of her programs and demonstrate their effectiveness helps secure the necessary funding. Her efforts ensure that the programs have the resources needed to grow and reach more children and families.

Emily understands the importance of collaboration in expanding and improving her programs. She builds strong partnerships with other organizations, such as schools, healthcare providers, and non-profits. These collaborations allow for resource sharing, coordinated services, and comprehensive support for children and families. Emily's ability to foster strong relationships with her partners enhances the effectiveness and reach of her programs.

Emily is committed to implementing best practices in her programs. She stays informed about the latest research and evidence-based approaches in social work and child welfare. Emily integrates these best practices into her programs, ensuring that they are effective and up-to-date. Her dedication to continuous improvement helps create programs that are both innovative and impactful.

Emily works tirelessly to expand the reach of her programs to serve more children and families. She develops outreach strategies to raise awareness about the available services and resources. Emily organizes community events, creates informational materials, and leverages social media to connect with a broader audience. Her efforts ensure that more families are aware of and can access the support they need.

Emily regularly evaluates the effectiveness of her programs to identify areas for improvement. She collects data, gathers feedback from participants, and assesses outcomes. Emily uses this information to make informed decisions about program enhancements and adjustments. Her commitment to evaluation and improvement ensures that the programs continue to meet the needs of the community and achieve positive outcomes.

Emily invests in the training and development of her team to ensure that they have the skills and knowledge needed to deliver high-quality services. She organizes training sessions, workshops, and professional development opportunities. Emily's focus on continuous learning helps her team stay updated with best practices and new developments in the field. This investment in her team's growth enhances the overall effectiveness of the programs.

Emily is always looking for innovative ways to enhance her

programs. She explores new approaches, technologies, and methodologies to improve service delivery. Emily's willingness to embrace innovation ensures that her programs remain dynamic and responsive to the changing needs of the community. Her creative initiatives help address emerging challenges and provide effective support to children and families.

Emily's efforts to expand and improve her programs highlight her dedication to making a positive impact. Her proactive approach, commitment to collaboration, and focus on continuous improvement ensure that her programs remain effective and responsive to the needs of vulnerable children and families.

As Emily sits in her cozy home, reflecting on her journey, she is filled with a sense of gratitude and fulfilment. Her path has been marked by challenges, growth, and profound moments of joy. Through her experiences, Emily has learned valuable lessons that have shaped her into the resilient and compassionate individual she is today.

One of the most significant lessons Emily has learned is the power of vulnerability. Opening up about her past and sharing her struggles has allowed her to connect deeply with others and build meaningful relationships. Emily has discovered that vulnerability is not a sign of weakness but a source of strength. It has enabled her to empathize with her clients, support her colleagues, and inspire those around her.

Emily's journey has taught her the critical importance of self care. She has learned that taking care of her mental, emotional, and physical well-being is essential for her to be effective in her role as a social worker. Emily's commitment to self-care practices, such as mindfulness meditation, regular exercise, and creative outlets, has helped her maintain balance and resilience. She understands that self-care is not a luxury but a necessity for sustaining her passion and dedication.

Emily's experiences have reinforced the value of resilience and perseverance. She has faced numerous challenges, from navigating the emotional demands of her job to overcoming personal struggles. Through it all, Emily has learned to stay focused on her goals and remain steadfast in her commitment to making a positive impact. Her resilience has enabled her to bounce back from setbacks and continue moving forward with determination.

Emily has come to appreciate the profound impact of supportive relationships. The love and encouragement she has received from the Johnson family, her friends, and her colleagues have been instrumental in her journey. These relationships have provided her with a sense of belonging, stability, and strength. Emily has learned that surrounding herself with supportive and understanding individuals is essential for her well-being and success.

Emily's commitment to continuous learning and growth has been a cornerstone of her journey. She has embraced opportunities for professional development, pursued advanced education, and stayed informed about the latest research and best practices. Emily's dedication to learning has enabled her to provide high-quality support to her clients and contribute to the advancement of the field. She understands that growth is a lifelong process and is committed to evolving both personally and professionally.

Reflecting on her journey, Emily is filled with a sense of fulfilment knowing that she has made a positive difference in the lives of vulnerable children and families. Her programs, advocacy efforts, and personal contributions have created lasting change and inspired others to take action. Emily's impact is a testament to the power of compassion, dedication, and the human spirit's capacity for growth and healing.

As Emily looks to the future, she is excited about the possibilities that lie ahead. She is committed to continuing her work, expanding her advocacy efforts, and developing new programs that address emerging challenges. Emily's journey has taught her the importance of resilience, love, and the power of supportive relationships. She is ready to embrace new opportunities and continue making a positive impact.

Emily's personal reflections on her journey highlight the lessons she has learned and the growth she has experienced. Her story is a testament to the strength of the human spirit and the importance of love, support, and advocacy. Emily's journey is far from over, and she looks forward to continuing her work and creating a brighter future for all children.

Emily's journey is filled with moments of celebration as she witnesses the positive changes her work has brought about. These successes are a testament to her dedication, resilience, and the impact of her efforts on the lives of vulnerable children and families.

One of Emily's most significant successes is the family support services program she developed. This program has helped countless families create safe and nurturing environments for their children. Emily celebrates the stories of parents who have gained confidence in their parenting skills, children who have thrived in stable homes, and families who have overcome challenges together. The positive feedback from participants and the visible improvements in their lives are sources of immense pride for Emily.

Emily's school-based intervention programs have made a remarkable difference in the lives of students. She celebrates the success stories of students who have improved their academic performance, developed better coping skills, and built positive relationships with their peers and teachers. The gratitude expressed by students, parents, and educators reinforces the impact of these programs. Emily takes joy in knowing that her efforts have contributed to creating a supportive and inclusive school environment.

The trauma-informed care programs Emily implemented have provided essential support to children who have experienced trauma. She celebrates the progress of children who have shown resilience, improved mental health, and emotional well-being. The success of these programs is evident in the positive outcomes for children, including their ability to heal and thrive. Emily's dedication to providing trauma-informed care has made a lasting impact on the lives of many children.

Emily's youth empowerment programs have inspired and motivated young people to reach their full potential. She celebrates the achievements of young individuals who have taken on leadership roles, pursued higher education, and made positive contributions to their communities. The success stories of these young people serve as a testament to the impact of Emily's initiatives. She takes pride in knowing that her efforts have empowered the next generation to become advocates for change.

Emily's community outreach programs have connected

families with essential resources and support services. She celebrates the success of resource fairs that have provided families with access to healthcare, housing assistance, legal aid, and other services. The positive feedback from participants, who report feeling more supported and empowered, highlights the impact of these programs. Emily's outreach efforts have created a more informed and connected community.

Emily's advocacy work has led to meaningful policy changes at both local and national levels. She celebrates the successes of campaigns that have secured increased funding for child welfare services, implemented trauma-informed practices, and improved access to mental health care. The recognition of her advocacy work by policymakers and community leaders highlights the impact of her efforts. Emily takes pride in knowing that her advocacy has driven positive changes that benefit vulnerable children and families.

Emily's dedication and success have been recognized through numerous awards and accolades. She celebrates these recognitions as milestones in her journey, reflecting the impact of her work and the difference she has made. The awards and honours she has received serve as a testament to her commitment to child welfare and her community. Emily's achievements are celebrated by her colleagues, friends, and the Johnson family, who take pride in her accomplishments.

Emily takes time to reflect on her journey and celebrate her personal growth and resilience. She acknowledges the challenges she has overcome, the lessons she has learned, and the progress she has made. Emily's ability to celebrate her successes and recognize her achievements reinforces her sense of purpose and motivation. Her reflections serve as a reminder of the positive impact she has made and the importance of her work.

Emily's celebrations of success highlight the positive changes she has helped bring about through her dedication and efforts. Her journey is marked by moments of joy, pride, and fulfilment, as she witnesses the impact of her work on the lives of vulnerable children and families.

As Emily reflects on her journey and the impact she has made, she looks to the future with hope and determination. Her experiences have shaped her into a resilient, compassionate, and empowered individual, ready to embrace new opportunities and continue making a positive difference.

Emily is committed to expanding her advocacy efforts to reach a broader audience and influence more significant policy changes. She plans to collaborate with national organizations and policymakers to advocate for comprehensive child welfare reforms. Emily's goal is to ensure that all children have access to the support and resources they need to thrive.

Emily is excited about developing new and innovative programs that address emerging challenges faced by vulnerable children and families. She aims to create initiatives that focus on mental health, educational support, and community engagement. Emily's vision includes leveraging technology and research to design programs that are both effective and accessible.

Building on her success in creating strong community partnerships, Emily plans to further strengthen these relationships and explore new collaborations. She envisions a network of organizations working together to provide holistic support to children and families. Emily's efforts will focus on enhancing coordination and resource sharing to maximize the impact of community services.

Emily is passionate about mentoring the next generation of social workers and advocates. She plans to establish mentorship programs that provide guidance, support, and professional development opportunities for students and new professionals. Emily's goal is to inspire and equip future leaders with the skills and knowledge they need to make a meaningful impact.

Emily is dedicated to continuous learning and professional growth. She plans to pursue advanced education, such as a doctoral degree in social work or public policy, to deepen her expertise and expand her influence. Emily's commitment to education reflects her desire to stay at the forefront of her field and contribute to the development of best practices.

Emily's journey has instilled in her a deep sense of confidence and determination. She is proud of the progress she has made and the positive impact she has had on the lives of vulnerable children and families. Emily's experiences have taught her the importance of resilience, empathy, and the power of collective action.

As she looks to the future, Emily is filled with hope and excitement for the possibilities that lie ahead. She is ready to embrace new challenges and opportunities, confident in her ability to make a difference. Emily's dedication to her work and her unwavering commitment to supporting children and families ensure that her impact will continue to grow.

Emily's story is a testament to the strength of the human spirit and the importance of love, support, and advocacy. With the support of the Johnson family, her colleagues, and her community, Emily is ready to continue her journey and create a brighter future for all children.

Chapter 16
Expanding Horizons

Emily's dedication and expertise have opened up exciting new opportunities in her career, allowing her to expand her horizons and make an even greater impact.

Emily's exceptional leadership skills and commitment to child welfare have led to her being offered several prominent leadership roles. She has been promoted to the position of Director of Child Welfare Services, where she oversees the development and implementation of programs that support vulnerable children and families. In this role, Emily is responsible for managing a team of social workers, coordinating with community partners, and ensuring that the organization's goals are met. Her leadership has been instrumental in driving positive change and improving the quality of services provided.

Emily is excited about leading new projects that address emerging challenges in child welfare. One such project involves the development of a comprehensive mental health support program for children and adolescents. This initiative aims to provide accessible and effective mental health services, including counselling, therapy, and support groups. Emily collaborates with mental health professionals, schools, and community organizations to create a holistic approach to mental health care. Her goal is to ensure that children and adolescents receive the support they need to thrive emotionally and mentally.

Emily is also involved in research projects that explore innovative approaches to child welfare. She collaborates with academic institutions and research organizations to conduct studies on the effectiveness of trauma-informed care, early intervention programs, and family support services. Emily's research contributes to the development of evidence-based practices that can be implemented on a broader scale. Her commitment to innovation ensures that the programs she develops are informed by the latest research and best practices.

Emily's advocacy work continues to expand as she takes on new roles in policy development and reform. She is invited to join advisory boards and committees that focus on child welfare policies at the local, state, and national levels. Emily's expertise and insights are highly valued, and she plays a key role in shaping policies that support vulnerable children and families. Her advocacy efforts aim to create systemic changes that improve access to resources, enhance service delivery, and promote the well-being of children.

Emily's reputation as a leader in child welfare has led to opportunities for international collaboration. She is invited to participate in global conferences and forums where she shares her experiences and learns from experts around the world. Emily collaborates with international organizations to develop programs that address child welfare issues in different cultural contexts. Her work on the global stage allows her to contribute to the advancement of child welfare practices worldwide.

Emily continues to prioritize her professional development by pursuing advanced education and training opportunities. She enrols in specialized courses and certification programs that enhance her skills and knowledge. Emily's commitment to continuous learning ensures that she remains at the forefront of her field and can provide the highest quality support to children and families. Her dedication to professional growth also inspires her colleagues and mentees to pursue their own development.

Emily's new opportunities also include increased community engagement. She organizes and participates in community events, workshops, and awareness campaigns that promote child welfare and support services. Emily's efforts to engage with the community help raise awareness about the importance of child welfare and encourage collective action. Her ability to connect with community members and stakeholders strengthens the impact of her work and fosters a sense of unity and collaboration.

Emily's new opportunities in leadership roles, new projects, research, policy advocacy, international collaboration, professional development, and community engagement reflect her dedication to expanding her horizons and making a positive impact. Her journey continues to be marked by growth, innovation, and a commitment to supporting vulnerable children and families.

Emily's dedication to child welfare extends beyond her local community, leading her to engage in international social work. Her involvement in global initiatives allows her to share her expertise, learn from diverse practices, and make a positive impact on children and families in different countries.

Emily partners with international organizations such as UNICEF, Save the Children, and World Vision to address child welfare issues on a global scale. These collaborations involve developing and implementing programs that provide essential support to vulnerable children and families. Emily's expertise in trauma-informed care, family support services, and advocacy is highly valued, and she contributes to the design and execution of initiatives that address the unique challenges faced by children in different cultural contexts.

One of Emily's key contributions to international social work is her involvement in training and capacity-building programs. She travels to various countries to conduct workshops and training sessions for social workers, educators, and healthcare providers. Emily's training programs focus on best practices in child welfare, trauma-informed care, and effective advocacy strategies. By sharing her knowledge and skills, she helps build the capacity of local professionals to provide high-quality support to children and families.

Emily understands the importance of developing programs that are culturally relevant and responsive to the needs of the communities they serve. She works closely with local partners to design initiatives that respect and incorporate cultural values and practices. Emily's ability to adapt her approaches to different cultural contexts ensures that the programs are effective and sustainable. Her commitment to cultural sensitivity and inclusivity enhances the impact of her work.

Emily's advocacy efforts extend to the international stage, where she works to influence policies that support child welfare. She participates in global forums and conferences, sharing her experiences and insights to inform policy discussions. Emily collaborates with international advocacy groups to raise awareness about child welfare issues and promote policy changes that benefit children worldwide. Her ability to articulate the needs of vulnerable children and families helps drive systemic change on a global scale.

In times of crisis, Emily's expertise is invaluable in providing emergency response and humanitarian aid. She has been involved in relief efforts following natural disasters, conflicts, and other emergencies that impact children and families. Emily works with international relief organizations to coordinate the delivery of essential services, such as shelter, food, medical care, and psychosocial support. Her ability to respond quickly and effectively to emergencies ensures that children and families receive the support they need during critical times.

Emily actively participates in international research projects that explore child welfare issues and best practices. She collaborates with researchers from different countries to conduct studies and share findings. Emily's involvement in research helps generate new knowledge and insights that inform the development of effective programs and policies. Her commitment to knowledge exchange ensures that the lessons learned from different cultural contexts are shared and applied to improve child welfare globally.

Emily's international work has allowed her to build a network of professionals and organizations dedicated to child welfare. These connections provide opportunities for collaboration, resource sharing, and mutual support. Emily's ability to foster strong relationships with her international partners enhances the effectiveness of her work and creates a sense of global solidarity in addressing child welfare issues.

Emily's involvement in international social work highlights her commitment to making a positive impact on children and families worldwide. Her collaborations with international organizations, training and capacity-building efforts, development of culturally relevant programs, advocacy and policy influence, emergency response, research, and knowledge exchange reflect her dedication to supporting vulnerable children and families across the globe.

Emily's involvement in international social work has provided her with rich cultural exchange and learning experiences. These opportunities have broadened her perspective, deepened her understanding of diverse cultures, and enhanced her ability to provide effective support to children and families.

Working abroad allows Emily to immerse herself in the local cultures of the countries, she visits. She takes the time to learn about the customs, traditions, and values of the communities she serves. Emily's willingness to embrace new experiences and adapt to different cultural contexts helps her build trust and rapport with the people she works with. This cultural immersion enriches her personal and professional life, providing her with a deeper appreciation for the diversity of human experiences.

Emily's international work exposes her to different approaches to social work and child welfare. She learns from the practices and methodologies used by her international colleagues, gaining new insights and ideas that she can incorporate into her own work.

Emily's openness to learning and adapting new approaches enhances her ability to develop innovative and effective programs. The exchange of knowledge and best practices fosters a collaborative environment where everyone benefits from shared experiences.

Emily's experiences abroad help her develop cross-cultural competence, an essential skill for working in diverse environments. She learns to navigate cultural differences, communicate effectively with people from various backgrounds, and provide culturally sensitive support. Emily's ability to understand and respect different cultural perspectives strengthens her relationships with clients and colleagues. This competence is invaluable in her work, as it ensures that her programs are inclusive and responsive to the needs of diverse communities.

Emily actively participates in cultural traditions and events in the countries she visits. Whether it's celebrating local festivals, attending traditional ceremonies, or participating in community gatherings, Emily embraces these opportunities to connect with the local culture. These experiences provide her with a deeper understanding of the cultural context in which she works and help her build meaningful connections with the people she serves.

Emily makes an effort to learn the languages of the countries she works in. She takes language classes, practices with native speakers and uses language learning apps to improve her skills. Emily's ability to communicate in the local language enhances her effectiveness as a social worker and helps her build stronger relationships with clients and colleagues. Language learning also provides her with a deeper insight into the culture and fosters mutual respect and understanding.

Emily's international experiences contribute to her personal growth and self-awareness. She reflects on the challenges and successes she encounters while working abroad, gaining valuable insights into her strengths and areas for improvement. Emily's ability to adapt to new environments, overcome obstacles, and embrace cultural differences strengthens her resilience and confidence. These reflections help her grow both personally and professionally, enriching her journey as a social worker.

Emily shares the cultural insights and experiences she gains from working abroad with her colleagues and community back home. She organizes presentations, writes articles, and participates in discussions to share her learnings. Emily's ability to convey the importance of cultural sensitivity and inclusivity helps raise awareness and promote best practices in her organization. Her efforts to share her experiences contribute to a more culturally competent and informed social work practice.

Emily's involvement in international social work provides her with valuable cultural exchange and learning experiences. These opportunities broaden her perspective, enhance her cross-cultural competence, and enrich her ability to provide effective support to children and families. Emily's journey is marked by a deep appreciation for cultural diversity and a commitment to continuous learning and growth.

Emily's commitment to child welfare has led her to build extensive global networks and partnerships, enhancing her impact and fostering collaboration across borders. These connections allow her to share knowledge, resources, and best practices, creating a unified effort to support vulnerable children and families worldwide.

Emily partners with renowned international organizations such as UNICEF, Save the Children, and World Vision. These collaborations involve joint projects, research initiatives, and advocacy campaigns aimed at improving child welfare globally. By working with these organizations, Emily gains access to a wealth of resources and expertise, which she leverages to enhance her programs and initiatives. These partnerships also provide opportunities for cross-cultural learning and the exchange of innovative ideas.

Emily regularly attends global conferences and forums focused on child welfare and social work. These events bring together experts, practitioners, and policymakers from around the world to discuss emerging challenges and share solutions. Emily's participation in these conferences allows her to stay updated on the latest developments in the field and build connections with like-minded professionals. She often presents her work and shares her experiences, contributing to the global dialogue on child welfare.

Emily is an active member of several professional networks and associations dedicated to social work and child welfare. These networks provide platforms for collaboration, knowledge sharing, and professional development. Emily's involvement in these networks helps her stay connected with peers, access valuable resources, and participate in joint initiatives. Her contributions to these networks are highly valued, and she often takes on leadership roles to drive collective efforts.

Emily works to establish cross-border partnerships with organizations and institutions in different countries. These partnerships involve collaborative projects, exchange programs, and joint research initiatives. By working together, Emily and her partners can address common challenges and develop solutions that are informed by diverse perspectives. These cross-border collaborations enhance the effectiveness of her programs and create a broader impact.

Emily is committed to the exchange of knowledge and best practices with her international colleagues. She organizes and participates in webinars, workshops, and training sessions that focus on key issues in child welfare. Emily's ability to share her expertise and learn from others fosters a culture of continuous improvement and innovation. These knowledge exchange initiatives help build the capacity of social workers and organizations worldwide.

Emily utilizes technology to facilitate collaboration and communication with her global partners. She uses online platforms, video conferencing, and collaborative tools to stay connected and coordinate efforts. Technology enables Emily to overcome geographical barriers and work effectively with her international colleagues. Her ability to leverage technology enhances the efficiency and reach of her collaborative initiatives.

Emily's advocacy efforts extend to the global stage, where she works to influence international policies that support child welfare. She collaborates with global advocacy groups to raise awareness about critical issues and promote policy changes that benefit children worldwide. Emily's ability to articulate the needs of vulnerable populations and advocate for systemic change helps drive global efforts to improve child welfare.

Emily's efforts to build global networks and partnerships create a sense of community and shared responsibility among child welfare professionals. These connections foster mutual support, collaboration, and a collective commitment to making a positive impact. Emily's leadership and vision inspire others to join the effort and contribute to the global movement for child welfare.

Emily's dedication to building global networks and partnerships enhances her impact and creates a unified effort to support vulnerable children and families worldwide. Her collaborations, knowledge exchange initiatives, and advocacy efforts reflect her commitment to making a meaningful difference on a global scale.

Emily's international work is both rewarding and challenging. She faces various obstacles, but her resilience, adaptability, and commitment to making a positive impact help her overcome these challenges.

One of the primary challenges Emily encounters is navigating cultural differences. Each country has its own customs, traditions, and social norms, which can affect how child welfare services are perceived and delivered. To overcome this, Emily invests time in learning about the local culture and building relationships with community leaders and stakeholders. She attends cultural events, participates in local traditions, and seeks guidance from her local partners. Emily's cultural sensitivity and respect for local customs help her build trust and effectively implement her programs.

Language barriers can pose significant challenges in communication and service delivery. Emily addresses this by learning the basics of the local language and working with interpreters and bilingual staff. She also uses visual aids and culturally relevant materials to ensure that her messages are understood. Emily's efforts to bridge language gaps demonstrate her commitment to effective communication and inclusivity.

In many countries, limited resources can hinder the implementation of child welfare programs. Emily faces challenges such as inadequate funding, lack of infrastructure, and scarcity of trained professionals. To overcome these constraints, she actively seeks funding from international donors, writes grant proposals, and collaborates with local organizations to pool resources. Emily's resourcefulness and ability to leverage partnerships help her secure the necessary support to sustain her programs.

Political instability and varying legal frameworks can impact the effectiveness of child welfare initiatives. Emily navigates these challenges by staying informed about the political and legal landscape of the countries she works in. She collaborates with local legal experts and policymakers to ensure that her programs comply with local regulations and advocate for necessary policy changes. Emily's ability to adapt to different political environments and work within legal constraints is crucial for the success of her initiatives.

Working in regions affected by conflict, natural disasters, or other crises can pose safety and security risks. Emily prioritizes the safety of her team and the communities she serves by conducting thorough risk assessments and developing contingency plans. She collaborates with local authorities and international organizations to ensure that safety protocols are in place. Emily's proactive approach to safety and security helps mitigate risks and ensures the well-being of everyone involved.

The emotional toll of working with vulnerable populations in challenging environments can lead to burnout and compassion fatigue. Emily addresses these challenges by prioritizing self-care and seeking support from her colleagues and mentors. She practices mindfulness, engages in regular exercise, and takes breaks to recharge. Emily also participates in peer support groups and professional supervision to process her experiences and maintain her emotional well-being.

Each country has its own work culture and organizational practices, which can differ significantly from what Emily is accustomed to. She adapts by being flexible and open-minded, learning from her local colleagues, and adjusting her approach as needed. Emily's ability to adapt to different work environments enhances her effectiveness and fosters positive relationships with her international partners.

Ensuring the sustainability of her programs is a key challenge for Emily. She addresses this by building the capacity of local organizations and communities to continue the work after her involvement ends. Emily provides training, resources, and support to local professionals, empowering them to take ownership of the programs. Her focus on sustainability ensures that the positive impact of her initiatives endures long after she has moved on to new projects.

Emily's ability to overcome the challenges of international work is a testament to her resilience, adaptability, and dedication. Her commitment to cultural sensitivity, effective communication, resourcefulness, safety, self-care, and sustainability ensures that she can make a meaningful and lasting impact on the lives of vulnerable children and families worldwide.

Emily's international work has been a profound journey of personal growth, enriching her life in numerous ways. The experiences she has gained from working in diverse cultural contexts have shaped her into a more resilient, empathetic, and insightful individual.

Emily's exposure to different cultures has significantly enhanced her cultural sensitivity. She has learned to appreciate and respect the unique customs, traditions, and values of the communities she serves. This cultural awareness has deepened her understanding of the diverse ways in which people live and interact, making her more empathetic and effective in her work. Emily's ability to navigate cultural differences with grace and respect has strengthened her relationships with clients and colleagues.

Working in various countries has honed Emily's communication skills. She has become adept at overcoming language barriers and finding creative ways to convey her messages. Emily's efforts to learn new languages and use visual aids have improved her ability to connect with people from different backgrounds. Her enhanced communication skills have made her a more effective advocate and social worker, capable of building trust and rapport with diverse populations.

The challenges Emily has faced in her international work have built her resilience. She has learned to adapt to new environments, overcome obstacles, and remain focused on her goals despite difficulties. Emily's experiences have taught her the importance of perseverance and flexibility, enabling her to navigate complex situations with confidence. Her resilience has become a cornerstone of her personal and professional growth, empowering her to tackle challenges head-on.

Emily's international work has broadened her perspective on social issues and human experiences. She has gained insights into the different ways in which societies address child welfare and the unique challenges faced by children and families in various cultural contexts. This expanded worldview has enriched Emily's understanding of global issues and inspired her to think creatively about solutions. Her broadened perspective has made her a more thoughtful and innovative social worker.

Emily's leadership abilities have been strengthened through her international collaborations. She has learned to lead diverse teams, manage cross-cultural projects, and coordinate efforts with international partners. Emily's experiences have taught her the importance of inclusive leadership and the value of diverse perspectives. Her ability to inspire and guide others has been enhanced, making her a more effective leader in her field.

Emily's work with vulnerable populations in different countries has deepened her empathy. She has witnessed the resilience and strength of children and families facing adversity, and these experiences have touched her profoundly. Emily's empathy drives her commitment to making a positive impact and fuels her passion for advocacy. Her ability to connect with others on a deep emotional level has become a defining aspect of her work.

Emily's international work has brought her a sense of personal fulfilment and purpose. The knowledge that she is making a difference in the lives of children and families around the world gives her a profound sense of satisfaction. Emily's dedication to her work and the positive impact she has made are sources of pride and motivation. Her journey has reinforced her belief in the importance of compassion, resilience, and the power of collective action.

Emily's personal growth through her international work is a testament to her resilience, empathy, and commitment to making a positive impact. Her experiences have enriched her life, shaping her into a more effective and compassionate social worker. Emily's journey continues to inspire her to embrace new challenges and opportunities, confident in her ability to make a meaningful difference.

Emily is deeply committed to sharing her knowledge and experiences with others, recognizing the importance of education and collaboration in advancing child welfare. Through workshops, seminars, and various educational initiatives, she empowers fellow social workers, advocates, and community members to make a positive impact.

Emily regularly conducts workshops on topics such as trauma informed care, child welfare policies, and effective advocacy strategies. These workshops are designed to provide practical skills and knowledge that participants can apply in their work. Emily's engaging teaching style and ability to connect with her audience make her workshops highly effective. She uses a combination of lectures, interactive activities, and case studies to ensure that participants gain a comprehensive understanding of the subject matter.

In addition to workshops, Emily leads seminars at universities, training programs, and professional conferences. Her seminars cover a wide range of topics, from the latest research in child welfare to innovative program development. Emily's ability to present complex information in an accessible and engaging manner makes her seminars valuable learning experiences. She encourages active participation and discussion, fostering a collaborative learning environment.

Emily has developed comprehensive training programs for social workers, educators, and healthcare providers. These programs are designed to build capacity and enhance the skills of professionals working with vulnerable children and families. Emily's training programs include modules on best practices, cultural competence, and self-care. She ensures that the content is relevant, up-to-date, and tailored to the needs of the participants. Her commitment to high-quality training helps improve the effectiveness of child welfare services.

Emily provides one-on-one mentoring and coaching to students, interns, and new social workers. She offers guidance, support, and practical advice to help them navigate their careers and develop their skills. Emily's mentorship is characterized by her genuine care and investment in the success of her mentees. She creates a supportive and nurturing environment where they can learn, grow, and thrive.

Emily collaborates with universities and training institutions to develop and deliver courses on child welfare and social work. She serves as a guest lecturer, curriculum advisor, and program developer. Emily's contributions help ensure that the next generation of social workers is well-prepared to address the challenges of the field. Her involvement in education reflects her commitment to fostering a knowledgeable and skilled workforce.

Emily shares her knowledge and experiences through writing. She regularly publishes articles in professional journals, magazines, and online platforms. Her articles provide valuable insights into best practices, research findings, and personal reflections on her work. Emily has also authored several books that delve into her experiences and the lessons she has learned throughout her career. Her writing serves as a resource for social workers, advocates, and anyone interested in child welfare.

Emily organizes community workshops and awareness campaigns to educate the public about child welfare issues. These workshops provide valuable information on topics such as parenting skills, mental health support, and accessing resources. Emily's efforts to engage the community help raise awareness and promote collective action. Her ability to connect with community members and provide practical support makes these workshops impactful and well-received.

Emily leverages technology to reach a wider audience through webinars and online courses. These virtual platforms allow her to share her knowledge with participants from different regions and backgrounds. Emily's webinars cover a variety of topics and provide opportunities for interactive learning and discussion. Her online courses offer flexible learning options for busy professionals, ensuring that they can access valuable training and resources.

Emily's efforts to share her knowledge and experiences through workshops, seminars, training programs, mentoring, writing, community workshops, and online platforms highlight her commitment to education and collaboration. Her dedication to empowering others ensures that her impact extends far beyond her immediate work, creating a ripple effect of positive change in the field of child welfare.

Emily's work has had a profound impact on child welfare practices globally, inspiring change and improvements that benefit vulnerable children and families. Her dedication, innovative approaches, and advocacy efforts have set new standards and influenced policies and practices worldwide.

Emily's development of innovative programs has served as a model for child welfare organizations globally. Her trauma-informed care programs, family support services, and school-based interventions have been widely recognized for their effectiveness. These programs have inspired other organizations to adopt similar approaches, leading to improved support for children and families. Emily's ability to design and implement programs that address the unique needs of vulnerable populations has set a new benchmark for best practices in the field.

Emily's advocacy work has led to significant policy changes that support child welfare. Her efforts to raise awareness about critical issues and influence policymakers have resulted in increased funding for child welfare services, the implementation of trauma-informed practices, and improved access to mental health care. Emily's ability to articulate the needs of vulnerable children and families has inspired other advocates to join the cause and drive systemic change. Her work has demonstrated the power of advocacy in creating lasting improvements in child welfare policies.

Emily's collaborations with international organizations and professionals have facilitated the exchange of knowledge and best practices. By working with partners such as UNICEF, Save the Children, and World Vision, Emily has contributed to the development of global initiatives that address child welfare issues. Her involvement in international conferences, research projects, and training programs has helped disseminate effective practices and foster a collaborative approach to child welfare. Emily's global network of partners and colleagues continues to drive improvements in the field.

Emily's commitment to training and capacity building has empowered social workers, educators, and healthcare providers worldwide. Her workshops, seminars, and training programs provide valuable skills and knowledge that enhance the effectiveness of child welfare services. Emily's efforts to build the capacity of professionals ensure that they are equipped to provide high-quality support to children and families. Her dedication to education and professional development has inspired others to prioritize continuous learning and improvement.

Emily's involvement in research and knowledge sharing has contributed to the advancement of child welfare practices. Her research projects explore innovative approaches and provide evidence-based insights that inform program development and policy decisions. Emily's publications, presentations, and participation in knowledge exchange initiatives help disseminate valuable information to a global audience. Her commitment to research and knowledge sharing has inspired others to adopt evidence-based practices and continuously seek ways to improve their work.

Emily's efforts to engage and empower communities have created a ripple effect of positive change. Her community workshops, awareness campaigns, and outreach programs have raised awareness about child welfare issues and encouraged collective action. Emily's ability to connect with community members and provide practical support has inspired others to get involved and make a difference.

Her work has demonstrated the importance of community engagement in driving sustainable improvements in child welfare.

Emily's achievements have been recognized through numerous awards and accolades, highlighting the impact of her work. These recognitions serve as a testament to her dedication and effectiveness in improving child welfare practices. Emily's success stories and the positive feedback from her clients, colleagues, and community members inspire others to
strive for excellence and make a meaningful impact in their own work.

Emily's work has inspired change and improvements in child welfare practices globally. Her innovative programs, advocacy efforts, global collaborations, training initiatives, research contributions, community engagement, and recognition have set new standards and influenced policies and practices worldwide. Emily's dedication to making a positive impact continues to inspire others and drive lasting improvements in the field of child welfare.

As Emily sits in her cozy home, surrounded by mementos from her travels and the warmth of her loved ones, she takes a moment to reflect on her achievements and the profound impact of her international work. Her journey has been filled with challenges, growth, and countless moments of fulfilment.

Emily reflects on the personal and professional growth she has experienced through her international work. She has become more resilient, empathetic, and culturally sensitive. Her ability to navigate diverse cultural contexts and build meaningful relationships has enriched her life and enhanced her effectiveness as a social worker. Emily's experiences have taught her the importance of adaptability, perseverance, and continuous learning.

Emily takes pride in the innovative programs and initiatives she has developed and implemented. Her trauma-informed care programs, family support services, and school-based interventions have made a significant difference in the lives of vulnerable children and families. Emily's ability to design and execute effective programs has set new standards in the field of child welfare. She is proud of the positive outcomes these programs have achieved and the lasting impact they have created.

Reflecting on her advocacy work, Emily feels a deep sense of fulfilment knowing that her efforts have led to meaningful policy changes. Her testimony before parliamentary committees, collaboration with policymakers, and participation in global advocacy campaigns have driven systemic changes that benefit children and families. Emily's ability to influence policy and raise awareness about critical child welfare issues has inspired others to join the cause and advocate for positive change.

Emily's international work has provided her with opportunities to collaborate with professionals and organizations worldwide. She reflects on the knowledge exchange and learning experiences that have enriched her understanding of child welfare practices. Emily's collaborations have fostered a sense of global solidarity and collective responsibility in addressing child welfare issues. She is grateful for the connections she has made and the shared commitment to making a positive impact.

Emily takes pride in her efforts to engage and empower communities. Her community workshops, awareness campaigns, and outreach programs have raised awareness about child welfare issues and encouraged collective action. Emily's ability to connect with community members and provide practical support has created a ripple effect of positive change. She is inspired by the resilience and strength of the communities she serves and is proud of the impact her work has had.

Emily's achievements have been recognized through numerous awards and accolades. These recognitions serve as a testament to her dedication and effectiveness in improving child welfare practices. Emily reflects on the moments of celebration and acknowledgment, feeling a deep sense of gratitude for the support and encouragement she has received from her colleagues, friends, and family.

Emily is proud of her efforts to inspire and mentor the next generation of social workers and advocates. Her workshops, seminars, and mentoring programs have empowered others to pursue careers in social work and advocacy. Emily's ability to share her knowledge and experiences has created a legacy of compassion and commitment that will continue to make a positive impact for years to come.

As Emily reflects on her achievements, she is filled with hope and excitement for the future. She is committed to continuing her work, expanding her advocacy efforts, and developing new programs that address emerging challenges. Emily's journey has taught her the importance of resilience, love, and the power of supportive relationships. She is ready to embrace new opportunities and continue making a positive impact.

Emily's reflections on her achievements and the impact of her international work highlight the profound difference she has made in the lives of vulnerable children and families. Her journey is a testament to the strength of the human spirit and the importance of love, support, and advocacy. Emily's story continues to inspire others and drive lasting improvements in child welfare practices globally.

As Emily reflects on her journey and the impact she has made, she looks to the future with hope and determination. Her experiences have shaped her into a resilient, compassionate, and empowered individual, ready to embrace new opportunities and continue making a positive difference.

Emily is committed to expanding her advocacy efforts to reach a broader audience and influence more significant policy changes. She plans to collaborate with national organizations and policymakers to advocate for comprehensive child welfare reforms. Emily's goal is to ensure that all children have access to the support and resources they need to thrive.

Emily is excited about developing new and innovative programs that address emerging challenges faced by vulnerable children and families. She aims to create initiatives that focus on mental health, educational support, and community engagement. Emily's vision includes leveraging technology and research to design programs that are both effective and accessible.

Building on her success in creating strong community partnerships, Emily plans to further strengthen these relationships and explore new collaborations. She envisions a network of organizations working together to provide holistic support to children and families. Emily's efforts will focus on enhancing coordination and resource sharing to maximize the impact of community services.

Emily is passionate about mentoring the next generation of

social workers and advocates. She plans to establish mentorship programs that provide guidance, support, and professional development opportunities for students and new professionals. Emily's goal is to inspire and equip future leaders with the skills and knowledge they need to make a meaningful impact.

Emily is dedicated to continuous learning and professional growth. She plans to pursue advanced education, such as a doctoral degree in social work or public policy, to deepen her expertise and expand her influence. Emily's commitment to education reflects her desire to stay at the forefront of her field and contribute to the development of best practices.

Emily's journey has instilled in her a deep sense of confidence and determination. She is proud of the progress she has made and the positive impact she has had on the lives of vulnerable children and families. Emily's experiences have taught her the importance of resilience, empathy, and the power of collective action.

As she looks to the future, Emily is filled with hope and excitement for the possibilities that lie ahead. She is ready to embrace new challenges and opportunities, confident in her ability to make a difference. Emily's dedication to her work and her unwavering commitment to supporting children and families ensure that her impact will continue to grow.

Emily's story is a testament to the strength of the human spirit and the importance of love, support, and advocacy. With the support of the Johnson family, her colleagues, and her community, Emily is ready to continue her journey and create a brighter future for all children.

Chapter 17
Personal Fulfilment

Emily's journey to find balance between her demanding career and personal life is a testament to her dedication to both her professional responsibilities and her well-being. She understands that achieving this balance is essential for maintaining her mental, emotional, and physical health.

Emily makes a conscious effort to set clear boundaries between her work and personal life. She establishes specific working hours and avoids checking work emails or taking work-related calls outside of these hours. By setting these boundaries, Emily ensures that she has time to rest, recharge, and focus on her personal interests and relationships.

Self-care is a crucial aspect of Emily's routine. She practices mindfulness meditation, engages in regular exercise and enjoys creative outlets such as painting and reading. These activities help her manage stress, stay grounded, and maintain a sense of balance. Emily's commitment to self-care ensures that she can approach her work with renewed energy and focus.

Emily prioritizes spending quality time with her loved ones. She schedules regular family gatherings, social outings with friends, and date nights with her partner. These moments of connection and joy are essential for her emotional well-being. Emily's efforts to nurture her relationships help her feel supported and fulfilled.

Emily makes time for hobbies and activities that bring her joy and relaxation. Whether it's hiking, cooking, or exploring new art techniques, these activities provide her with a sense of fulfilment and help her unwind. Emily's dedication to pursuing her passions outside of work contributes to her overall well-being and happiness.

Emily recognizes the importance of seeking support when needed. She continues to work with her therapist, Dr. Collins, to navigate the emotional demands of her job and her personal life. Regular therapy sessions provide her with a safe space to explore her feelings, develop coping strategies, and gain insights into her experiences. Emily's willingness to seek support ensures that she can maintain her mental health and well-being.

Emily practices effective time management to balance her professional and personal responsibilities. She uses tools such as planners and digital calendars to organize her tasks and commitments. By prioritizing her activities and managing her time efficiently, Emily ensures that she can meet her work deadlines while also making time for herself and her loved ones.

Emily understands that achieving balance requires flexibility. She is open to adjusting her schedule and priorities as needed to accommodate unexpected events or changes. Emily's ability to adapt to different situations helps her maintain a sense of balance and prevents her from feeling overwhelmed.

Emily takes time to reflect on her achievements and the progress she has made in both her career and personal life. She acknowledges her successes and celebrates her milestones, no matter how small. This practice of self-reflection helps Emily stay motivated and appreciate the journey she is on.

Emily's efforts to find balance between her demanding career and personal life highlight her commitment to maintaining her well-being and happiness. Her dedication to setting boundaries, prioritizing self-care, nurturing relationships, engaging in hobbies, seeking support, managing her time effectively, embracing flexibility, and reflecting on her achievements ensures that she can navigate the demands of her career while also enjoying a fulfilling personal life.

Emily's pursuit of personal passions and hobbies plays a vital role in her overall well-being and fulfilment. These activities provide her with joy, relaxation, and a sense of accomplishment, enriching her life beyond her professional responsibilities.

Emily has a deep love for art and painting. She finds solace and creative expression in her artwork, often spending hours in her home studio experimenting with different techniques and mediums. Painting allows Emily to unwind and channel her emotions into something beautiful. Her artwork is not only a personal passion but also a way to connect with others, as she occasionally participates in local art exhibitions and shares her creations with friends and family.

Emily enjoys spending time outdoors, exploring nature through hiking and other activities. She finds peace and rejuvenation in the natural world, often taking weekend trips to nearby trails and parks. Hiking allows Emily to disconnect from the demands of her career and immerse herself in the beauty of the environment. These outdoor adventures provide her with a sense of freedom and adventure, contributing to her overall well-being.

A voracious reader, Emily finds joy and inspiration in literature. She enjoys exploring a wide range of genres, from classic novels to contemporary fiction and non-fiction. Reading provides Emily with an escape from the stresses of daily life and allows her to explore new ideas and perspectives. She often participates in book clubs and literary discussions, sharing her thoughts and insights with fellow book enthusiasts.

Emily has a passion for cooking and experimenting with new recipes. She enjoys exploring different cuisines and creating delicious meals for herself and her loved ones. Cooking is a therapeutic activity for Emily, allowing her to express her creativity and nurture those around her. She often hosts dinner parties and gatherings, where she can share her culinary creations and enjoy the company of friends and family.

Emily practices yoga and mindfulness as part of her self-care routine. These practices help her stay grounded, manage stress, and maintain a sense of balance. Yoga provides Emily with physical and mental benefits, enhancing her overall well-being. She often attends yoga classes and workshops, connecting with a community of like-minded individuals who share her commitment to mindfulness and self-care.

Emily has a passion for travel and exploring new cultures. She enjoys visiting different countries, experiencing their traditions, and learning about their history. Travel provides Emily with a sense of adventure and broadens her perspective on the world. Her international work has allowed her to combine her love for travel with her commitment to child welfare, creating meaningful and enriching experiences.

Emily finds joy in gardening and nurturing plants. She has a small garden at home where she grows flowers, herbs, and vegetables. Gardening allows Emily to connect with nature and experience the satisfaction of watching her plants thrive. This hobby provides her with a sense of accomplishment and tranquillity, contributing to her overall well-being.

Emily's pursuit of personal passions and hobbies brings her joy, fulfilment, and a sense of balance. These activities enrich her life, providing her with opportunities for creative expression, relaxation, and personal growth. Emily's dedication to her passions ensures that she can navigate the demands of her career while also enjoying a fulfilling and well-rounded personal life.

Relationships play a pivotal role in Emily's life, providing her with love, support, and a sense of belonging. She understands the importance of nurturing these connections and makes a conscious effort to maintain and strengthen her relationships with family, friends, and colleagues.

Emily's relationship with the Johnson family is the cornerstone of her support system. The love and stability they have provided since her adoption have been instrumental in her growth and success. Emily nurtures these bonds by spending quality time with her family, participating in family traditions, and celebrating special occasions together. She values the open communication and mutual respect that define her relationship with the Johnsons, ensuring that they remain a close-knit and supportive unit.

Emily cherishes her friendships and the companionship they offer. She maintains a close-knit group of friends who share common interests and provide emotional support. Emily makes an effort to stay connected with her friends through regular meet-ups, phone calls, and social activities. Whether it's attending social events, exploring new hobbies, or simply catching up over coffee, Emily values the time spent with her friends and the joy they bring to her life.

Emily's relationships with her colleagues and mentors are essential to her professional growth and success. She fosters a collaborative and supportive work environment by building strong connections with her peers. Emily regularly seeks guidance from her mentors, participates in peer supervision groups, and engages in professional development activities. Her ability to build and maintain positive professional relationships enhances her effectiveness as a social worker and contributes to a supportive work culture.

Emily's involvement in community activities and volunteer work allows her to build meaningful connections with community members. She participates in local events, supports community initiatives, and collaborates with local organizations. Emily's efforts to engage with her community create a sense of unity and collective responsibility. These connections provide her with a broader support network and enrich her life with diverse perspectives and experiences.

Emily's romantic relationship is another important aspect of her life. She values the love, companionship, and support she shares with her partner. Emily makes an effort to nurture this relationship by spending quality time together, communicating openly, and supporting each other's goals and aspirations. Her commitment to maintaining a healthy and loving relationship contributes to her overall happiness and well-being.

Emily understands the importance of maintaining a balance between her personal and professional relationships. She prioritizes self-care and sets boundaries to ensure that she can give her best to her loved ones and her work. Emily's ability to manage her time effectively and stay organized helps her maintain this balance and nurture her relationships.

Emily celebrates the milestones and achievements of her loved ones, recognizing the importance of these moments in strengthening relationships. Whether it's a birthday, anniversary, or professional accomplishment, Emily makes an effort to acknowledge and celebrate these special occasions. Her thoughtfulness and appreciation for the people in her life reinforce the bonds she shares with them.

Open and honest communication is a key aspect of Emily's relationships. She values transparency and actively listens to the needs and concerns of her loved ones. Emily's ability to communicate effectively helps her build trust and understanding in her relationships. She is always willing to offer support and encouragement, creating a positive and nurturing environment for those around her.

Emily's dedication to building and nurturing relationships highlights the importance of love, support, and connection in her life. Her efforts to maintain strong bonds with family, friends, colleagues, and her community contribute to her overall well-being and fulfilment. Emily's story is a testament to the power of relationships in providing a sense of belonging and enriching one's life.

Emily understands the importance of self-care in maintaining her well-being and ensuring she can continue to support others effectively. She has adopted a variety of self-care practices that help her manage stress, stay grounded, and maintain a healthy balance between her personal and professional life.

Emily practices mindfulness and meditation regularly. These practices help her stay present, manage stress, and cultivate a sense of inner peace. She sets aside time each day for meditation, using guided sessions or simply focusing on her breath. Mindfulness techniques, such as mindful breathing and body scans, are integrated into her daily routine to help her stay centred and calm.

Regular physical exercise is a key component of Emily's self care routine. She enjoys activities such as yoga, hiking, and jogging, which provide both physical and mental benefits. Yoga helps Emily improve her flexibility, strength, and relaxation, while hiking and jogging allow her to connect with nature and clear her mind. Exercise is a vital part of Emily's routine, helping her maintain her physical health and reduce stress.

Emily finds joy and relaxation in creative activities such as painting and writing. These outlets allow her to express her emotions and thoughts in a constructive way. Painting provides Emily with a sense of accomplishment and a way to unwind, while writing helps her process her experiences and reflect on her journey. Engaging in creative activities is an essential part of Emily's self-care, providing her with a sense of fulfilment and relaxation.

Emily prioritizes healthy eating as part of her self-care routine. She focuses on a balanced diet that includes plenty of fruits, vegetables, whole grains, and lean proteins. Emily enjoys cooking and experimenting with new recipes, which allows her to nourish her body with wholesome and delicious meals. Maintaining a healthy diet helps Emily feel energized and supports her overall well-being.

Getting enough quality sleep is crucial for Emily's well-being. She establishes a consistent sleep routine, aiming for 7-8 hours of sleep each night. Emily creates a relaxing bedtime environment by minimizing screen time before bed, using calming essential oils, and practicing relaxation techniques. Quality sleep helps Emily recharge and ensures she can approach each day with clarity and focus.

Emily values her social connections and makes an effort to nurture her relationships with family, friends, and colleagues. Spending time with loved ones, engaging in meaningful conversations, and participating in social activities provide Emily with emotional support and a sense of belonging. These connections are an important part of her self-care, helping her feel supported and connected.

Emily continues to work with her therapist, Dr. Collins, to navigate the emotional demands of her job and personal life. Regular therapy sessions provide her with a safe space to explore her feelings, develop coping strategies, and gain insights into her experiences. Emily's commitment to therapy ensures that she can maintain her mental health and well-being.

Emily makes time for relaxation and leisure activities that bring her joy and help her unwind. Whether it's reading a good book, watching a favourite movie, or spending time in nature, these activities provide Emily with a sense of relaxation and enjoyment. Taking time for leisure helps her recharge and maintain a healthy balance in her life.

Emily sets clear boundaries between her work and personal life to ensure she has time for self-care. She establishes specific working hours and avoids checking work emails or taking work-related calls outside of these hours. By setting boundaries, Emily ensures that she can focus on her well-being and personal interests.

Emily's self-care practices are essential for maintaining her well-being and ensuring she can continue to support others effectively. Her commitment to mindfulness, physical exercise, creative outlets, healthy eating, quality sleep, social connections, therapy, relaxation, and setting boundaries helps her navigate the demands of her career while also enjoying a fulfilling personal life.

Emily's journey has not been without its personal struggles. However, her resilience and the unwavering support of her network have helped her overcome these challenges and emerge stronger.

At one point in her career, Emily experienced burnout due to the emotional demands of her work. The constant exposure to trauma and the pressure to support vulnerable children and families took a toll on her mental health. Recognizing the signs of burnout, Emily sought help from her therapist, Dr. Collins. Through therapy, she learned to set boundaries, prioritize self-care, and develop coping strategies. Emily's willingness to seek support and make necessary changes allowed her to recover from burnout and continue her work with renewed energy.

Emily faced a significant personal loss when her beloved grandmother passed away. The grief and sadness were overwhelming, and Emily struggled to cope with the loss. During this difficult time, she found strength in her support network. The Johnson family, her friends, and her colleagues provided her with emotional support and comfort. Emily also attended grief counselling sessions, which helped her process her emotions and find ways to honour her grandmother's memory. The love and support she received from her network helped her navigate this challenging period and find healing.

Balancing the demands of her career with her personal life has been an ongoing challenge for Emily. There were times when she felt overwhelmed by her responsibilities and struggled to find time for herself and her loved ones. Emily addressed this challenge by setting clear boundaries between work and personal life, practicing effective time management, and prioritizing self-care. She also leaned on her support network for encouragement and advice. By making these adjustments, Emily was able to achieve a healthier balance and maintain her well-being.

Throughout her journey, Emily has faced moments of self doubt and uncertainty about her abilities. These feelings were particularly strong when she took on new leadership roles and responsibilities. To overcome self-doubt, Emily sought mentorship from experienced colleagues and participated in professional development programs. The guidance and encouragement she received helped her build confidence in her skills and capabilities. Emily's support network played a crucial role in helping her recognize her strengths and embrace new challenges with confidence.

Working with vulnerable populations can lead to compassion fatigue, a condition characterized by emotional exhaustion and reduced empathy. Emily experienced compassion fatigue during particularly challenging periods in her career. To address this, she implemented self-care practices such as mindfulness meditation, regular exercise, and creative outlets. Emily also sought support from her peers and participated in peer supervision groups, where she could share her experiences and receive feedback. These strategies helped her manage compassion fatigue and continue providing compassionate care to her clients.

Emily's involvement in community activities and volunteer work has provided her with a sense of purpose and connection. During times of personal struggle, she found strength in the support and camaraderie of her community. Emily's ability to give back and make a positive impact on others has been a source of fulfilment and resilience. The relationships she has built within her community have provided her with a strong support network that she can rely on during difficult times.

Emily's journey of overcoming personal struggles highlights her resilience, determination, and the importance of a strong support network. Her willingness to seek help, prioritize self-care, and lean on her loved ones has enabled her to navigate challenges and emerge stronger. Emily's story is a testament to the power of support and the human spirit's capacity for growth and healing.

Emily's journey is marked by numerous milestones, each representing a significant achievement in her personal and professional life. These celebrations highlight her dedication, resilience, and the positive impact she has made on the lives of vulnerable children and families.

Emily's achievement of advanced certification in trauma informed care was a significant milestone in her career. This certification recognized her expertise and commitment to providing specialized support to children who have experienced trauma. Emily celebrated this accomplishment with her colleagues and mentors, who acknowledged her dedication and hard work.

Emily's promotion to Director of Child Welfare Services was a moment of pride and celebration. This leadership role reflected her exceptional skills and the trust her organization placed in her. Emily's colleagues organized a surprise celebration to honour her promotion, expressing their admiration and support for her new role.

Emily was honoured with the prestigious Social Worker of the Year award by the National Association of Social Workers (NASW). This recognition celebrated her outstanding contributions to the field of social work and her impact on child welfare. The award ceremony was a memorable event, attended by her family, friends, and colleagues who celebrated her achievements with pride.

Emily celebrated the successful implementation of several innovative programs, including family support services, school-based interventions, and trauma-informed care initiatives. These programs made a significant difference in the lives of children and families, and their positive outcomes were a source of immense pride for Emily. She celebrated these milestones with her team, acknowledging their collective efforts and dedication.

Emily's graduation from her master's program in Social Work was a significant personal milestone. She celebrated this achievement with her family and friends, who supported her throughout her educational journey. Emily's pursuit of advanced degrees and continuous learning has been a source of pride and fulfilment.

Emily's ability to build and maintain strong relationships with her family, friends, and colleagues is a testament to her compassionate and empathetic nature. She celebrates the milestones in these relationships, such as anniversaries, birthdays, and special occasions, with joy and gratitude. These celebrations strengthen her bonds and provide her with a sense of belonging and support.

Emily's journey of personal growth and resilience is marked by numerous milestones. She celebrates her ability to overcome challenges, navigate difficult situations, and maintain a healthy work-life balance. Emily's reflections on her personal achievements and growth provide her with a sense of fulfilment and motivation.

Emily's involvement in community engagement and volunteer work has been a source of pride and celebration. She celebrates the positive impact of her efforts on the community and the relationships she has built through her volunteer work. Emily's dedication to giving back and making a difference is celebrated by her community and loved ones.

Emily values the importance of celebrating milestones with her loved ones. Whether it's a professional achievement or a personal milestone, she ensures that these moments are shared with the people who have supported her along the way. Emily's celebrations often include gatherings with family and friends, where they share stories, express gratitude, and create lasting memories.

Emily's journey is filled with celebrations of important milestones that highlight her dedication, resilience, and the positive impact she has made. These celebrations provide her with a sense of fulfilment and motivation, reinforcing the importance of her work and the support of her loved ones.

Emily's commitment to giving back to her community is a testament to her dedication to making a positive impact. Her efforts to support others and contribute to the well-being of her community are driven by her compassion and desire to create lasting change.

Emily actively volunteers her time and skills to support various community initiatives. She participates in local food drives, organizes clothing donations, and helps with community clean-up projects. Emily's hands-on involvement in these activities allows her to connect with community members and address immediate needs. Her dedication to volunteering reflects her commitment to making a tangible difference in the lives of those around her.

Emily is passionate about mentoring and supporting young people in her community. She volunteers as a mentor for at-risk youth, providing guidance, encouragement, and support. Emily's mentorship helps young individuals build confidence, develop essential life skills, and pursue their goals. Her efforts to empower the next generation are a vital part of her commitment to giving back.

Emily organizes and leads community workshops on various topics, such as parenting skills, mental health awareness, and financial literacy. These workshops provide valuable information and resources to community members, helping them navigate challenges and improve their well-being. Emily's ability to share her knowledge and expertise in an accessible and engaging manner makes these workshops impactful and well-received.

Emily collaborates with local non-profit organizations to support their missions and initiatives. She volunteers her time, donates resources, and helps with fundraising efforts. Emily's involvement with non-profits allows her to contribute to a wide range of causes, from homelessness prevention to educational support. Her commitment to supporting these organizations amplifies her impact and helps create a stronger, more resilient community.

Emily is actively involved in advocacy and awareness campaigns that address critical issues affecting her community. She participates in campaigns that promote child welfare, mental health awareness, and social justice. Emily's ability to raise awareness and advocate for positive change helps drive community-wide efforts to address these issues. Her advocacy work inspires others to get involved and take action.

Emily is dedicated to creating safe and inclusive spaces for community members to come together and support one another. She organizes support groups, community gatherings, and events that foster a sense of belonging and connection. Emily's efforts to build a supportive community environment help individuals feel valued and understood. Her commitment to inclusivity and support is a cornerstone of her work.

Emily's educational outreach efforts extend to schools and community centres, where she provides workshops and presentations on topics such as trauma-informed care, child welfare, and effective advocacy. Her ability to educate and inspire others helps build a more informed and compassionate community. Emily's outreach efforts ensure that valuable knowledge and resources are accessible to all.

Emily collaborates with community leaders and stakeholders to address systemic issues and develop solutions that benefit the community. She participates in community planning meetings, advisory boards, and task forces, where she shares her insights and expertise. Emily's collaborative approach helps create a unified effort to address challenges and improve the quality of life for community members.

Emily's efforts to give back to her community highlight her

dedication to making a positive impact and supporting others. Her involvement in volunteering, mentoring, organizing workshops, supporting non-profits, advocacy, creating safe spaces, educational outreach, and collaboration reflects her commitment to creating lasting change. Emily's story is a testament to the power of compassion and the importance of giving back to the community.

As Emily sits quietly, reflecting on her journey, she is filled with a profound sense of gratitude and fulfilment. Her path has been marked by challenges, growth, and countless moments of joy. Through her experiences, Emily has learned valuable lessons that have shaped her into the resilient and compassionate individual she is today.

One of the most significant lessons Emily has learned is the power of vulnerability. Opening up about her past and sharing her struggles has allowed her to connect deeply with others and build meaningful relationships. Emily has discovered that vulnerability is not a sign of weakness but a source of strength. It has enabled her to empathize with her clients, support her colleagues, and inspire those around her.

Emily's journey has taught her the critical importance of self care. She has learned that taking care of her mental, emotional, and physical well-being is essential for her to be effective in her role as a social worker. Emily's commitment to self-care practices, such as mindfulness meditation, regular exercise, and creative outlets, has helped her maintain balance and resilience. She understands that self-care is not a luxury but a necessity for sustaining her passion and dedication.

Emily's experiences have reinforced the value of resilience and perseverance. She has faced numerous challenges, from navigating the emotional demands of her job to overcoming personal struggles. Through it all, Emily has learned to stay focused on her goals and remain steadfast in her commitment to making a positive impact. Her resilience has enabled her to bounce back from setbacks and continue moving forward with determination.

Emily has come to appreciate the profound impact of supportive relationships. The love and encouragement she has received from the Johnson family, her friends, and her colleagues have been instrumental in her journey. These relationships have provided her with a sense of belonging, stability, and strength. Emily has learned that surrounding herself with supportive and understanding individuals is essential for her well-being and success.

Emily's commitment to continuous learning and growth has been a cornerstone of her journey. She has embraced opportunities for professional development, pursued advanced education, and stayed informed about the latest research and best practices. Emily's dedication to learning has enabled her to provide high-quality support to her clients and contribute to the advancement of the field. She understands that growth is a lifelong process and is committed to evolving both personally and professionally.

Reflecting on her journey, Emily is filled with a sense of fulfilment knowing that she has made a positive difference in the lives of vulnerable children and families. Her programs, advocacy efforts, and personal contributions have created lasting change and inspired others to take action. Emily's impact is a testament to the power of compassion, dedication, and the human spirit's capacity for growth and healing.

As Emily looks to the future, she is excited about the possibilities that lie ahead. She is committed to continuing her work, expanding her advocacy efforts, and developing new programs that address emerging challenges. Emily's journey has taught her the importance of resilience, love, and the power of supportive relationships. She is ready to embrace new opportunities and continue making a positive impact.

Emily's personal reflections on her journey highlight the lessons she has learned and the growth she has experienced. Her story is a testament to the strength of the human spirit and the importance of love, support, and advocacy. Emily's journey is far from over, and she looks forward to continuing her work and creating a brighter future for all children.

Emily's journey is characterized by her ability to embrace change and seize new opportunities with optimism and enthusiasm. Her willingness to adapt and grow has been a driving force behind her success and the positive impact she has made.

Emily's career has seen her take on various roles and

responsibilities, each presenting unique challenges and opportunities. Whether it was transitioning from a frontline social worker to a leadership position or taking on international projects, Emily has always approached these changes with a positive mindset. She views each new role as an opportunity to learn, grow, and make a difference. Emily's adaptability and willingness to embrace change have enabled her to thrive in diverse environments and drive positive outcomes.

Emily is always on the lookout for new projects that align with her passion for child welfare and advocacy. She eagerly takes on initiatives that address emerging challenges and provide innovative solutions. Emily's enthusiasm for exploring new projects is fuelled by her desire to create meaningful change and support vulnerable populations. Her ability to embrace new opportunities with optimism ensures that she remains at the forefront of her field and continues to make a positive impact.

Emily's commitment to continuous learning and professional development is a testament to her willingness to embrace change. She actively seeks out opportunities to expand her knowledge and skills, whether through advanced education, workshops, or conferences. Emily's dedication to learning ensures that she stays updated with the latest research and best practices, allowing her to provide high-quality support to her clients. Her optimism and enthusiasm for learning inspire those around her to pursue their own professional growth.

Emily's involvement in international social work has exposed her to diverse cultural contexts and new ways of addressing child welfare issues. She embraces these opportunities with an open mind and a willingness to learn from others. Emily's ability to adapt to different cultural environments and collaborate with international partners has been instrumental in her success. Her optimism and positive attitude help her navigate the complexities of international work and build strong relationships with her global colleagues.

Emily recognizes the importance of leveraging technology to enhance her work and reach a broader audience. She embraces technological advancements and incorporates them into her programs and initiatives. Whether it's using digital platforms for training and outreach or implementing data-driven approaches to improve service delivery, Emily's willingness to embrace technology ensures that her work remains relevant and effective. Her optimism about the potential of technology to drive positive change is a key factor in her success.

Emily's journey of personal growth is marked by her ability to embrace change and reflect on her experiences. She regularly takes time to assess her progress, celebrate her achievements, and identify areas for improvement. Emily's willingness to embrace change and adapt her approach as needed has been crucial to her personal and professional development. Her optimism and positive outlook on life help her navigate challenges and continue moving forward with confidence.

Emily's ability to embrace change and new opportunities with optimism serves as an inspiration to those around her. Her positive attitude and enthusiasm for growth encourage her colleagues, mentees, and community members to embrace change in their own lives. Emily's leadership and example demonstrate the power of optimism and adaptability in achieving success and making a positive impact.

Emily's journey of embracing change and new opportunities with optimism highlights her resilience, adaptability, and commitment to making a difference. Her willingness to learn, grow, and explore new possibilities ensures that she continues to thrive and inspire others. Emily's story is a testament to the power of optimism and the importance of embracing change in creating a brighter future.

As Emily reflects on her journey and the impact she has made, she looks to the future with confidence and a deep sense of fulfilment. Her experiences have shaped her into a resilient, compassionate, and empowered individual, ready to embrace new opportunities and continue making a positive difference.

Emily is committed to expanding her advocacy efforts to reach a broader audience and influence more significant policy changes. She plans to collaborate with national organizations and policymakers to advocate for comprehensive child welfare reforms.

Emily's goal is to ensure that all children have access to the support and resources they need to thrive.

Emily is excited about developing new and innovative programs that address emerging challenges faced by vulnerable children and families. She aims to create initiatives that focus on mental health, educational support, and community engagement. Emily's vision includes leveraging technology and research to design programs that are both effective and accessible.

Building on her success in creating strong community partnerships, Emily plans to further strengthen these relationships and explore new collaborations. She envisions a network of organizations working together to provide holistic support to children and families. Emily's efforts will focus on enhancing coordination and resource sharing to maximize the impact of community services.

Emily is passionate about mentoring the next generation of social workers and advocates. She plans to establish mentorship programs that provide guidance, support, and professional development opportunities for students and new professionals. Emily's goal is to inspire and equip future leaders with the skills and knowledge they need to make a meaningful impact.

Emily is dedicated to continuous learning and professional growth. She plans to pursue advanced education, such as a doctoral degree in social work or public policy, to deepen her expertise and expand her influence. Emily's commitment to education reflects her desire to stay at the forefront of her field and contribute to the development of best practices.

Emily's journey has instilled in her a deep sense of confidence and determination. She is proud of the progress she has made and the positive impact she has had on the lives of vulnerable children and families. Emily's experiences have taught her the importance of resilience, empathy, and the power of collective action.

As she looks to the future, Emily is filled with hope and excitement for the possibilities that lie ahead. She is ready to embrace new challenges and opportunities, confident in her ability to make a difference. Emily's dedication to her work and her unwavering commitment to supporting children and families ensure that her impact will continue to grow.

Emily's story is a testament to the strength of the human spirit and the importance of love, support, and advocacy. With the support of the Johnson family, her colleagues, and her community, Emily is ready to continue her journey and create a brighter future for all children.

Chapter 18
Continuing the Mission

Emily's unwavering commitment to supporting vulnerable children and families drives her to continually seek out and develop new initiatives. These initiatives are designed to address emerging challenges, leverage innovative approaches, and create lasting positive change.

Recognizing the growing need for mental health support, Emily has launched a comprehensive mental health program for children and adolescents. This initiative provides accessible counselling, therapy, and support groups, addressing issues such as anxiety, depression, and trauma. Emily collaborates with mental health professionals, schools, and community organizations to create a holistic approach to mental health care. The program aims to reduce stigma, promote mental well-being, and ensure that young people receive the support they need to thrive.

Emily is passionate about ensuring that all children have access to quality education. She has developed educational enrichment programs that provide tutoring, mentorship, and extracurricular activities for students from underserved communities. These initiatives aim to bridge the educational gap, enhance academic performance and foster a love for learning.
Emily's programs also focus on building essential life skills, such as critical thinking, problem-solving, and leadership.

To provide comprehensive support to families, Emily has established community resource centres in various neighbourhoods. These centres offer a wide range of services, including parenting workshops, financial literacy classes, job training, and access to healthcare resources. Emily's goal is to create a one-stop hub where families can receive the support and resources, they need to build stable and nurturing environments for their children. The centres also serve as a space for community members to connect, share experiences, and support one another.

Emily continues to advocate for trauma-informed care practices across all child welfare services. She has developed a training program for social workers, educators, and healthcare providers, equipping them with the knowledge and skills to support children who have experienced trauma. The training covers topics such as recognizing signs of trauma, creating safe and supportive environments, and implementing effective interventions. Emily's efforts aim to ensure that all professionals working with children are equipped to provide compassionate and effective care.

Emily believes in the power of empowering young people to become advocates for change. She has launched youth empowerment programs that focus on leadership development, civic engagement, and social justice. These programs provide young individuals with the tools and opportunities to make a positive impact in their communities. Emily's initiatives encourage youth to take on leadership roles, participate in community service, and advocate for policies that support their well-being.

Emily is leveraging technology to enhance the delivery of child welfare services. She has introduced digital platforms that provide virtual counselling, online educational resources, and remote support for families. These platforms ensure that services are accessible to those who may face barriers to in-person support. Emily's use of technology also includes data-driven approaches to track program outcomes and continuously improve service delivery.

Emily is actively involved in collaborative research projects that explore innovative approaches to child welfare. She partners with academic institutions and research organizations to conduct studies on topics such as early intervention, family support, and mental health. The findings from these research projects inform the development of evidence-based practices and policies. Emily's commitment to research ensures that her initiatives are grounded in the latest knowledge and best practices.

Emily continues to advocate for policy changes that support vulnerable children and families. She works with policymakers, advocacy groups, and community leaders to promote legislation that addresses issues such as child welfare funding, access to mental health services, and educational equity. Emily's advocacy efforts aim to create systemic changes that improve the lives of children and families on a broader scale.

Emily's new initiatives reflect her dedication to addressing emerging challenges and creating lasting positive change. Her innovative programs, collaborative efforts, and commitment to advocacy ensure that she continues to make a meaningful impact on the lives of vulnerable children and families.

Emily's dedication to community engagement is a cornerstone of her mission to support vulnerable children and families. She actively works to raise awareness about child welfare issues and foster a sense of collective responsibility within the community.

Emily organizes various community events to bring people together and raise awareness about child welfare. These events include family fun days, resource fairs, and awareness walks. By creating opportunities for community members to gather and learn about important issues, Emily fosters a sense of unity and collective action. These events also provide valuable information and resources to families in need.

Emily regularly hosts workshops and seminars on topics such as parenting skills, mental health awareness, and child safety. These educational sessions are designed to empower parents and caregivers with the knowledge and tools they need to support their children effectively. Emily's engaging and informative workshops help build a more informed and supportive community.

Emily collaborates with local organizations, schools, and healthcare providers to address child welfare issues comprehensively. These partnerships allow for coordinated efforts and resource sharing, ensuring that families receive holistic support. Emily's ability to build strong relationships with community partners enhances the effectiveness of her initiatives and
expands their reach.

Emily is a passionate advocate for child welfare and

frequently speaks at public events, conferences, and community meetings. She uses these platforms to raise awareness about critical issues, share her experiences, and inspire others to take action. Emily's compelling storytelling and advocacy efforts help mobilize community support and drive positive change.

To ensure that valuable information is accessible to all, Emily creates and distributes informational materials such as brochures, flyers, and newsletters. These materials cover a wide range of topics, from available resources to tips for supporting children's well-being. Emily's efforts to disseminate information help families stay informed and connected to the support they need.

Emily leverages social media to reach a broader audience and raise awareness about child welfare issues. She uses platforms like Facebook, Twitter, and Instagram to share important updates, success stories, and educational content. Emily's social media presence helps engage the community, promote her initiatives, and encourage collective action.

Emily believes in the power of youth advocacy and actively engages young people in her efforts. She organizes youth-led initiatives, such as peer mentoring programs and advocacy campaigns, to empower young individuals to become advocates for change. Emily's efforts to involve youth in her work help create a new generation of informed and passionate advocates.

Emily works to build a supportive network within the community, where families can connect, share experiences, and support one another. She facilitates support groups, community forums, and peer mentoring programs that provide a safe space for individuals to seek help and offer support. Emily's efforts to create a strong community network help foster a sense of belonging and mutual support.

Emily's community engagement efforts highlight her commitment to raising awareness about child welfare issues and fostering a sense of collective responsibility. Her ability to organize events, host workshops, collaborate with local organizations, advocate for change, create informational materials, leverage social media, engage youth, and build a supportive community network ensures that her impact extends far beyond her immediate work.

Emily's dedication to child welfare extends beyond direct service provision, she is deeply involved in advocacy and policy work to drive systemic changes that benefit vulnerable children and families. Her efforts in this area are characterized by her passion for justice, her ability to mobilize support, and her commitment to creating lasting impact.

Emily actively works to influence policy changes at local, state, and national levels. She collaborates with policymakers, advocacy groups, and community leaders to promote legislation that addresses critical child welfare issues. Emily's advocacy efforts focus on securing increased funding for child welfare services, implementing trauma-informed practices, and improving access to mental health care. Her ability to articulate the needs of vulnerable children and families helps drive policy changes that create a more supportive and
equitable system.

Emily frequently testifies before legislative bodies to provide expert insights and advocate for policy reforms. Her testimony is informed by her extensive experience in the field and her deep understanding of the challenges faced by children and families. Emily's compelling and evidence-based testimony helps shape legislative decisions and garner support for child welfare initiatives. Her ability to communicate effectively with policymakers is a key factor in her advocacy success.

Emily understands the power of collective action and works to build coalitions with other advocacy organizations, community groups, and stakeholders. These coalitions amplify the voices of those advocating for child welfare reforms and create a unified front to address systemic issues. Emily's leadership in coalition-building ensures that diverse perspectives are represented and that advocacy efforts are coordinated and impactful.

Emily is dedicated to raising public awareness about child welfare issues and the importance of policy changes. She engages in public speaking, writes articles, and participates in media interviews to highlight critical issues and advocate for solutions. Emily's ability to connect with the public and convey the urgency of child welfare reforms helps mobilize community support and drive collective action.

Emily develops and leads advocacy campaigns that focus on specific child welfare issues. These campaigns include public awareness initiatives, grassroots mobilization, and lobbying efforts. Emily's strategic approach to advocacy ensures that campaigns are well-organized, impactful, and achieve their goals. Her campaigns often result in increased public support, policy changes, and improved outcomes for children and families.

Emily collaborates with research institutions to conduct studies that inform policy decisions and advocacy efforts. These research projects provide valuable data and insights into the effectiveness of child welfare programs and the needs of vulnerable populations.

Emily's commitment to evidence-based advocacy ensures that her efforts are grounded in research and best practices. The findings from these studies help shape policy recommendations and drive systemic improvements.

Emily is an active member of professional associations dedicated to social work and child welfare. She participates in association meetings, contributes to policy discussions, and serves on committees that focus on advocacy and policy development. Emily's involvement in these associations allows her to stay informed about emerging issues, share her expertise, and collaborate with other professionals to advance child welfare policies.

Emily is passionate about mentoring the next generation of advocates and social workers. She provides guidance, support, and training to students and new professionals who are interested in advocacy work. Emily's mentorship helps build a strong pipeline of future leaders who are equipped with the skills and knowledge to drive positive change. Her efforts to inspire and empower others ensure that the impact of her advocacy work will continue for years to come.

Emily's involvement in advocacy and policy work highlights her commitment to creating systemic changes that benefit vulnerable children and families. Her ability to influence policy, build coalitions, raise public awareness, develop advocacy campaigns, collaborate with research institutions, engage with professional associations, and mentor future advocates ensures that her efforts have a lasting and meaningful impact.

Emily understands that achieving her mission requires a collaborative effort, and she is dedicated to building a team of passionate and skilled professionals who share her vision. Her approach to team-building is characterized by inclusivity, mentorship, and a commitment to excellence.

Emily begins by identifying the key roles needed to support her initiatives. These roles include social workers, mental health professionals, educators, community outreach coordinators, and administrative staff. Emily carefully considers the specific skills and expertise required for each position, ensuring that her team is well-rounded and capable of addressing the diverse needs of the children and families they serve.

Emily is committed to recruiting individuals who are not only highly skilled but also passionate about making a difference. She conducts thorough interviews and seeks candidates who demonstrate a deep commitment to child welfare and a genuine desire to support vulnerable populations. Emily values diversity and inclusivity, ensuring that her team reflects the communities they serve and brings a variety of perspectives and experiences to the table.

Emily creates a collaborative and supportive work environment where team members feel valued and empowered. She encourages open communication, active participation, and mutual respect. Emily's leadership style is inclusive and participatory, allowing team members to contribute their ideas and take ownership of their work. This collaborative approach fosters a sense of unity and shared purpose within the team.

Emily is dedicated to the continuous professional development of her team. She organizes regular training sessions, workshops, and seminars to enhance their skills and knowledge. These opportunities for learning and growth ensure that team members stay updated with the latest research, best practices, and innovative approaches in child welfare. Emily's commitment to professional development helps her team provide high-quality support to children and families.

Emily takes on a mentorship role, providing guidance and support to her team members. She offers one-on-one coaching, shares her experiences and helps them navigate challenges. Emily's mentorship fosters a culture of learning and growth, where team members feel supported and encouraged to reach their full potential. Her ability to inspire and motivate her team is a key factor in their success.

Emily understands the importance of work-life balance and promotes a healthy and supportive work environment. She encourages her team to prioritize self-care, set boundaries, and take time for themselves. Emily's efforts to create a balanced work environment help prevent burnout and ensure that team members can sustain their passion and dedication over the long term.

Emily believes in recognizing and celebrating the achievements of her team. She acknowledges their hard work, dedication, and contributions through regular appreciation events, awards, and public recognition. Celebrating successes boosts team morale and reinforces the value of their work. Emily's efforts to celebrate achievements create a positive and motivating work environment.

Emily also focuses on building strong partnerships with other organizations, community groups, and stakeholders. These partnerships enhance the team's ability to provide comprehensive support and access additional resources. Emily's collaborative approach ensures that her team can leverage the strengths and expertise of their partners to achieve their goals.

Emily's efforts to build a team of dedicated professionals highlight her commitment to collaboration, inclusivity, and excellence. Her ability to recruit passionate individuals, foster a supportive work environment, provide ongoing training, offer mentorship, encourage work-life balance, celebrate achievements, and build strong partnerships ensures that her initiatives are well-supported and impactful.

Emily's work in child welfare is fraught with challenges, but her resilience, resourcefulness, and unwavering commitment help her overcome these obstacles and continue making a positive impact.

One of the most significant obstacles Emily faces is securing adequate funding for her programs and initiatives. Limited financial resources can hinder the implementation and sustainability of essential services. To overcome this challenge, Emily actively seeks grants, donations, and partnerships with philanthropic organizations. She writes compelling grant proposals, organizes fundraising events, and leverages her network to secure the necessary funds. Emily's ability to advocate for her programs and demonstrate their impact helps attract financial support and ensure their continuity.

Navigating bureaucratic processes and regulations can be a daunting task. Emily often encounters delays and obstacles when trying to implement new programs or advocate for policy changes. To address this, she builds strong relationships with key stakeholders, including policymakers, government officials, and community leaders. Emily's ability to communicate effectively and collaborate with these stakeholders helps streamline processes and overcome bureaucratic hurdles. Her persistence and strategic approach ensure that her initiatives move forward despite administrative challenges.

Working in diverse communities, Emily encounters cultural barriers that can impact the effectiveness of her programs. Different cultural norms, values, and practices require tailored approaches to child welfare. Emily addresses this by engaging with community leaders, conducting cultural competency training for her team, and incorporating culturally relevant practices into her programs. Her commitment to cultural sensitivity and inclusivity helps build trust and ensures that her services are effective and respectful of the communities she serves.

The emotional toll of working with vulnerable children and families can lead to compassion fatigue and burnout. Emily recognizes the importance of self-care and mental health support for herself and her team. She implements regular debriefing sessions, provides access to counselling services, and encourages a healthy work-life balance. Emily's proactive approach to addressing the emotional challenges of her work helps maintain the well-being and resilience of her team, ensuring they can continue to provide high-quality support.

Implementing new programs and advocating for policy changes often meet resistance from those who are accustomed to the status quo. Emily faces opposition from individuals and organizations resistant to change. To overcome this, she uses data and evidence to demonstrate the effectiveness of her initiatives. Emily also engages in open dialogue, listens to concerns, and addresses misconceptions. Her ability to build consensus and foster a collaborative environment helps mitigate resistance and drive positive change.

Limited access to resources such as trained professionals, facilities, and technology can hinder the delivery of services. Emily addresses this by building partnerships with local organizations, educational institutions, and healthcare providers. She leverages these partnerships to access additional resources, provide training opportunities, and enhance service delivery. Emily's resourcefulness and ability to mobilize support ensure that her programs have the necessary resources to succeed.

Working in areas affected by conflict, natural disasters, or other crises poses safety and security risks. Emily prioritizes the safety of her team and the communities they serve by conducting thorough risk assessments and developing contingency plans. She collaborates with local authorities and international organizations to ensure that safety protocols are in place. Emily's proactive approach to safety and security helps mitigate risks and ensures the well-being of everyone involved.

Ensuring the sustainability of her programs is a key challenge for Emily. She addresses this by building the capacity of local organizations and communities to continue the work after her involvement ends. Emily provides training, resources, and support to local professionals, empowering them to take ownership of the programs. Her focus on sustainability ensures that the positive impact of her initiatives endures long after she has moved on to new projects.

Emily's ability to overcome obstacles in her work is a testament to her resilience, resourcefulness, and dedication. Her strategic approach, commitment to self-care, cultural sensitivity, and focus on sustainability ensure that she can navigate challenges and continue making a meaningful impact on the lives of vulnerable children and families.

Emily's initiatives have achieved remarkable successes, creating a positive and lasting impact on the lives of vulnerable children and families. These successes are a testament to her dedication, innovative approaches, and collaborative efforts.

Emily's comprehensive mental health support programs have significantly improved the well-being of children and adolescents. The accessible counselling, therapy, and support groups provided through these programs have helped reduce anxiety, depression, and trauma-related symptoms. Many participants have reported improved mental health, better coping skills, and enhanced emotional resilience. The success of these programs has been recognized by mental health professionals and community leaders, leading to increased support and funding.

The educational enrichment programs developed by Emily have made a substantial difference in the academic performance and overall development of students from underserved communities. Through tutoring, mentorship, and extracurricular activities, these initiatives have helped bridge the educational gap and foster a love for learning. Students who participated in these programs have shown significant improvements in their grades, increased school attendance, and higher levels of engagement. The positive outcomes have garnered praise from educators and parents alike.

The establishment of community resource centres has provided families with essential support and resources. These centres offer a wide range of services, including parenting workshops, financial literacy classes, job training, and access to healthcare resources. Families who have utilized these services report increased stability, improved parenting skills, and better access to necessary resources. The success of the community resource centres has led to the expansion of these services to additional neighbourhoods, further extending their positive impact.

Emily's trauma-informed care training programs have equipped social workers, educators, and healthcare providers with the knowledge and skills to support children who have experienced trauma. The training has led to the implementation of trauma-informed practices across various child welfare services, resulting in more compassionate and effective care. Participants in the training programs have reported increased confidence in their ability to support traumatized children and a deeper understanding of trauma's impact. The success of these training programs has been recognized by professional associations and has influenced policy changes.

The youth empowerment programs launched by Emily have inspired young individuals to become advocates for change. These programs focus on leadership development, civic engagement, and social justice, providing youth with the tools and opportunities to make a positive impact in their communities. Participants have taken on leadership roles, organized community service projects, and advocated for policies that support their well-being. The success of these programs has been celebrated by community leaders and has inspired other organizations to adopt similar approaches.

Emily's use of technology to enhance child welfare services has led to increased accessibility and efficiency. Digital platforms providing virtual counselling, online educational resources, and remote support have ensured that services are available to those facing barriers to in-person support. The data-driven approaches implemented by Emily have improved program outcomes and service delivery. The success of these technological innovations has been recognized by industry experts and has set a new standard for child welfare services.

Emily's involvement in collaborative research projects has generated valuable insights and evidence-based practices that inform program development and policy decisions. The findings from these research projects have led to the implementation of effective interventions and the improvement of child welfare services. The success of these research initiatives has been acknowledged by academic institutions and research organizations, further validating the impact of Emily's work.

Emily's advocacy efforts have resulted in significant policy changes that support vulnerable children and families. Her work with policymakers, advocacy groups, and community leaders has led to increased funding for child welfare services, the implementation of trauma-informed practices, and improved access to mental health care. The success of these advocacy efforts has created systemic changes that benefit children and families on a broader scale.

Emily's initiatives have achieved remarkable successes, creating a positive and lasting impact on the lives of vulnerable children and families. Her dedication, innovative approaches, and collaborative efforts have set new standards in child welfare and inspired others to join the cause. Emily's story is a testament to the power of compassion, resilience, and the importance of collective action in creating meaningful change.

Emily's dedication and passion for child welfare have a profound ripple effect, inspiring others to get involved and make a difference. Her work serves as a beacon of hope and motivation for individuals and organizations alike.

Emily's colleagues are continually inspired by her commitment and innovative approaches. Her leadership and mentorship encourage them to pursue their own initiatives and strive for excellence in their work. Many of her team members have taken on leadership roles in their own right, developing new programs and advocating for policy changes. Emily's ability to foster a supportive and empowering work environment motivates her colleagues to push boundaries and achieve their goals.

Emily's community engagement efforts attract a diverse group of volunteers who are eager to contribute to her mission. Her passion and dedication resonate with volunteers, inspiring them to give their time and skills to support vulnerable children and families. Emily's ability to connect with volunteers on a personal level and show the tangible impact of their efforts keeps them motivated and committed. Many volunteers have gone on to pursue careers in social work and advocacy, inspired by their experiences working with Emily.

Emily's youth empowerment programs have a lasting impact on the young individuals who participate. Her mentorship and support help them develop leadership skills, confidence, and a sense of purpose. Many of these young people become advocates for change in their own communities, organizing events, leading initiatives, and raising awareness about child welfare issues. Emily's ability to inspire and empower youth ensures that the next generation is equipped to continue the fight for social justice and child welfare.

Emily's efforts to raise awareness and engage the community have inspired countless individuals to take action. Her public speaking, workshops, and community events highlight the importance of collective responsibility and the power of community support. Many community members have been inspired to get involved, whether through volunteering, donating, or advocating for policy changes. Emily's ability to mobilize community support creates a strong network of individuals dedicated to making a positive impact.

Emily's advocacy work has not only led to policy changes but also inspired policymakers to prioritize child welfare issues. Her compelling testimony and evidence-based recommendations have influenced legislators to take action and support initiatives that benefit vulnerable children and families. Emily's ability to articulate the needs and challenges faced by these populations inspires policymakers to champion child welfare reforms and allocate resources to support these efforts.

Emily's innovative programs and successful initiatives serve as a model for other organizations working in the field of child welfare. Many organizations have adopted her approaches and implemented similar programs, inspired by the positive outcomes she has achieved. Emily's willingness to share her knowledge and collaborate with other organizations fosters a culture of learning and continuous improvement. Her work inspires others to innovate and strive for excellence in their own efforts to support children and families.

Emily's impact extends beyond her immediate work, creating a lasting legacy of compassion, resilience, and advocacy. Her story inspires others to believe in the power of one person to make a difference and motivates them to take action in their own lives. Emily's dedication to her mission and her ability to inspire others ensure that her work will continue to create positive change for years to come.

Emily's work inspires others to get involved and make a difference by empowering colleagues, motivating volunteers, engaging the community, influencing policymakers, inspiring other organizations, and creating a lasting legacy. Her dedication, passion, and innovative approaches serve as a powerful example of the impact one person can have on the lives of vulnerable children and families.

Emily's journey in child welfare has been a profound catalyst for her personal growth and development. Through her continued efforts, she has evolved in numerous ways, gaining invaluable insights and skills that have enriched both her professional and personal life.

Emily's work with vulnerable children and families has

strengthened her emotional resilience. She has learned to navigate the emotional demands of her job, developing coping strategies to manage stress and prevent burnout. Emily's ability to maintain her emotional well-being while supporting others is a testament to her resilience and dedication.

Emily's experiences have deepened her empathy and compassion. Working closely with children and families facing significant challenges has given her a profound understanding of their struggles and strengths. This empathy drives her commitment to making a positive impact and fuels her passion for advocacy. Emily's ability to connect with others on a deep emotional level has become a defining aspect of her work.

Through her various roles and responsibilities, Emily has honed her leadership skills. She has learned to lead diverse teams, manage complex projects, and inspire others to achieve their goals. Emily's inclusive and participatory leadership style fosters a collaborative environment where everyone feels valued and empowered. Her growth as a leader has been instrumental in the success of her initiatives.

Emily's international work has significantly enhanced her cultural competence. She has gained a deep appreciation for diverse cultures and learned to navigate cultural differences with sensitivity and respect. Emily's ability to work effectively in diverse environments has enriched her personal and professional life, making her a more effective and compassionate social worker.

Emily's involvement in advocacy and policy work has strengthened her ability to influence change. She has developed skills in public speaking, coalition-building, and strategic planning. Emily's ability to articulate the needs of vulnerable populations and advocate for policy changes has been a key factor in her success. Her growth as an advocate has enabled her to drive systemic changes that benefit children and families.

Emily's dedication to continuous learning has been a cornerstone of her personal growth. She actively seeks out opportunities for professional development, pursues advanced education, and stays informed about the latest research and best practices. Emily's commitment to learning ensures that she remains at the forefront of her field and continues to provide high-quality support to her clients.

Emily's journey has fostered a deep sense of self awareness. She regularly reflects on her experiences, acknowledges her strengths and areas for improvement, and sets goals for personal and professional growth. Emily's ability to engage in self-reflection and embrace feedback has been crucial to her development. This self-awareness helps her navigate challenges with confidence and resilience.

Emily's work in child welfare has sharpened her problem solving skills. She has learned to think critically, develop innovative solutions, and adapt to changing circumstances. Emily's ability to address complex issues and find effective solutions has been a key factor in the success of her initiatives. Her growth as a problem-solver ensures that she can navigate challenges and continue making a positive impact.

Emily's journey has brought her a profound sense of personal fulfilment. The knowledge that she is making a difference in the lives of vulnerable children and families gives her a deep sense of satisfaction and purpose. Emily's dedication to her work and the positive impact she has made are sources of pride and motivation. Her journey has reinforced her belief in the importance of compassion, resilience, and the power of collective action.

Emily's personal growth and development through her continued efforts highlight her resilience, empathy, leadership, cultural competence, advocacy skills, commitment to learning, self-awareness, problem-solving abilities, and personal fulfilment. Her journey is a testament to the transformative power of dedication and the profound impact one individual can have on the lives of others.

As Emily sits in her quiet study, surrounded by mementos of her travels and the heartfelt letters from the children and families she has helped, she takes a moment to reflect on her journey. The path she has walked has been filled with challenges, triumphs, and countless moments of growth and learning.

Emily feels a deep sense of gratitude for the journey she has undertaken. She is thankful for the opportunities she has had to make a difference in the lives of vulnerable children and families. Each step of her journey has been a learning experience, shaping her into the resilient and compassionate individual she is today. Emily's reflections are filled with appreciation for the support she has received from her family, friends, colleagues, and the communities she serves.

Reflecting on the impact she has made, Emily is filled with a sense of fulfilment and pride. She recalls the faces of the children who have found hope and healing through her programs, the families who have gained stability and support, and the communities that have come together to create positive change. Emily's work has touched countless lives, and the stories of transformation and resilience inspire her to continue her mission. She is proud of the tangible outcomes her initiatives have achieved and the lasting positive impact they have created.

Emily's journey has been one of profound personal growth and development. She has learned to navigate challenges with resilience, embrace vulnerability, and lead with empathy and compassion. Emily's experiences have deepened her understanding of the complexities of child welfare and the importance of cultural sensitivity and inclusivity. Her commitment to continuous learning and self-reflection has enabled her to grow both personally and professionally, making her a more effective advocate and leader.

As Emily reflects on her journey, she is mindful of the legacy she is building. Her work has inspired others to get involved, advocate for change, and support vulnerable populations. Emily's ability to empower and mentor the next generation of social workers and advocates ensures that her impact will continue to grow. She is proud of the strong network of professionals, volunteers, and community members who share her vision and are committed to making a difference.

Emily's reflections are not just about the past but also, about the future. She is excited about the new initiatives she is developing, the partnerships she is building, and the opportunities to expand her advocacy efforts. Emily's journey has taught her the importance of resilience, love, and the power of collective action. She looks to the future with confidence, knowing that she has the skills, support, and determination to continue making a positive impact.

Ultimately, Emily's reflections are filled with a deep sense of fulfilment. The knowledge that she has made a difference in the lives of vulnerable children and families gives her a profound sense of purpose and satisfaction. Emily's journey is a testament to the strength of the human spirit and the importance of compassion, resilience, and advocacy. Her story continues to inspire others and drive lasting improvements in child welfare practices globally.

Emily's reflections on her journey highlight the impact she has made, the personal growth she has experienced, and the legacy she is building. Her story is a powerful reminder of the difference one individual can make and the importance of continuing to strive for positive change.

As Emily reflects on her journey and the impact she has made, she looks to the future with hope and determination. Her experiences have shaped her into a resilient, compassionate, and empowered individual, ready to embrace new opportunities and continue her mission of supporting vulnerable children and families.

Emily is committed to expanding her advocacy efforts to reach a broader audience and influence more significant policy changes. She plans to collaborate with national organizations and policymakers to advocate for comprehensive child welfare reforms. Emily's goal is to ensure that all children have access to the support and resources they need to thrive.

Emily is excited about developing new and innovative programs that address emerging challenges faced by vulnerable children and families. She aims to create initiatives that focus on mental health, educational support, and community engagement. Emily's vision includes leveraging technology and research to design programs that are both effective and accessible.

Building on her success in creating strong community partnerships, Emily plans to further strengthen these relationships and explore new collaborations. She envisions a network of organizations working together to provide holistic support to children and families. Emily's efforts will focus on enhancing coordination and resource sharing to maximize the impact of community services.

Emily is passionate about mentoring the next generation of social workers and advocates. She plans to establish mentorship programs that provide guidance, support, and professional development opportunities for students and new professionals. Emily's goal is to inspire and equip future leaders with the skills and knowledge they need to make a meaningful impact.

Emily is dedicated to continuous learning and professional growth. She plans to pursue advanced education, such as a doctoral degree in social work or public policy, to deepen her expertise and expand her influence. Emily's commitment to education reflects her desire to stay at the forefront of her field and contribute to the development of best practices.

Emily's journey has instilled in her a deep sense of confidence and determination. She is proud of the progress she has made and the positive impact she has had on the lives of vulnerable children and families. Emily's experiences have taught her the importance of resilience, empathy, and the power of collective action.

As she looks to the future, Emily is filled with hope and excitement for the possibilities that lie ahead. She is ready to embrace new challenges and opportunities, confident in her ability to make a difference. Emily's dedication to her work and her unwavering commitment to supporting children and families ensure that her impact will continue to grow.

Emily's story is a testament to the strength of the human spirit and the importance of love, support, and advocacy. With the support of the Johnson family, her colleagues, and her community, Emily is ready to continue her journey and create a brighter future for all children.

The End.

Made in the USA
Middletown, DE
19 January 2025